Sudan Days
1926-1954

Sudan Days
1926-1954

A Memoir

by

Richard Owen

Edited by Duff Hart-Davis

Matador
9 Priory Business Park,
Wistow Road, Kibworth Beauchamp,
Leicestershire. LE8 0RX
Tel: 0116 279 2299
Email: books@troubador.co.uk
Web: www.troubador.co.uk/matador
Twitter: @matadorbooks

ISBN 978 1785890 246

British Library Cataloguing in Publication Data.
A catalogue record for this book is available from the British Library.

Printed and bound by CPI Group (UK) Ltd, Croydon, CR0 4YY
Typeset in 12pt Bembo by Troubador Publishing Ltd, Leicester, UK

Matador is an imprint of Troubador Publishing Ltd

Family Tribute

As son and nephew, we have felt moved, sixty years after his retirement, to publish Richard Owen's memoir of his time in the Sudan Political Service. It provides a fascinating and amusing personal record of a distinct part of late British Imperial history, and a vivid picture of the many and varied peoples and cultures of the Sudan. In particular, it sheds light on the conditions which prevailed in the Southern Sudan in the period preceding independence. This was followed by fifty years of bloody conflict between North and South, which finally led to their separation in 2011. Tribal conflicts still plague the South.

Robert Owen,   David Lyon
December 2015.

CONTENTS

GLOSSARY

ambatch	cork-like shrub
andot	game played with camel pellets
angareb	bed
araki	illicitly brewed liquor
aro	tribal spirit
baati	revenant
bazunkw	local banjo
dambari	man with power to deflect locust swarms
fiki	holy man
fuzzy-wuzzies	the Beja tribes
gamloon	village idiot
ghafir	watchman
hakeem	doctor
hukuma	government
hulal	stick for scratching head
imma	turban
jebel	hill or mountain
kadi	religious leader
khanjar	curved knife
khor	grass valley
kujur	witch doctor
mamur	administrative assistant
mek	chief
merissa	locally-brewed hooch
merkaz	headquarters
mirikh	broom-like shrub
mudir	governor
nahas	copper drums
nazir	local leader

omda	mayor or other local official
sarraf	cashier
sheikh	an eminent man
shelegai	Baggara spear
sitt	lady
syce	groom
tiffa	thatch of fuzzy hair
ulema	local council

EDITOR'S PREFACE

Richard Owen was born at Ashendene in Hertfordshire (his mother's family home) on 23 May 1903, the son of Colonel Charles Owen and his wife Gwendoline, formerly Hornby. He grew up in the shadow of the First World War, during which his father worked in the War Office. After Sandroyd prep school he went to Repton, and then read Classics at Corpus Christi College, Oxford. In 1926 he joined the Political Service of the Sudan, which was then a condominium administered jointly by Britain and Egypt (although in practice largely by the British). At the time the Sudan Political Service was viewed, rather like the Indian Civil Service, as an elite corps: it was said that the Sudan was a land of blacks ruled by blues.

His first posting was as Assistant District Commissioner at Wau, capital of Bahr al-Ghazal province, the mainly Dinka country in the far south. In 1928 he moved to Geteina and Ed Dueim in the White Nile Province, and in 1932 to Sinkat, in Kassala, where he was Deputy Commissioner. From 1936 to 1939 he was Deputy Assistant Civil Secretary in the Government offices in Khartoum. During and after the Second World War he was District Commissioner in the central, largely Arab state of Kordofan, and in 1945 he returned to Wau as Deputy Governor of Bahr al-Ghazal – a promotion which he described as 'the greatest bit of luck.' Finally, for five years from 1948, he was Governor of the province.

A tall, slim man, he spent months among tribes who went what he called 'starko' and fought each other with spears or sticks. Out in the wilds, his life was generally one of extreme privation. The heat was formidable – often 114 F. Food was rough, washing facilities minimal – hence his propensity for plunging, as starko as any native, into crocodile-free pools or rivers. Poisonous snakes, lions, leopards, scorpions and other noxious insects abounded. Yet he seems to have been impervious to discomfort, and never wrote a word of complaint.

Often he sat as a magistrate in provincial courts, and he was firm in sentencing minor criminals to floggings or terms in prison. Yet he was compassionate in dealing with primitive people, and saw that the most valuable task he could perform was to lead them slowly towards civilisation – a policy which led to many a clash with Central Government in Khartoum, which always wanted changes made quickly. It now seems extraordinary to reflect that in far-flung outposts all over the British Empire hundreds of men with much the same background as Owen were engaged in similar endeavours, in equally primitive surroundings.

A dedicated fisherman and a keen naturalist, he was happiest out on trek, visiting Government outposts, police stations, schools and so on. During his trips he took hundreds of photographs of people, wild life and scenery. After his retirement he published *Hunting Big Game with Gun and Camera in Africa*, a book which describes his safaris, more often with a camera than with a rifle – and he loved watching animals more than shooting them. Once, during a voyage up the Nile, he reported to his mother:

> The hippos were in great force and most entertaining, sometimes gambolling and playing about in the water within 25 yards of the ship, rolling over with their legs in the air and splashing and chasing each other with most palpable enjoyment.

In the evenings he had plenty of time to write, and his output of words was prodigious. Every page of his diaries was crammed with information and ideas, recorded in very small, neat italic writing, and he fired off long letters at least once a week to his father and mother, his sister Elizabeth or other members of the family. Often, having just declared, 'There is nothing much to report from here,' he carried on full steam ahead for six or seven more pages.

He acquired such fluent Arabic that on the telephone he was often taken for a native. Early in 1936, when he was preparing to marry Margaret Fletcher (whose father Albert owned and ran a brewery in Walsall), all his Arab friends wanted to know was (a) was she nice and fat? and (b) how much bride-price had he had to pay? What he did not tell them was that he thought his life was coming to a premature end. He was suffering from some mysterious heart ailment, so debilitating that he feared he would not survive until the wedding.

Survive he did. Returning to England on leave in April, he sought treatment, which resolved whatever his problem had been, and he married Margaret in August 1936. Their son Robert was born in London in 1940, and by the time their daughter Janet arrived in Khartoum in 1943, the family was so immersed in Sudanese life that young Robert was surprised to find that his sister was white rather than black.

In 1954, at the age of fifty-one, the author resigned in disgust from the Political Service, believing that when, in the near future, the Sudan became independent, the Southern Sudan should receive a high degree of autonomy in the new constitution. He was over-ruled by the Foreign Office, who gave in to pressure from the Egyptians. As he added in a footnote to his memoir:

> Owing to the extreme difficulty of communications, the poorness of natural resources and the formerly primitive nature of the inhabitants, the Government had adopted a policy, up to 1945, which meant that the South, economically and politically, lagged behind the North. The South's inclusion in the single, independent Sudan republic… was against the wishes of most of the populace, and full of danger for them.

In retirement he wrote *Sudan Days,* a record of everyday life in happier times – the second quarter of the 20th century. He completed the book in 1961, but until now it has never seen the light of day. It is an affectionate account of working among the Arabs and Africans whose lives he strove to regulate, and whom he came to love. His classical education shines in his writing, and his agreeably dry humour comes out equally in his letters home. Inevitably, many details of his narrative are now out of date, but he left a fascinating picture of British attempts to organise a vast country, since ravaged by revolution and war.

To broaden the picture he created, I have included excerpts from his letters between the chapters of the book.

Duff Hart-Davis, Uley, Gloucestershire, June 2015.

Written c. 1961

The Sudan is an unbelievably miscellaneous country, and I have attempted to build up a picture of it in the second quarter of the 20th century, as seen through the eyes of a British administrator. I have tried to do what Impressionist artists do – to fashion an overall picture from a jumble of independent and often seemingly irrelevant dabs of paint: to give the reader some feeling of the immense variety, the salient features of life and character, and the daily problems which beset those who laboured in the vineyard.

Of the several motives which have impelled me to write, I think the main one is love of the country and its people. In selecting an officer for service overseas, the first quality I should look for would be a capacity for liking people: judgment, initiative, brains, self-confidence and the whole gamut of virtues can be nullified by a lack of warmth. Some of the most successful colonial administrators were *not* the most brilliant men, but men who loved the country and the people they were serving, and were loved by them.

I know that my colleagues were not all paragons; that the Government we served made errors; that I personally made some gross ones; and that among the Sudanese themselves, from the highly-civilised urban intellectual to the bush-living primitive, there were thugs and scoundrels, as there are from Chicago to Vladivostok. Yet in nearly all that kaleidoscopic mass of humanity there were contrasting virtues. Above all there was *character*, a character which you do not find elsewhere in Africa – that colour and positive humanity and responsiveness which evoke personal affection and cover a multitude of defects. One's surroundings in the Sudan were, by most standards, ghastly; conditions of life were often uncongenial; frustrations were as common as elsewhere in the world. Yet, looking back, I know I was privileged to serve in the finest administrative service the earth can show, and among a most lovable people.

Geologically, the country varies from flat wastes and impenetrable marshes to mountains which top 10,000 feet. Climatically, it varies from the arid Nubian desert of the Egyptian frontier, where rain is a phenomenon seen once in five years, to a sixty-inch fall and tropical forest on the Uganda borders. Racially, the country is a veritable continent, despite having a total population of not much over ten million. [By 2014 it had risen to forty million].

On the Nile, in the extreme north, the people have strong Egyptian affinities, and their own language. Along the eastern side, southwards to Eritrea, live the Hamitic tribes of the Beja, known to the world as 'the Fuzzies' – pastorals, and in origin hill men, again with their own obscure tongue. Westwards lie people with much West African blood in them, and, in some cases, with their own speech. Southwards, up the Nile and on either side of it, are highly-developed riverain Arabs. In the capital, Khartoum-and-Omdurman (which face each other across the rivers where the Blue and White Niles join) are all the paraphernalia of a civilised, polyglot modern city.

Further south, a settled population of cultivating Arabs lives on the irrigated schemes from the Blue Nile and in the precariously-watered vistas west of the White Nile. Next come large elements of West Africans, immigrants earlier in the century and now resident. Then comes the great pagan block of the Nuba mountains in central Kordofan, with its babel of tongues and kaleidoscope of differing units. Beyond that lie Fung and semi-African and semi-Ethiopian elements on the Abyssinian border, again with their own speech. Southwards again lies the deep belt of the Baggara, the cattle-owning Arabs who live on a fifteen to thirty-inch rainfall and speak their own racy, spicy patois of Arabic. Finally in the Southern Sudan we come to the Nilotic bloc of Shilluks, Nuer and Dinka, with their cattle and their bogs, and beyond them the Bantu tribes of the deepest south.

In the northern provinces, despite the diverse racial ingredients and the surviving local languages, there is the unifying influence of an Islamic culture and tongue. Although the actual blood of Arabia may run thin, this is fundamentally an Arab civilisation, and therefore largely an Asiatic one in essentials. In the southern provinces, the onlooker is in Africa – the real Africa. The tribal divisions are innumerable, as are the languages, and the outlook is pagan. The whole culture and outlook are divergent from the Arab culture of the north.

Until 1820 the Sudan knew no unity. The tribes lived, warred, moved as they listed, and the outside world's knowledge of the country was next to nothing. Then in 1821 Ismail, son of Mohammed Ali, the great Khedive of Egypt, conquered most of what is now termed the Sudan, which was attached to Egypt and administered by a governor-general and provincial governors. In the middle of the century a few traders began to penetrate the south and west. In the 1860s and 1870s Sir Samuel Baker and General George Gordon were employed by the Khedive Ismail to suppress the slave trade in the southern provinces, and Gordon himself acted as Governor General from 1877 to 1880, but resigned when he saw his work thwarted by apathy and opposition.

In 1882 came revolt, the result partly of resentment against a government which was felt to be under foreign and Christian influence, partly as a protest against sheer maladministration, and partly driven by a genuine revivalist movement. Under the religious leader, the Mahdi Mohammed Ahmed, the country rose against Egyptian authority, and Egyptian forces were defeated. By 1884 little authority remained to Egypt outside Khartoum and a few beleaguered garrisons.

By then, as the result of a financial collapse, and the assumption of control in conjunction with France, England had assumed a considerable responsibility for Egyptian affairs; and at that critical point Gordon was sent to the Sudan with the principal objective of extricating the garrisons and foreign communities – a well-nigh impossible task. After evacuating some 2,000 personnel, Gordon was cut off in Khartoum and besieged there. A British relief force was organised, and its gunboats pushed up the Nile but arrived too late, to find that the city had fallen and Gordon had been killed on 26 January 1885.

The expedition withdrew. Operations began against the Dervishes (or tribesmen) around Suakin port, where the British troops had landed, and several fierce actions fizzled out, though Suakin remained in British hands. The Mahdi established his capital at Omdurman, and when he died in that same year – 1885 – his place was taken by the Khalifa Abdullahi. In 1894 the Abyssinian army invaded Southern Egypt, but was repulsed by Egyptian troops under British leadership, in operations which culminated in Kitchener's advance and the battle of Omdurman on 2 September 1898. Thousands of native troops were killed, and Kitchener entered Khartoum in triumph. When the Khalifa himself died a brave death at the battle of Um Debeikerat in 1899, the Anglo-Egyptian reoccupation was complete.

The campaign had been fought largely with Egyptian money and with a large proportion of Egyptian troops, with considerable additions of British forces, and the whole under British leadership. The Sudan was accordingly declared to be a condominium between Britain and Egypt, administered by a Governor General selected by H.M.G. and appointed by the Khedive, and financially dependent to no small extent on the British Treasury.

Thus opened the 20th century. Over-simplification is dangerous in historical affairs; but it is fairly accurate to separate the first and second quarters of the century, and to say that the main objective of the first was the establishment of order, sound administration and economic stability, whereas that of the second was political advance leading up to self-government. The first quarter involved a very direct form of administration, and its culmination was the inception, in 1923, of the great Gezira cotton-growing scheme, which sealed the Sudan's economic independence. The second began with the devolution of authority known as the 'native administration', which gave way to a progressive system of local government, and so, in turn, to a Governor General's (Sudanese) Advisory Council, to a Legislative Assembly, and thus on to independence.

It is of this country in this second quarter of the 20th century that I indite my experience. In 1898 the Sudan's million square miles held a population which probably did not exceed three million, divided by the curse of Babel, the scorn of race for race and the enmity of tribe to tribe, living in precarious uncertainty and economic chaos, without education, communications or social services. In fifty-six years it rose to take its place in the modern world as a viable, self-respecting, democratic national unit. Can any other territory on earth show a similar record? Only a virile and adaptable people could have achieved it – a people whom it was a privilege to serve.

CHAPTER ONE

The Daily Round

The great bulk of existence is made up of small things. Sensational events and memorable happenings are rare. Let us therefore live together the ordinary day of an ordinary District Commissioner, in the central or west-central portion of the country, shortly after the close of the war in 1945.

Rising with the sun is no virtuous work of supererogation in the tropics; nor is it irksome; it is only common sense, for the first two hours of the day are for most of the year the best. We have been called at six o'clock, and since this happens to be Thursday, which is the day for the weekly police parade, we have mounted our ponies and are on the parade ground by a quarter to seven. This is January and the weather is cold, and since cold has a more numbing and fuddling effect upon Arab and African alike than upon the European, the movements of the foot police, and especially their arms drill, lack the precision of a Guards' display but improve with improving circulations.

There is rather more to be seen on the air strip a few hundred yards away, where our twenty-five mounted police are doing their evolutions. The police officer is an old nugget whose father was an Emir of the Khalifa and his mother a slave woman. As a mere lad he fought at Omdurman and was shot through the eye and left for dead. He is of the old school, loyal, primitive, quite unteachable, and how he has survived the scrutiny of the Establishments Office in Khartoum, and remained in service until he is over sixty, while progressive, well-educated and efficient young police officers are filling vacancies and climbing the ladder all around him, nobody quite knows. He drills his police somewhat as if they were the Khalifa's cavalry and he was back at Omdurman. His one gimlet eye seems to descry an enemy hovering in the background, and the manoeuvres appear to lead up, in a slow crescendo, towards a devastating charge which shall obliterate him.

Police uniform, though smart and impressive, was not designed for charging. This applies especially to the *imma*, or turban. The *imma* comprises nearly five yards of material, and I have seen it, when unrolled, effectively used for bandaging a wound, securing a refractory prisoner, forming a substitute for a rifle sling, tying together the legs of four hens, and rescuing a man who had fallen off the quay and into the harbour at Port Sudan. But when rolled up and worn on the head it is apt to abandon its human perch with any sudden movement of its owner or his mount. That necessitates the rider dropping out of line and dismounting, which in turn disturbs other horses in the line.

To aggravate dislocation on this particular morning, the syce [groom] of the *omda* [the mayor] has seen fit to bring his master's most seductive mare on exercise, past the parade ground just as the force is performing 'At the halt, on the left, form platoon', and two *immas* have already fallen off. This is too much for the horses, and the resulting final evolution resembles a cavalry-rout, a horse-fair and a stud-farm combined.

The police officer makes a bee-line for the offending syce, impugning his ancestry and threatening everything from disembowelling downwards. Since time is in any case nearly up, I give the word to dismiss, and, mounted and foot, the police march back to barracks. The cavalry are blown home by their bugler, the infantry led by their piper, Baiyin, who can play three tunes (today it is *The Flowers of the Forest*) on bagpipes presented by one of my predecessors, a Scot who was no mean performer. When Baiyin plays, one realises why the Germans call the bagpipes *ein Dudelsack*. He is, moreover, the heaviest drinker among the police, and were anyone rash enough to put his mouth to the chanter, he would receive an alcoholic backhander of memorable vigour. Last night had been a thick one for Baiyin: and since the mounted bugler also is still out of breath from his Balaclava efforts, the result is *'une coupe d'oreille magnifique.'*

On our way back we turn aside to join our No. 2, the Assistant District Commissioner, who is just completing the weekly inspection of the *merkaz* [headquarters] animals – the donkeys which carry the water to the dispensary and girls' school, the camels which pull the conservancy (or, by a euphemism, 'night soil') carts, and the bulls which contentedly and ruminatively pull the rubbish carts.

It is now eight o'clock, and we return for breakfast, and afterwards, about nine o'clock, move to the office in the *merkaz* buildings. Office hours are from 9 till 2, after which routine closes down. These hours are wise, and though there are individuals who will sit on at their desks till any time in the afternoon, acquiring a feeling of virtue and being a burden to their subordinates, this type of mortification of the flesh leads to spiritual and mental desiccation, and sometimes to physical breakdown; and the sensible official returns to his lunch at 2. After five hours non-stop in a temperature which may, in the hot weather, be 114 F in the shade, no man is fit to come to an administrative decision or listen unjaundiced to a case – and many an error has been perpetrated by trying to do so.

The first hour or two of this morning are already booked. January is the time when the annual assessment of business profits tax takes place. A trader may, if he cares, submit his books and full accounts; then he is placed on the Financial Secretary's List, and his year's profits are assessed for taxation by experts in Khartoum. In fact only companies and a very few of the largest and most opulent private businesses adopt this method. Practically no ordinary trader – Arab, Greek or Syrian – keeps any record that would pass for accounts, and their profits are assessed by a district board, approved by the Governor and presided over by the District Commissioner.

The board will comprise the *mamur* (the District Commissioner's administrative assistant, and usually the man of premier prestige in Sudanese official circles), the Chief Merchant, the *omda* of the town and two or three of the most reputable (not necessarily the most wealthy) merchants themselves. The basis for the assessment is last year's list, and in the almost total absence of reliable accounts the board's normal method is to see what the man paid last year, consult such figures as it may have of his transactions in the gum market, melon seed market, grain and animal markets, smell out his general reputation (which his fellow merchants know fairly accurately), listen to his expostulations, agree to raise, lower or leave his tax at what they believe to be a fair figure, work out backwards from the tax what the profits must have been, inform him – and then judge from his expression whether their guess has been a good one. The entire process is amateur, expeditious and equitable.

The whole of the previous day has gone in this exacting pastime, but there are still a dozen names to be dealt with, and the *mamur,* reliable and admirable as ever, has got the lists and market figures at his elbow and the other members of the board in their places at ten minutes past nine. The first name called is that of Ahmed Babikr, whose business is mainly that of a cattle-dealer and whose profits at last year's assessment had been fixed at a sum which represented a tax of £20. Ahmed does not appear, being sick, but a petition from him is read out by the *mamur,* in which he claims that his profits are nil, his losses considerable and his children starving. He did not expect the board to believe this, but there is no harm in trying anything on the dog. The members are consulted, and the consensus is that although Ahmed is painting the lily, there is a distinct substratum of truth.

'His purchases in the market here have gone down by forty per cent,' the *mamur* observes. 'Yes,' says one of the merchant members, 'and there was that big consignment of cattle he sent through Um Shukr. The herdsman broke the quarantine regulations, and twenty of the beasts caught rinderpest and died on him.' We all look virtuous, knowing how shocking it is to break veterinary rules of quarantine, though many merchants and cattle owners will do so if it suits their purpose.

'I think I heard,' says another of the merchants, 'that he also had half a dozen animals eaten by hyenas.'

'Talking of hyenas,' says the *omda,* who is a born raconteur, 'I once knew a West African who could turn himself into a hyena. He would go to an ant-hill and roll at the foot of it, and when he got up, lo and behold he…' But at this point I recall them to Ahmed Babikr.

'I think,' says Merchant No. 1, after a pause, 'I am right in saying that he has seven children.'

'Eight,' says the *omda,* 'and all daughters.'

'And I understand,' says Merchant No. 2, 'that he has been bitten by a dog suspected of rabies and is in hospital under treatment.'

'Talking of dogs,' says the *omda,* 'I had a little white bitch; she could even catch a gazelle, and once …'

I recall him and sum up, and we agree that what Ahmed can afford to pay is about £10, and that his profits should be assessed at a figure which will result in that sum to the exchequer.

After him comes Mr Anaxagoras Papadopoulos, the richest but not the most popular of the local Greek merchants. Mr Papadopoulos appears in person. He is stout; he wears a shirt with a collar stud but no tie; and there is something essentially oleaginous about his figure and rather muddy complexion. He carries a book of *soi-disant* accounts, but they are of little use to the board. The modern descendant of Pericles does not speak or write his ancestors' matchless tongue in their fashion; and since in any case Arabic is the official language – or else English – his hieroglyphics are 'not evidence.'

Last year he paid a tax of £150, and there was every reason to think that that had been an under-assessment. This year it appears that everything has gone wrong with him. He has bought produce at the highest rate, and the bottom has dropped out of the market just as he was going to sell. Animals he bought to send eastwards to the city meat-markets have either died of mysterious diseases or encountered a curious and inexplicable abstinence among the urban populations, which has caused the demand for meat to drop and prices of sheep and bulls to shrink. His retail grocery in the town is not paying, owing to the general lack of cash. His bakery and soda-water factory have failed, owing to the dishonesty of an employee. His son's education in far-away Khartoum is expensive, and his wife has had twins.

The board listens politely, declines, in the absence of a Rosetta Stone, to examine the hieroglyphics in his book, and invites him to retire while it deliberates. There is silence for a moment.

'He has just added a verandah and three rooms to his already extensive house,' the Head Merchant observes at last. 'I happen to know the contractor, who charged him £700. I cannot help thinking that the past year has not been an unprofitable one for him.'

The *mamur*, always fair-minded, knows that Mr Papadopoulos is not a popular figure with his fellow-merchants. He produces all available facts and records from the clerk of the market and the returns received from other big centres. Mr Papadopoulos's retail shop's profit can be roughly calculated, since the custom of every shop in the town is a matter of common knowledge

'Thinking of soda water,' interpolates the *omda,* taking advantage of a pause while the *mamur* is adding up figures, 'a friend of mine once nearly lost an eye opening a ginger beer bottle. In those days ginger beer was new …'

5

'Ten ... sixteen ... twenty-three ... thirty-one,' breathes the *mamur*. That makes three-one-four-six. His profits cannot have been less than about £3,146, or shall we say £3,000 – which would mean a tax figure of £220. Does the board agree? Mind you, I think we are being lenient.'

The board does, and Mr Papadopoulos is recalled. On being apprised of the board's assessment his eyes roll upwards and there is a quivering about the gills. He begins an expostulation, but then checks it, and with a final *mort de ma vie* kind of shrug he turns and shuffles out of the room – from which we deduce that we have erred if anything on the side of mercy, and that he will, at most, put in a petition of remonstrance to the Governor, for form's sake, and then pay up.

So it continues. In an hour and a half the dozen traders have been dealt with, the whole list is handed to the clerk for preparation and forwarding to the *mudiria,* the provincial headquarters. We thank the members of the Board and leave the room to repair to our own office and continue the day's miscellaneous work.

The *mamur* is just ushering in a rather furtive little man whom I recognise as Hamid Effendi, the second *sarraf,* or cashier, who has come to take leave before going to Khartoum for treatment. His case has been an interesting one. Three months ago he began to have hallucinations, heard voices in his ears and saw butterflies flitting through the keyhole of the Government safe. I knew that both the voices and the lepidoptera had a partly alcoholic origin, but there was more to it than that. He had accordingly been given a month's leave and sent home, to be treated by a local *fiki,* or holy man.

The methods of suggestion and exorcism used by the *fikis* are often extremely effective in simple psychological cases, and should never be scornfully passed over. But they are the methods applied to a simple and uneducated folk, and though Hamid Effendi is young and has only an elementary education, he has become too sophisticated for them to succeed and is being sent to Khartoum, to the recently-appointed Government psychiatrist, for Freud and Jung to be given their innings.

I wish him good luck and recovery, and then send for the police officer and ask him whether there is any judicial work waiting. There is: the case of a woman arrested in possession of a still for brewing *araki,* the illicitly-distilled Blue Ruin which in various forms pervades most countries of the world. In this instance the police had been advised by an informant, probably the owner of a rival still. Their arrival to search the house had been unheralded, yet by the time a frightened girl had opened the door to them, all trace of illicit apparatus had disappeared, and a search of the premises – even a judicious prodding of the ground (incriminating evidence is often interred) – revealed nothing.

During the investigations the owner, a shocking hag with gold ear-rings and a pock-marked face, had sat unmoved on her *angareb* – a bed with wooden legs and twisted palm-fronds. She looked extremely pregnant, and when the unavailing search was finished she sneeringly asked the policeman if he were a gentleman and would condescend to leave her in peace, seeing the condition she was in. The bashful young private began to withdraw. But the police officer in charge, with whom loyalty to professional duty overrode any dictates of gallantry, overheard the words, fixed her with his one gimlet eye, estimated her age at fifty and asked whether she wanted a midwife to assist – he himself being well versed in the craft. Before she could remonstrate he had rudely disturbed the folds of her gown and brought to birth a large jorum with dregs of *araki* still in it and a two-foot pipe used in the process of distilling.

Araki cases can be tried by the town court, and this one is sent to them. But cases of illicit firearms are reserved for the District Commissioner, since few courts, Arab or African, will treat the arms problem seriously or regard the unlicensed holding or misuse of firearms as anything but a formal offence. In this instance a man of Nuba extraction has been arrested by a zealous young policeman. The weapon in question is an old Remington rifle, and though the hammer is held by wire and the foresight has been removed (many locals aver that a foresight merely obstructs the vision), it is none the less a lethal weapon, and an illegal one. The accused fortunately pleads guilty – though he will not divulge the source whence he procured the firearm – and the proceedings are quickly over.

Next comes a meeting at the Arab Girls' School, to select the annual intake of new pupils. *Sitt* [Lady] Nefisa has raised our school to a pitch of popularity which is even now proving embarrassing. It had been agreed that a proportion of the vacancies will be reserved for daughters of tribesmen outside the 'capital', and the remainder distributed among the administrative quarters of the town. But the selection of girls to fill these quotas is not so easy. Some can be eliminated as too old (there are one or two visible in the crowd whom one would guess to be of marriageable age). Some are too small; others have failed to pass the intelligence test through which *Sitt Nefisa* has put them all. Yet after these siftings there are still too many little girls – wide-eyed, clad in their best frocks and embroidered slippers and earrings, with their black hair plaited and braided, pathetically keen to be accepted, and not comprehending what the difficulty is all about. Nearly all are accompanied by their fathers, and a few by their mothers, though in elite circles many of the best women do not appear in public.

In a country where the privileges of position and birth are traditional, the barren and mechanical justice of pure competitive examination is neither thinkable nor desirable. An *omda,* a sheikh of a quarter, a senior official – such men are entitled by prestige and position to some consideration. The selection board has to steer a middle course between the granting of such arbitrary priorities and following the results of the intelligence test. The method of selection is, in fact, one of privilege tempered by examination. The results are probably as much in the public interest as any selection ever is, but it is not easy to persuade the parents of rejected children of this; and though parental intransigence can be firmly met, it is much more distressing to see some of the little candidates themselves sobbing quietly at finding themselves shut out of paradise.

We return to the office, harrowed and rather hot, to find a missionary waiting for us. He is Father Carnera, from the big Italian mission which works with the Dinka in the south of the district and in the next province. He has brought the annual returns of game shot on licence by the Mission stations, and since he is passing through, he thought he would visit me and present them in person. Being personally very interested in game, I take a quick glance through the returns. What strikes me is that, while waterbuck, cob and other inoffensive animals have been shot in some numbers, there is no record of lion, leopard, wild dog or other ravening predator being killed, which would help pay for the hoofed victims and maintain the balance. I mention this to the Father and receive the disarming and ingenuous reply: 'Sir – the Bishop does not approve of his Fathers hunting lions. They might be hurt. We are under orders not to see lions.'

There seems no answer to this, for I know the Bishop – and if I were a Father, would rather face a lion than His Lordship when disobeyed.

Before I can think of anything suitable to say, the Father adds that he has a question to ask: do I remember the well dug last year at one of their stations? I remember it clearly. The enterprising lay-brother had dug down to a certain depth and there encountered rock. In response to a request I had sent a skilful Arab expert with some dynamite. The lay-brother had admitted that he was not gifted with the *dono di coraggio,* and had run very fast when the explosions were due. This did not surprise me, for in my last district – a hilly one – we had used explosives, and the instructions which accompanied them contained seventeen paragraphs, the last of which read: 'Then light fuse and run like hell.' At all events, the explosion had created access to an excellent supply of sweet water, and the resulting well was now known as Bir Boomp.

Father Carnera informs me that his colleague Father Ignatio – a highly qualified dowser – thinks he has found water at the site of a proposed new station. The situation, however, is rocky; would I be able to oblige them with a fresh supply of dynamite? Father Ignatio's dowsings are well known. It is generally held that if a bottle of whisky were buried, he would feel its magnetism from half a mile away; his nose for water is less reliable. Nevertheless, since any increase in water supplies is a public benefaction, and since the Mission is notable for its practical enterprise and energy, I promise that if digging is started, and provided a water expert bears out Father Ignatio's intuitive prognostications, I will arrange for the necessary explosives when the time comes.

The Father departs, and the office orderly announces that two sheikhs from a section of the Baggara, or cattle-owning Arabs who stretch across the Sudan from West Africa to the Nile, are outside and would like to pay their compliments. This is a welcome interlude. Both are old friends; coffee is called for, and the next twenty minutes go in hearing and giving news – but mainly hearing. The news is about personalities and tribal politics, serious and scurrilous, grave and Rabelaisian. It drifts on to the prospects of elephant- hunting down on the river, and other things blissfully divorced from offices, education, finance, law and the whole gamut of concerns with which civilisation depresses itself.

In fact there is more to talk about than we can well deal with at the moment, so I invite them to come to tea at the house in the afternoon. To finish the morning I pick up a little sheaf of petitions which lies on the desk. The petition is largely a relic of the days of direct administration. It costs the petitioner five piastres, or one shilling, unless he can write, in which case it costs him three piastres, the price of a stamped Government sheet of paper on which the subject is inscribed; the other two piastres go to the petition-writer, who sits outside the offices and earns a livelihood by scribing for the illiterate. Petitioners are usually suspect and unwelcome. But the institution has its merits; first because there is the occasional injustice or malpractice going on which is thus brought to light and put right; and second, because complaints and applications flooding in to headquarters from the perimeter give one very useful indications of the happiness or unhappiness, prosperity or indigence, the political trends or administrative needs in many a quarter of the district.

First today we have two or three building petitions. When a man wishes to erect a new building or add to his house in the town, there are various aspects to be considered – availability of site, public health, and whether he had a real *raison d'être* in the town at all (for here, as elsewhere, the drift to urban centres is a persistent problem and has to be guarded against). One notes the place and quarter and tells the petitioner to be on the spot at 7 a.m. on Monday, when the weekly Town Ride is held and when these matters will be decided on the spot, with the necessary experts present - the *omda*, the police officer, a medical representative, and the indispensable *mamur*. These are the hard-working deities who guard the populace against overcrowding, uproar, unsightliness, bad hats, stinks and all other goblins which menace urban amenities. If the petition passes their scrutiny, it will be approved.

Next comes a merchant who wishes to raise a suit against another for a considerable sum. The man is a reasonable citizen; the defendant is reputed to be a twister. This is a straightforward case for the law, the petition itself a necessary formality, and the petitioner is allowed to file a suit, to be heard on his next visit by the district judge.

Here comes an Arab, from a village on our Northern borders where the desert meets the sown, and his plea is damage to his crops by the hordes of camels of our nomad neighbours in the next District. It is the age-old cry, heard since the days of Abraham and Lot, the cry of a man who has a stake in the unrewarding soil under a spasmodic and meagre rainfall, and who sees his hard-won livelihood reduced or even annihilated by the animal wealth of the shiftless Ishmaelites, to whom there are no boundaries, no ties of the soil and who, when grazing or water are exhausted in one quarter, may seek them 200 miles in another direction and at another neighbour's expense.

The nomad may be a romantic figure, but he is on the whole more of a destroyer than a producer, and his very mobility makes him the headache of the administrator and the plague of his often unwilling host. The only chance of obtaining redress is at the annual inter-district meeting, where officers and sheikhs, complainants and defendants from both sides of the border meet for several days. The meeting is already fixed for March, and we send our man back with a letter to his *omda* to have him, and any other similar complainants, fit and smiling in the ring at the appointed time, while we write to his neighbour's district asking him to do the same on his side. Redress cannot be prompt, but with patience it may be obtained.

What is the next complaint? About an *omda*? The petitioner is a sour-visaged man with a grizzled goatee beard and an expression that would curdle milk, and his very dirty jibba is not savoury. It appears that the *omda* who reigns over the hilly north-west corner of the district and has more scallywags per square mile to cope with than any other similar authority, has taken all his animals, imprisoned him unjustly, beaten him illegally and razed his house to the ground. Asked what is the cause of this barbarous and shocking treatment, he replies that he has not a notion – the *omda* 'just did it'.

When a petitioner refuses to assign any reason for the events of which he complains, it is an almost certain sign that (a) he is lying, and (b) he is in the wrong and, knowing it, fears to reveal too much. Besides, this man's name, Ibrahim el Kinein, is vaguely familiar. I know the *omda* for a good one, wily, sometimes unscrupulous in method but honest in purpose, loyal to the Nazir and with most engaging manners as well as no mean powers of blarney, a strong and valuable personality. I rapidly extract from the confidential cupboard a file which contains the records and personality sheets of every notable in the district and look him up to see the opinions of my predecessors. 'A wise and vigorous ruler, though I would not always guarantee his methods, A.K.F. 1933.' 'A mixture of Falstaff, Mulvaney, and a company promoter, but a most valuable man. T.B.M. 1938.' One predecessor has even burst into doggerel in the margin:

> *In El Mardi Iman*
> *There are subtle attractions.*
> *I find definite charm*
> *In El Mardi Imam,*
> *And his manners disarm*
> *My mistrust of his actions...*

Ah, here we have it: 'Has suffered much from the dissident faction of the Kinein family; needs backing; see File 45 for full details. S.T.B. 1939.' The petitioner is told that he can be given a letter to the Nazir if he likes, with a request for a full inquiry and report, but that if his charges prove baseless or exaggerated, he will go before the tribal court on a charge of false accusation and fomenting disloyalty. Knowing what he would get, he retires with a few final expostulations and a scowl.

I send for File 45, and with that and sundry letters which will require the drafting of answers, I leave the office with a sigh of relief, since the clock has struck two and it is time for lunch and that brief siesta which wiser men normally seek of an afternoon at Latitude 12 in the tropic of Cancer.

To his sister Elisabeth   June 1927

I've just been sitting on a court at my first murder trial, an interesting though far from pleasant procedure. It was over a woman ... and the man, a Dinka, had eventually murdered, under particularly nasty circumstances, both a man and a boy. Even such a solemn procedure as this you have to hold in the most informal way possible – in your shirtsleeves, in an open room, with the witnesses giving their evidence sitting in their place, and all the neighbourhood sheikhs crowding round, to get an idea of Government methods.

There is no repeating of formulas, or counsel's speeches or assumption of the black cap, and so on. The reason is that the savage, though perfectly honest (he hasn't the brains for scientific lying) is amazingly stupid, and if brought up outside his ken or put suddenly

12

in strange surroundings, will merely lose his head and say the first thing that comes into it.

The oath is administered on the spear which, though they have nothing you could term a religion, is not unnaturally an important object in their daily life, hedged round with lots of superstitions and symbolic significance. The witness licks the spear, then spits on his chest and draws the point of the spear across his chest, passes it round his head, and the oath is complete.

Diary 26 July 1928

Morning nearly all taken up with a case of hashish etc. One prisoner, a tall, powerful bad-hat of an Egyptian, had got his guard to go and obtain hash for him, and was found raving, with rolling eyes and violent convulsions, in his ward room. That was all plain – and the bloke in the suk who possessed the hashish was pinched, and he too pleaded guilty; but there was also evidence that the policeman, and the prisoner too, had been drinking araki; and the policeman anyway was a rotter and had misconducted himself with the prisoners. Got it pretty well established that the guard had been for araki, and jugged him as well as the others.

To his father   16 January 1933
Sinkat

Ibex come down to the lower slopes to feed by night, retiring upwards to the cloud-line to spend the day; so you have got to start off by night and take up your position well above them.

Up at 3.30, therefore, and off before 4, with an elderly Fuzzy as guide, and a younger ditto to carry field-glasses, water-bottle, a sweater and a Jaeger dressing gown. The latter may sound odd paraphernalia for hunting, but Sanders (who is a Bisley shot) on Jebel Akareiriba a fortnight ago missed three shots running at an ibex simply because he was too cold to hold the rifle properly – and very glad was I later for having had the warning!

We climbed up a precipitous peak at one end of the *jebel* to within 200 feet of the top (which is 5,000 feet) and there chose our shelter. It was only just after five, and still quite dark, with the Southern Cross still showing, and the clouds were settling down fast on the hill tops. At about sunrise (6 a.m.) the thirty Fuzzies who had been scraped up overnight began their manoeuvrings from a mile and two miles away.

Nothing at all happened for an hour; the clouds swept down on us, and the mist thickened and faded intermittently. And then there was the clatter of one loose stone, and the old man, Musa, pointed down the precipitous slope, and there were two ibex, stock still. I might have had a shot at over 200 yards, but refrained – luckily, for as the ram skipped off, he displayed a half-grown head.

Nothing more for a full hour, save that one could hear the Fuzzies working the hillside and corries, and coming nearer, and I began to fear it was going to be a frost. And then quite suddenly they were there: three clattered by far below, two others came loping towards the gully over which we sat and looked as if they were going to turn up it and come right under us, but tacked and went over a spur.

Quite without warning a ram appeared straight ahead and a bit above us, followed by a larger one. The smaller one turned up hill, the larger disappeared, walking towards us into a little dip that hid him. A breathless moment … and he was there, a frontal shot at 120 yards, his heavy head a grand sight. The bullet took him fairly at the base of the neck, and he slid down thirty feet of rock and never stirred. A pretty head, of only average length, just under thirty-six inches, but of fine shape and thickness. I've seldom had a more exciting or enjoyable morning.

To his sister Elizabeth   26 April 1933
Sinkat

The Setit is lovely country, no positive mountains, but the river running under high, steep banks and often thickly-wooded, precipitous hillsides with great crags of limestone rock jutting out among them and reminding me of nothing so much as the Seven Sisters stretch of the Wye near Symonds Yat. There are running shallows, over pebbly ground, where you can enjoy a good wallow, though you can't venture into deep water for a swim, owing to the crocs.

Bird life is abundant – great fishing eagles with snowy breasts and chocolate-coloured wings, white egrets that fly in wedge formation like geese and turn all pink in slanting evening sun, herons, ibis, smaller birds of colours as pure and vivid as those of a Saxon illuminated text, and guinea fowl innumerable, which here represent an easily acquired and very toothsome meal.

CHAPTER TWO

The Rest of the Day is Your Own

The afternoon siesta is not a mere foible of the Mediterranean race. In a tropical climate the most Nordic individual is well advised to pander to his own weakness and take that short period of hot-hour oblivion which makes a big difference to health and staying power. You can take a file or two to bed with you to study, if conscience needs any laying – and the soporific effect of urgent Government correspondence is irresistible.

Today, when this interlude is over, the first necessary activity is to have the monthly haircut. High-class barbers are not easily found outside Khartoum, and not always there. But in most stations there will be one or two practitioners, and the District Commissioner's head is a scalp for which there will be competition. Barbers are on the whole a likeable if rather eccentric race.

One of whom I was fond was periodically in gaol, for beating his wife or for assaulting his *bête noire,* the chief butcher, and used to be sent for from the prison, whence he would come with gyves on his wrist and operate, on my verandah, with a guard standing beside him with a fixed bayonet. The clanking of the handcuffs was slightly disturbing, but his manipulation of the scissors was unaffected. When for any reason he was unprocurable, his place had to be taken by an amateur, and there were two alternatives. One was the *bête noire* himself, who tackled a mop of hair with the same zeal, and in much the same style, as he would cut up a bullock. The other, slightly preferable one, was the chief accountant. Yaisi Effendi was always ready to oblige a fellow official. But I think there was a streak of the sadist or the paranoiac in his particular form of barberism. He had been passed-over for promotion, and the way he handled the horse-clippers (he despised scissors) suggested that he was trying to get his own back on Life for the wrong it had done him.

He never actually mutilated me; but when he could not make the hair come right, he did what he always did with his accounts - made it come wrong. One usually emerged looking like one of those old-fashioned Japanese dolls, with a flat mat of hair sticking out like a sweep's brush from the crown and a shaven skull underneath it. Since most of the hair from the crown had been dropped down inside the shirt-collar, one had a very good notion of what the old-time penitent or palmer endured who habitually wore a hair-shirt next to the skin.

Our present barber's only weakness is for the bottle (he is not a Muslim, but a semi-Christian from the south). For patronising his services a mid-week day must be chosen, because on Friday he will be preparing for Saturday, on Saturday he will be drunk, on Sunday drunker, on Monday not emerged and on Tuesday emerging. On Thursdays his head is clearest and his hand steadiest, but on Wednesdays his tongue is most loosened, and I hear a deal of gossip, scandal and rumour which no intelligence service would afford.

The ordeal over, I issue, and since it will be a little time before the two sheikhs come for tea, walk past the aerodrome to the football ground. The corners of the landing-field, which it is the duty of the *merkaz* to keep up, are very white indeed, and closer inspection will show that they are not made of cement with a coat of whitewash but from accumulated bones. We once told an American airman that they were the bones of pilots who had tried to land on the ground - and not tried again. He was inclined to believe us. Actually they were the bones of camels, gathered by prisoners and arranged tastefully by the *mamur*. Nothing is quite so glisteringly white as dry bones.

On the football ground there is a match in progress, the *merkaz* team playing against a side from an Intermediate school thirty miles away. As I arrive, play is held up, the ball having been lofted and landed in an acacia tree of the tallest variety, and since brickbats have failed to disengage it, one of the players has ascended the tree to recover it. This achieved, the game progresses and there is some fast and accomplished football: many Sudanese schools turn out skilful and very competent teams.

The *merkaz* team however, with its extra weight and on a sandy ground, is one goal up at present. At this moment an apparent equalizing goal is scored, but is given off-side. It did not look to me to be off-side and during the half-time interval which follows soon afterwards, I say as much to the police officer who is refereeing, but his reply – 'I was not certain myself, Sir. I therefore considered it my duty to give the benefit of the doubt to Government' – admits of neither criticism nor argument.

Early on in the second half the equalizing goal cannot be gainsaid. The weakest link in the *merkaz* team is the goal-keeper, who is the head dresser at the hospital and whose principal virtue as a player is that he as nearly fills the goal as is humanly possible. He had taken a previous goal-kick and had been enveloped in a cloud of sand and dust, on whose dissolution the ball was seen to be reposing unmoved. He had therefore tried punting the next, but the ball had described a parabola over his left shoulder and trickled through the corner of the goal. But with honours even and the onlookers feverishly excited, I must leave the game and return to the house to meet my two Baggara guests.

Teacups loosen the tongue, and talk ranges over many things: giraffe-hunting, tribal customs, history and personalities. I ask why a certain young man, a cousin of the Nazir's, has become a clerk to one of the courts, and receive the nonchalant answer, 'Oh, the Nazir found that he couldn't catch a giraffe on horseback, so he was sent to school instead!' This leads us on to the question of courage and of 'guts', and here, embarking on a story myself, I find myself landed in a language difficulty on realizing that there is no colloquial Arabic translation for 'moral courage'. The very idea is foreign to ordinary Arab temperament, and to express it one has to get round it. What I want to ask my friends is whether, in common with most of humanity, they are greater moral cowards than physical? – not that I have any doubt of the true answer, for there can be few braver or more daring races than the Baggara.

The realisation of my own abject moral cowardice was first brought home to me by a snake. The place was a large rest-house in the Eastern Sudan, and I had made the usual after-breakfast pilgrimage. I had closed the door behind me and was enthroned, when something caught my eye. Looking at the door, six feet in front of my face, I beheld a large, saw-scaled viper, the species which causes more deaths than any other in the Northern Sudan and was probably the prototype of Conan Doyle's

Speckled Band. He had been lying along the top of the door when I entered underneath him, and when the door closed he had nipped between door and lintel. His head and a foot of him were wriggling venomously above the latch. The other foot, of tail, was lashing out towards the hinge.

Now there were two courses open. One was to lift the latch, gingerly open the door and try to scuttle through it before he dropped down my neck. The other was to remove the bucket from beneath me and emerge through the bucket-hole, stern first, in front of my servants in the kitchen block just behind the house. Probable death? Or certain dishonour? Moral cowardice prevailed. I chose the former, and survived, *grace à dieu*. The snake did not.

My guests agree that, like me, they would certainly have faced the serpent. In fact they do not worry very much about serpents. The only snake that they have been taught to fear is the *um guttiya,* 'he of the crest', which inhabits the larger hills of the Nuba mountains some way to the east of us. I know something about *um guttiyas.* When, after the battle of Omdurman, the Khalifa escaped southwards, he took up his residence on the edge of the Nuba mountains.

On one occasion he was thinking of making a raid with his cavalry upon the big, southernmost hill of Elliri. A Nuba merchant, one Daldum, recounted to me how he had visited the Khalifa and dissuaded him from any such move (to the salvation of Elliri), on the grounds that, glad as the people would be to welcome him, they were infested by a particularly dangerous and aggressive breed of serpents. These were three times as long as a man, could erect a crest on their heads, moved faster than a horse and left tracks of burnt grass behind them. Their only ally was the firefly, which would attach itself to their forehead, like a miner's torch, when they were hunting in the deep caves, and in return was never molested. If there was one thing calculated to rouse these monsters and bring them on the warpath, it was the galloping of a horse.

Without taking friend Daldum too seriously, there was no question of the people's belief in this monster, and their fear of it. A doctor, who was also a celebrated ophiologist, had offered a reward for any specimen, but nothing had been forthcoming. In 1939, however, when I was staying at Elliri, the dresser in the dispensary casually informed me that a dead *um guttiya* had just been brought in. It had attacked three men who were hunting hyrax, or rock-rabbits, up the mountain side. It had bitten two, both of whom had died rapidly, but the third had killed it with a timely back-hander from his spear. Would I like to see it?

It was an evil-looking, blackish-brown serpent, thin and well over eight feet long, though reputed to be quite a small specimen. It was placed in pickle and sent to our expert in Khartoum, from whom a jubilant letter came a week or two later to say that this was the first genuine Black Mamba, *Dendroaspis angusticeps,* obtained from the Sudan.[1]

After a good deal more chat and exchange of news, the two guests take their leave and I am free to have a bath. This is not to be a peaceful evening, for my wife and I have been invited to the christening of the daughter of the head of the Syrian Community. The Community is a most friendly and worthy one, comprising some of the best of the merchants, and we have gratefully accepted. The priest, *Père* Emilienne, is an old acquaintance, with a deep and impressive beard, lively eyes and a vast nose rising above the foliage like a shoulder of Lebanon through its cedar forests.

At these ceremonies one is always struck, by the mixture of the refined and beautiful with the tawdry. The priest's cope is of an intricate embroidery, which is exquisite. The altar cloth in the church is always seemly. On the altar itself are a couple of dirty tin candlesticks and a candle stuck in an old beer bottle. The address is in fine, lucid Arabic, every word intelligible; the prayers largely a rigmarole of a monkish variety which I am glad to find foxes quite a lot even of the Syrians. Doubtless if Cicero had been condemned to listen to a High Mass in medieval Latin, he would not have recognised in it the finest flowers of the language he had wielded.

The proceedings of the christening itself are held in the house, not the church. We are dressed as for a dance, rather than as for a religious function. A kitchen table stands in the middle with a tin bath on it. The godmother, wearing a silk dress of an apoplectic plum colour and draped in a towel, holds the baby, a most complacent and cheery little lady. After reading the service, *Père* Emilienne takes her, christens her with holy oil on

---

1   *Dendroaspis angusticeps* is now classed as the Eastern Green Mamba, a separate species from the Black Mamba, *Dendroaspis polylepis.*

forehead, eyes, mouth, chest, stomach and legs, then plunges her firmly into the bath and sponges her down. Since even that produces scarcely a protest, she is pinched to make her emit a yowl sufficient to drive the devil out. After that she is handed around to be kissed and admired, and then we settle down to coffee, nuts, sweet and sticky cakes and excellent brandy.

There is entertainment as well. A speech of welcome is well and clearly recited by a very fat little girl dressed in a boy's shirt, tight knickers and a cardboard Greek military helmet. There is singing, by a visitor from Provincial Headquarters with a really fine bass voice. There is also a sword-dance by Naaman, the Syrian brother-in-law of our host. Naaman had fought in the French army in various parts of Africa and in various bloody battles, but, according to his own ingenuous tales, he had run away more swiftly than anybody else, and so had survived every encounter. His most military activity now is a sword dance. With half a bottle of brandy inside him he is worth watching, and his virtuosity, with feet and sword arm simultaneously, a delight to follow. It constantly looks if his own or somebody else's ear or head must be sliced off, but nobody is any the worse at the end of it.

The usual elite of the commercial and official community are all gathered here, and I find myself discussing the possibility of a locust invasion, of which we have been warned. The locust breeds in the early rains. When his eggs hatch out after several weeks, there emerge 'hoppers', no larger than big, blackish ants. In the course of the next six weeks the hordes of hoppers march, grow and change their yellowish garments several times until, as full-grown, winged and now purplish locusts four inches long, they inflate themselves and float off into the sky in their billions to carry desolation across the map of Africa.

I know of no more devastating phenomenon, nothing more calculated to drive man to manic depression, than the sight of those evil purple clouds hanging low upon the horizon, in wisps and streaks and masses, and to ride the next day and see sterile dearth where the finest corn in twenty years had smiled a few hours before. The courage, fatalistic and yet optimistic, of the populace always won my admiration, and they would pass the disaster off with the proverbial saying 'Year of the locusts, year of grain in plenty' – which has a substratum of truth, for the heavy rains needed to hatch out the predatory swarms also ensure a heavy and full-headed millet crop.

Up to the middle 1920s there was no method of meeting the enemy better than to attack the hoppers with branches and brooms, or drive them into trenches and bury them – a method which left a hundred survivors for every victim. Driving them on to bushes in a dense mass, pouring petrol over the bush and setting light to it in an *auto da fé* was clumsy at best, wasteful of fuel, wasteful of vegetation, and all-but cost one valuable human life at least.

Grievous as are the visitations of the common or Desert Locust, more serious still is the rarer but all-voracious Hairy-chested Locust. The Chief Merchant recalled the invasion of this pest in 1929: 'I was cultivating that year, and I had gone out to my plot and put my clothes down (it was a hot day) and set to work to hoe. At that moment down came the locusts. They settled on my grain, and stayed there two hours. I was distraught. At the end of that time they all rose and passed on – and do you know? They had never touched a head or a stalk of grain. But when I went for my clothes, I couldn't find them, and had to go home in my pants. The locusts had eaten every shred.'

Hearing this, the irrepressible *omda* lent across and said, 'That's nothing. They came again in 1931. I was visiting a relation at Sennar, and I went out with him to help cultivate – just like you. We became a bit sleepy and lay down under a tree, and the brutes came and settled on our cultivation for three hours. They were all round us and all over us. They never touched a head of millet, but when I woke after my snooze and got up to go, I found they had shaved my beard clean off.'

The *omda* is a difficult man to cap, but after a second of stupefied silence the doctor says he has heard that there is a Western tribe who have an occult power over the locusts and are employed to keep them off. They are known as *dambaris*, and are more of a guild than an actual tribe, and their power is hereditary. A reputable practitioner, in a year when locusts are expected – i.e. one of heavy rains and moist conditions, for which the *dambaris* seem to have an uncanny nose in advance – will wander eastwards and take up residence with some community, who welcome and reward his services.

Certain taboos are laid on the village – food, plants and other things which the people must not touch during the critical months. The *dambari* himself must eat no new food, only last year's grain and old vegetables, and even old eggs; he must also, like Sampson, let no razor touch his head or beard until the danger is past. He sleeps on the open hillside or sand-dunes, and can hear the locusts coming from afar.

I once had personal experience of a *dambari* at work. The time was September, when the mature hoppers are spreading their wings and moving eastwards in search of vegetation to devour. The normal procedure for a swarm is to rise and fly when the sun grows warm, to alight on their prey in the late afternoon, and to spend the night ravaging.

At about 4 pm I rode into a village just as the *dambari* who had been induced to reside there was ascending the rocky knoll above the houses. He was a small, insignificant man. In one hand he carried his beads, and in the other his wand, which was festooned with fowls' feathers, papers bearing Koranic texts and one or two fine ostrich feathers at the tip. A swarm of locusts was already approaching from the north-west, and, standing on the knoll he prayed and gently waved his wand across their path.

The swarm came flying low, as it does when looking for an area to settle on, then slowly descended upon the acacia scrub in the wadi, blotting out the foliage beneath its myriads. A second approaching swarm was already visible, and this too he waved at, almost like a policeman directing traffic. The mass passed over the cultivations and dropped onto the bare sand dune beyond them, the dune turning dark purple under them. Then there was a considerable interval. But as the sun fell low a third powerful swarm appeared, coming from due north. Once more he executed his passes. On reaching the village the swarm swerved off westwards and disappeared into the sunset. Sheer chance? Possibly. But what influence sent the swine down the declivity at Gadara? Next day I was intrigued to find that a neighbouring village and a different *dambari* were complaining about our practitioner, because whenever locusts were about, he infallibly re-directed the swarms into their territory.

From locust magic we turn to occult fire-raising, which is another of those phenomena which leave the inquirer half-sceptical, half-wondering. There are occasional *fikis* or holy men who are credited with the power of wishing a fire upon the house of any person, however distant, who has crossed them or who merits divine visitation, and some of the cases are hard to explain away. At other times fires occur, usually at regular intervals, which seem to pursue certain persons and are put down to the agency of spirits.

Such a series had just been taking place in the *merkaz*. Admittedly fires are easily enough and frequently enough caused where only the better houses are of solid material and the humbler habitations are built of wood, grass, and dry millet stalks. But even so a fire must have someone to kindle it. A police corporal, Ahmed Omar, had married a young woman who had a reputation for being fey. Two years ago exactly the hut she was sleeping in went up in flames, without assignable reason. The following year, on the anniversary of the previous holocaust, 15 January, the hut she used as a kitchen again went up in smoke. This would be likely enough, in the case of a kitchen, except that there was no fire lit in it and the hut was disused.

Three days ago, on 16 January, at 1.30 pm her kitchen hut, which again was unused since they were messing with friends, once more caught fire. The woman had no particular enemies or ill-wishers; people were all round about the hut at the time, and nobody had been seen to enter. We had heard the fire-bugle from the offices and had run to the police lines, to find the fire well under weigh. The corporal, feeling unsafe, sagely removed his chattels from his living hut and parked them under a tree until such time as this be-devilment should cease.

Yesterday we had again heard the fire-bugle, at exactly 1.30, and sure enough there was Ahmed Omar's hut roaring to high heaven. The burnt-out lady had been sitting in it chatting with two other police wives. It was empty of stuff. A moment before the half hour, a third neighbour had looked in and said, 'Well, praise be, the fires seem to be finished now.' She had scarcely begun to speak on some other subject when they looked up: the roof was alight at the peak, and though they rushed out and shrieked for assistance, it was too late. Perhaps when psychical investigation has explained poltergeists, usually associated with adolescents and unhappy relations in a house, we may have a clearer notion of what kindled the fires.

The doctor diverts us from speculation by describing the conditions in Saudi Arabia, where he has been at Jeddah, working on secondment during the annual pilgrimage with the Sudan Medical Mission, which helps to look after Sudan and other pilgrims and has won golden opinions in the medical world. He had not actually met the great King Ibn al Saud, but had dealt mainly with the King's sixth son (out of a reputed 137) who was titular Minister for War but despite his martial duties proved of so religious a cast that it was difficult to transact mundane business with him – until at a reception he got his teeth stuck in a piece of Turkish delight and the whole set came out, after which the other-worldly facade had vanished and business had gone smoothly.

But by this time it is getting late. The refreshments have been good, the company enjoyable. Our hostess, who has paid personal attention to every guest of whatever creed, race or status, must be feeling somewhat worn (the little lady who provided the occasion for the gathering has long since been whisked off to her well-deserved cot). We take our leave and plod homewards through the sandy side-streets under a luminous full moon and go thankfully to bed.

To his father   4 June 1933
Sinkat

Native court punishments are sometimes of an unorthodox kind. Two young women of the Gemilab section of the Hadendowa tribe gallivanted with two young irresponsibles of another section. While the men each got a year [in gaol] from the Nazir, it is hard to know what to do with the women. Prison is unsuitable and demoralizing for nomad women, and would be considered a great disgrace by the tribe. On the other hand, if they were allowed to go back unpunished, they would almost certainly be killed by their brothers – whose duty by tribal custom is to strangle women who deliberately go wrong.

The Nazir solves it by shaving the women's heads! It is the biggest disgrace in the eyes of the tribe that a woman can suffer; it does not subject them to a demoralizing period, like prison, by taking them away from the tribal atmosphere and associating them with men and with the female riff-raff of Kassala, old hags doing time for distilling illicit liquor and black Sudan's courtesans.

25

To his father   17 September 1933
Sinkat

It is a standing puzzle to our sheikhs why we do not go and conquer
Eritrea, seeing that it a pleasant and very healthy hilly territory, and
fertile in spots. 'You have got the Eastern Arab Corps sitting there
in Kassala,' they say, 'and British troops at Gegeit. What's the use of
them? If you'd like Eritrea, why not go over and take it?'

CHAPTER THREE

The Arab Leader

I think the best way of looking at the Arab population of the Northern Provinces is to visit a few of the chief men of the tribes and local governments. For one thing, although a District Commissioner had to be accessible to all, and should – and did – associate with men of every stratum of society, in the nature of things his most important and frequent contacts were with these big men. For another, the government of a nation or the head of a community is a very good mirror of that community's aspirations, standards, and outlook. Some of the Arabs have a proverb, 'A dead fish begins stinking at the head first', the purport of which is roughly the same as Bonaparte's when he said that 'There is no such thing as a bad army. There are only bad officers'. It is the leaders who count. If they are rotten, the body politic will rot, and if they are sound, the flock need not fear.

Arab organization sixty years ago was exceedingly loose. The word 'sheikh' denoted the head of a section or an eminent man, without reference to size or importance: the section might be a mere half-dozen nomadic families, or a great and powerful tribe. The word could also denote a man of learning and was, in fact, virtually a title of respect. In all the works of the old travellers the word is thus found in its true, and loose, significance. One sheikh might owe allegiance to another, but the title did not differentiate between them.

Closer administration and organization demanded something rather more defined, and there gradually arose a system throughout the provinces whereby the word 'sheikh', though it still might pertain to a man of greater or more meagre weight, and was still used as a courtesy title, represented in the official hierarchy the smallest administrative unit, a single village or a single clan. Next above him came the *omda*, a term imported from Egypt, with variant terms in some Provinces such as Shartai or Sheikh el Khatt, whose authority extended over a number of sheikhs. Above him, at the apex of the pyramid, came the Nazir, a really big man whose command might cover a wide territorial area or a great tribe.

Good administration does not break. It adapts and modifies. When the time came, about the close of the first quarter of the century, to end direct administration and to devolve powers and responsibilities as the first step in the process which would lead to self-administration and eventual independence, these Arab authorities were the primary and most obvious channels for such devolution and were successfully used. But conditions are not static. Most of the Nazirs, and virtually all the old ones, were uneducated men. That made them none the less respected or effective under the conditions of previous days; but would they be able to move with the times, to cope with more complicated machinery and heavier responsibility, to survive against an increasingly-powerful urban intelligentsia, to maintain their status while the tribalism of a past generation metamorphosed itself steadily into a territorial set-up of local governments?

That they did successfully go through this process was due partly to the sheer character and adaptability of these remarkable men, partly to the loyalty and respect felt by their people for their persons and for the divinity which (as Hamlet says) 'doth hedge a king', and partly because the rising generation of potential leaders, the sons and relatives of the reigning houses, went through the educational mill and came out, for the most part, a generation of Januses who could look to their tribesmen and had not lost their touch and sympathy, yet through their education could also look at the demands of modern civilization and politics without flinching.

Tribalism has immense survival value and will remain for decades or even centuries the basis of Arab life. But more and more the big Nazirs have ceased to be mere traditional tribal nabobs and tended to become the corner-stone of amalgamations of differing peoples fusing together in large local government units.

A word about the Arab conception of headship. It has never been formalized, never rationalized into a political theory, and is one of the most elusive ideas, defying close definition. Its bases are in the Arab character, a deep feudal loyalty, a firm belief in the hereditary principle (though not necessarily primogeniture) a powerful attraction to personality rather than office, a deference to public opinion and reputation, and a strong sense of obligation in the ruler towards his subjects – all set in that background of belief in brotherhood and common humanity which is the gift of Islam.

These elements produce a hybrid system, which partakes of feudalism yet with much greater liberty to the individual than was ever the mark of European feudalism. It might best be summed up as autocracy tempered by public opinion. Provided the head of a tribe upheld the tribe's interests and exhibited the qualities traditionally admired – courage, generosity, equity, and above all sheer personality – there was little that his subjects would not endure from him. If he failed in those qualities, loyalty would wane, ties loosen and either the headship would pass through pressure of public opinion to more acceptable and competent hands, or else the tribe would split and new swarms would hive off under different leaders. No better example of this Semitic tendency can be found than the history of early Israel, where the popularity of a David or the wisdom of a Solomon could unite a fissile people, yet the moment such a personality ceased to exist, the exactions of a Rehoboam split the kingdom in two.

Let us therefore look at a few of these individuals who are the pivots of society and one of the pillars of administration. The first is one of the old school, Radi Kambal, Nazir of the Aulad Hemeid, a section of the Baggara or cattle-owning Arabs West of the White Nile. His people, like all Baggara, are seasonally nomadic; in the dry season, fly-free and droughty, they move southward to the river where watering is easy, where the rich, short grass grows, and where they border on the Shilluk and Dinka of the Southern Provinces.

In the summer when rains and flies drive them north, they will move across two hundred miles of country to the undulating, sandy central Sudan, among settled Arab villages, where they will purvey milk to the towns and hubs of population. But the Nazir's command, once confined to his own tribe, has now taken in other elements, and is itself the bigger half of a still larger and viable Local Government unit. In that command are included another Baggara tribe, the Hawazma, cousins to the Aulad Hameid and, as so often with cousins, usually at odds with them. There is also a considerable group of settled and cultivating Arabs, the Kawahla; and a further group of half-cultivating, half-pastoral Arabs, the Kenana; a body of arabicized ex-slaves, a rather debased half-Arab, half-negroid crew; and several little isolated hills of Nuba – the black, negroid, pagan race who seem as nearly impervious to Islam, Christianity, and progressive civilization as human material can be.

Radi Kambal, who fought against the British at Omdurman, is now nearing seventy, and his type will not be found again. Loyalty is its keynote, and patriarchy its creed. He always has been and still is a perfectly honest friend of and believer in the Government he serves. Politics as such do not interest him. He has worked with the British, trusts them and will go on doing so. When war broke out in 1939 he sent a telegram of loyal adherence to the Governor. It ran, 'God is with the democracies. I am on His side'.

To be with him in his encampment in the early years of the war was a memorable experience. At the time of the evening prayer his henchmen and tribesmen would line up with their prayer-mats and he would lead them. In addition to the dignified devotions of his creed he would utter special prayers for the success of the Allied cause and call down celestial blessing on the heads of Choorch-heel, Rooss-feel and other leaders. Then, transferring his stance from Mount Ebal to Mount Gerizim, he would launch into a commination service and invoke such a blistering curse upon the heads of Hitler and his gang as a mediaeval Pope could not have bettered. Whether it was all canonically correct according to the code of Islam, I have never been certain, but it was spontaneous and impressive.

Loyalty with him extended to every personal relation. I once went hunting along with a keen young man who was a clerk in Radi's entourage. I was armed with a small-bore rifle, as Radi knew. The boy, El Safi, carried a twelve-bore shotgun. We were lucky enough to stumble on a lioness at close quarters. She was sitting behind a thin bush, and a grey ant-tump, between us and her, suddenly rose from the short grass and disclosed itself as a lion. While the lady made off, I shot the lion, very fortunately (and by an inaccurate snapshot) through the spine.

Only afterwards did I learn from the lad that the fowling-piece was Radi's; that he was under minute instructions, when the lion charged the

District Commissioner, to wait until he could see the whites of its eyes and then discharge the right barrel into its left eye and the left barrel into its right. If anything happened to the District Commissioner, he would be held personally responsible and might be skinned.

Radi's patriarchy extended to his people and was perhaps most marked in his dealings with the Nuba, whom he treated as backward and slightly comic children, to be borne with, cared for and jollied along into the proper course. In administrative matters his word was law. If the presence of rinderpest made it inadvisable for his tribe to go as far as the Province capital in the rains, he would issue instructions accordingly, and if any clan were rash enough to disobey him, his reaction was likely to be to impose a heavy fine of cattle on the offending section. Whether it was legal, no sea-lawyer ever queried. It was expedient, and it was just - and it was Radi's word.

Probably a Radi regime is the nearest thing to successful feudalism that the world has to show. Of course it is passing, and probably has passed, with the old man himself, by now. Yet it has been a potent factor in the making of the modern Sudan and the spirit which inspired it is still active, modified to meet modern needs.

Let us look at another type, another old-school instance but a contrast to Radi. When the head of the Hassania, who live a mainly settled life on both sides of the White Nile, died in the twenties with 'devolution' impending as a policy, the authorities were in a quandary. The main stem of the royal house was almost dead, and any survivor impossible, even in the tribe's eyes. In accepting a head, the people would not go further than the cadet branch of the royal house; and a leader, however able or loyal, cannot function effectively if he is a mere 'dog of the Government' and has not at least a measure of acceptance from his subjects. Youth and brains were, at that period, still somewhat suspect in Arab eyes; yet among the elders of the family there was never a man with the qualities of leadership. Government was in a difficulty.

The man pitched on is AbdelGader. He is the senior man of the family and the only one whom the tribe will unitedly accept, and we find him in his mud-built village East of the Nile. He is already elderly and it is unlikely that his reign will be a very long one. It is an 'off' hour in the afternoon, with no press of business, and AbdelGader emerges from his house with a large plate of cat's-meat in his hand and the Arabic equivalent of, 'Puss, puss' on his lips accompanied by an entourage of eleven cats, which keep down not only mice but scorpions and other noxious pests in his quarters. For AbdelGader is the kindliest of men and one of the holiest, and will shortly be at his most natural and his happiest leading the prayers. Of the art of ruling he has little, and of the temper of the ruler nothing. Subordinate *omdas* and sheikhs also doubtless have the feeling that with a weak man at the wheel they will have a very much better time of it.

The Nazir is probably seen to best advantage when sitting in court. Even here he can cause headaches, for his nature is one which carries compromise to extremes. In all disputes compromise is of the essence of Arab procedure, but when there has been a serious killing, one cannot in the twentieth century expect all the parties to pay £100 of blood-money and shake hands all round as if nothing more need be done. AbdelGader's favourite method in any case, civil or criminal, is to avoid a clear-cut decision, to gather a force of *fikis*, whose aura of slightly musty sanctity commands respect, and to negotiate an agreed conclusion in which neither party gets quite what they want but nobody is badly done down. Unsuitable though this may be to our hard, legal minds, most of what appear to us criminal cases are regarded by the Arabs as torts, or civil wrongs, and the AbdelGader method usually secures fair equity and is not on the whole unpopular.

But although there is little enough of the *Führer* about the Nazir, the withered stem has green shoots. His brother is a rake, but his son and his nephew alike have character and ability and are being given education. Moreover there are trustworthy elders who will help him with counsel and support. He has, with a good deal of pressure, been persuaded to delegate powers to the younger scions of the house, who will serve their apprenticeships thus. He will fulfill the purpose and tide us over the difficult period; and when in the fullness of time his place is vacant, the new occupant will be a man of greater vigour and education who can move with the times.

A generation with a twentieth-century education tends to look slightly superciliously at any leader who is uneducated, conservative and puritan, in the Sudan as in Britain. Yet these qualities are no disadvantage in the eyes of the public. Moreover, wisdom is not the same as cleverness, and some of these leaders have wisdom in a high degree and the ability to distinguish what matters from the flashy parade of false values of the mere snobbishness of modernity.

There was another Nazir of a big amalgam of peoples in the West, who was of a religious disposition more unyielding than AbdelGader's, and of high repute for character and justice. Towards the end of the Second World War he and a number of his subordinates went to the Province capital to see the film 'Desert Victory'. Meeting them on their return, I asked one of these sheikhs what had impressed him most. The answer was, 'The tanks. They came r-r-rolling at you out of the screen, like a charging elephant' – here he cowered dramatically – 'until you thought you would be crushed'. I asked the same question of a second, and his reply was, 'The aeroplanes. They dived and shot - *takh-takh-takh,* like the rain. Nothing could live'. I then turned to the Nazir and asked him what had most impressed him. He mused for a moment and then thoughtfully replied, 'The date-trees beside the Suez canal. Never have I seen such fine dates grow anywhere'. Happy and sage philosopher!

By way of a change let us move again south and west and take another Nazir. He again is the head of a great Baggara tribe, richer and more powerful than Radi's; and like him, his command includes hill units of Nuba, various settled Arab elements, some debased semi-West-African people called the Daju, and even a pocket of the Nilotic Dinka, who live north of their brethren and outside the Southern Provinces. Osman is a different type from the old men. He is in his thirties and the prime of life, vigorous and with a fair education behind him. He is a man of imagination, a born raconteur and the best company in the district; his farmyard imitations – the distinctions between a dog barking at a hyena, at a lion, at a thief; an overloaded camel grumbling; two old women quarrelling – are inimitable. He is exactly the type Shakespeare would have loved to meet, and chunks of his racy style would have appeared in the mouth of the Second Gravedigger or Lancelot Gobbo a month later.

He has sat on the Governor General's Advisory Council, is versed in the main currents of politics, has married a well-educated wife and can hold his own with any of the intelligentsia. Fairly good, though not outstanding, in court, he understands his intriguing, colourful, lawless tribesmen perfectly, and with his ability, charm and progressive spirit is the one man who can hold together and steer such a huge and motley amalgam.

For, motley they are, and as for the Baggara themselves, intrigue is the breath of their nostrils. They are everlastingly engaged in faction, fiery, good companions, unquiet spirits. Let us assume that there is a vacancy for an *omda* which has to be filled, and the clans concerned have been summoned to decide who should be appointed. We sit with the Nazir under a large acacia tree, and representatives of each section of the clan are interviewed in turn.

We have already agreed that of the several possible candidates a number will have to be vetoed, but there are two probables, and of these one is preferable, a peaceable and average soul called El Dom, one of the ruling house. The Nazir's agents have in fact already done a good deal of quiet canvassing on his behalf. The appointment is therefore a kind of semi-democratic, indirect election by acclamation, with the Nazir as a sort of not-very-detached Upper House and the Government, represented by the District Commissioner, in the background as final arbiter.

The first section, that of the evicted *omda*, wish to retain the headship, and put forward a grey-bearded old scallywag, Ahmed Chow, with a deep scar across his cheek caused by an elephant's tusk in a hunting escapade, well known to us all as about the third-wickedest man in the tribe and with a brazen scurrility as his most engaging asset. Prepared to put in a veto, but hoping not to have to do so, we proceed with the other sections. Luck is in. The old tale of the election of Themistocles as Athenian admiral is more or less re-enacted. That is to say, every man of substance thinks that he himself would undoubtedly best fill the billet and is therefore inclined to vote for himself, but puts El Dom second and would accept him as a *pis aller.*

On the declaration of the poll there is a moment's silence, then pandemonium. The Ahmed Chow party arises with shouts, imprecations, furious grimaces and brandishing of spears, asseverating that never, NEVER would they accede to El Dom. They would leave the tribe. They would leave the district rather than do so. Just as we are wondering whether to call up the forces of public security, there is a sudden lull. In a moment everything has subsided, and while we mop our brow everybody smiles, congratulates each other and El Dom and says they have never known so speedy and peaceful an election. Eatanswill [2] was much less civilized.

How long El Dom will last, we may well ponder. Cattle-owning Arabs are seldom happy unless engaged in some type of intrigue. Allegiances fluctuate and tempers mount and die away with uncommon rapidity. In a large section of this same great tribe, a section called the Aulad Surur, I experienced a particular outburst which was typical though more than usually violent. The *omda* was a fiery, tactless but colourful and effective man and a loyal one, twenty-five years in the saddle, a most surprising period for any Baggara *omda*. The malcontents had been sowing discord and working up revolt for a long time, led by a one-eyed scoundrel with a face of crab-apple sourness and two other confederates. The discord had issued in wild complaints and demands for the *omda*'s dismissal, and the Nazir and I met the tribe to listen to them.

There was no substance in the complaints, only noisy intransigence, and the dissident faction were told that without a proved grudge they would be given no further hearing, and until they could produce a case – or agreed to drop it altogether – the three ringleaders would be kept under arrest. A retainer was sent to arrest them, but never reached them. The next thing we saw was a phalanx of two hundred Aulud Surur advancing, with *shelegais* (the great, broad-bladed, twelve-foot Baggara spears) uplifted and pointed, upon our tree. A number of the main tribe, seeing what was happening, rushed up to protect their Nazir and repel the attack; the two lines formed up a few yards apart with a deafening din and itching weapons, and the three armed retainers of the Nazir began to stuff cartridges into the chambers of their rusty old Remingtons.

When I tried to get between the opposing armies, I was seized by the shoulders by two more brawny retainers and pulled back into a deck-chair, from which seat in the stalls, since intervention was precluded, I watched comfortably for full five minutes while clamour and passions seemed to be working themselves into a climax. At the critical moment there burst through from behind us a bevy of grey-beards, who threw

---

2   The election in Dickens's *The Pickwick Papers*.

themselves upon the most bellicose core of the Aulad Surur braves and after two minutes of objurgation and admonition and pushing forced them away and back to their trees.

The Nazir and I then fed, in my tent, while a partisan Heaven came in on our side by discharging a short but torrential downpour which caught the Aulad Surur unprotected and in the open, and when we visited them twenty minutes later, we found them in a very *dégonflé* condition. The three men were arrested without difficulty, and a heavy cattle fine was levied for their disgraceful behaviour. To this day I have never known whether the whole uproar could not have gone beyond a mere rude demonstration intended to intimidate, or whether we were within an ace of death. Tribal opinion tends to the latter view, but probably the Aulad Surur themselves were the last people to know. So quick are their kind to flare up, so quick to subside.

Let us take one more look at a big figure. This time we will go to the Eastern Sudan, where the barren and austere Red Sea Hills rise, with the red and purple lights of the evening sun reflected on their granite turrets and battlements, among plains and wadis bearing scattered thorn-scrub and tussocky grass. Here the Beja tribes, the Fuzzy-Wuzzies, graze their cattle and camels. Of Hamitic stock but of Arab civilization, they are courageous, independent, staunch Muslims, wild, yet with that strength of character which can make the most valuable citizens out of barbarous elements within a generation or two.

Their Nazir, Mohammed Tirik, is I suppose of the old school again, and yet in truth he is timeless. He was ancient in the land of Uz, and he will be still directing his people two centuries hence; for with the old traditional qualities he combines a political astuteness which can sail with any wind, and he knows that no politician and no bureaucracy will ever be able to maintain control over his men. His Old Testament charm is irresistible. Yet under the frank, desert bonhomie of an Abraham he hides the guile of a Macchiavelli. He is not above playing off tribe against Government and Government against tribe, for he knows neither can do without him. He is prone to the universal Arab infirmity of trusting only his own blood and treating suspiciously, even scurvily, potential loyal subordinates from other houses. Yet his influence is immense.

How he ever sleeps I scarcely know, for he is accessible to the meanest member of his people at any time of night or day, and for the most trivial plaint or appeal. His pocket is always open. I once attempted, as a matter of interest, to work out an approximate private budget for him, but was defeated. His revenue was partially assessable: with his salary, official dues received from market sales and from his cotton holdings in the big irrigated scheme at the south end of his domain he received over £4,000 a year. But this was augmented by the cash and, more particularly, the animal wealth presented to him (or lifted by him) from his subjects, and was as unfathomable and irregular in dimensions as in origin.

Let no one speak of 'bribes' or even of 'exactions', for as to his expenditure, all one could say with certainty was that it was always slightly in advance of his revenue and, with hundreds of cattle and herds of she-camels not far beyond call, I have lent him a bob to meet the needs of a beggar-woman because he had not a penny in his pocket. Was there a big case toward, and twenty witnesses to be fed for a week pending the hearing? The Nazir fed them. Had some scoundrel been sentenced to a fine of £40 or prison in default? The Nazir headed the subscription list (even sometimes when he had imposed the fine). Women, *fikis* and the deserving and undeserving poor were always with him, and no solicitation went unsatisfied.

He afforded the perfect example of the head of an Arab tribe's financial functions and privileges; for he was the distribution centre of the wealth of the tribe; all flowed in to him, and provided that it flowed out again for the purposes and in the channels approved by tradition, all was well, and no exactions were resented or regarded as unconstitutional. Only if he failed in his duties would public support be withdrawn, his behests be regarded as oppressive and his whole position be in danger. He was, as I have said, that paradox, an autocrat dependent on public opinion.

Leadership in the religious brotherhood of Islam added powerfully to the respect felt for any great sheikh by his people. Mahommed Tirik once added notably to his prestige in this quarter. A new mosque was to be built, and a mosque should traditionally be sited so as to point to Mecca, just as a church points eastwards. A junior Sudanese surveyor, with his panoply of theodolite and other instruments and the requisite maps, laid out the site. The Nazir regarded it with a cold eye and said impassively, 'You have got it wrong. Mecca isn't that way. It is there' (pointing to a quarter at least twenty degrees north of the surveyor's alignment).

The official was piqued and retorted that he had all the proper instruments, that Science *said* Mecca was in that direction and that therefore it *must* be. How did the Nazir know that it was in a different direction? The laconic answer was, 'I can smell it.' The matter was left in abeyance. By singular good luck the Director of Surveys chanced to be on a tour of inspection and visited the centre only a few days afterwards. I therefore asked him, of his courtesy, if he would cut the Gordian knot for us by personally deciding the alignment. He kindly did so. The Nazir was correct to within one degree and a half.

The alien administrator in his benevolent impatience is always apt to forget the importance of tempo. There is, in a rapidly emerging country, always a big gap between the progressive pace the Government wishes to keep up and the capacity of a conservative and scarcely-educated public for absorbing new ideas and playing the game as laid down. It is the big leaders who have to bridge that gap. They have to be sufficiently twentieth-century to retain Government's confidence, and be competent vehicles for its policy; yet if they once step too far out of the traditional atmosphere and become strangers to their people, their influence is undermined and their very value to Government as policy-vehicles is lost. Only great men can fulfil this dual role.

The simplest and most benevolent Government measure has to be interpreted to the populace and may be misconstrued, or at least fail to interest and elicit response. I remember watching the exasperation of a well-intentioned agricultural officer who was doing research work into the stem-borer, the evil worm which destroys so much of the fine millet grown on the receding Nile flood. Surely the people would know something of the nature, origin and causes of such a pest, or at least have theories on the subject? He therefore set about catechising a group of Arabs. The most popular theory elicited that there was no knowing and no telling. The second most popular was that the worms die at the end of the season, and God creates more the next year. Beyond this we could not penetrate. The spirit of scientific questing must not be looked for.

Superstition survives among the most enlightened and eminent leaders, just as it does among us who take our hat off to a magpie or a sweep, throw salt over one shoulder and avoid walking under a ladder. When I offered my rifle to a young Arab, an able and most intelligent man and a nephew of the Nazir, to have a shot at a bustard, he declined – not on the grounds that he had not taken out a game-licence, but because his wife was expecting a child, and if he killed or hurt any creature the effect might be reproduced in the baby.

An even more striking example of the same belief occurred when a young *omda* told me that he was expecting his wife to produce their first child and he was somewhat worried. He had, when she was some three months on in pregnancy, bought a sheep and brought it home, and had proceeded to put his personal brand on it by cutting a nick in the left ear. His wife had protested, on the grounds of long-standing custom and taboo. He had told her that in these days of enlightenment one did not observe such superstitions, and had carried out his purpose, but she remained unconvinced. Some weeks after he had recounted this I was privileged to see the newly-arrived infant. She was a delightful little lady, but in the lobe of her left ear was a perceptible and quite deep nick – and how the deformity had come we must leave to the experts.

Suppose again that a census or a routine check of animals for herd-tax has to be carried out. The leader is held responsible by Government for its execution, or at least its facilitation. But what are his people's views? Nobody loves the income tax authorities in any case, but it does not end there. Exact counting and numbers are abhorrent to most simple folk. Never will an Arab be found who will say, 'I have six cows and seventy-three sheep'. His reply will be rather, 'God has prospered me; my sheep have increased,' or, 'The cattle are dead. Only a few are left'. For numbering brings the evil eye and can be the harbinger of disaster. One may compare King David's ill-advised census of Israel, recorded in 2 Samuel xxiv, which was visited by the judgment of a calamitous plague.

How do these leaders get on together and regulate their relations in official matters? The relations are somewhat like those of European kings in the days of crowned heads. They might be cordial. They might be, and often were, veiledly hostile, and occasionally the veil was very transparent, but the leaders were 'cousins', with a similarity of interests and understanding of the dignity and courtesy due from each to his opposite number. At some periods and in some districts their behaviour was superior to that of their respective district commissioners, who could become grossly partisan and possessive. A particular feud between two tribes in neighbouring provinces, which had resulted in bitter salvoes from H.Q. and Governor to Governor, finally reached the Civil Secretary in Khartoum and elicited the following firman:

> This correspondence will now cease. The days have passed when the people in one's neighbour's District were automatically a set of conscienceless knaves egged on by an incompetent nincompoop.

For obvious geographical reasons, the regulation of inter-tribal relations and the hearing of disputes presented practical difficulties. These were least when all parties were of settled communities. They were greatest when one side or both were of a nomadic way of life. The nomad has flourished extremely under the *Pax Britannica* (once admirably mis-typed by a solemn Province Headquarters clerk as *Pox Britannica*); his herds are still vulnerable to the adventurous rustlers who, armed or unarmed, may drive off one or more beasts, take them hundreds of miles over desert country and dispose of them, possibly in French territory. But the big-scale, organized raiding of animal wealth is a thing of the lawless past, and the nomad's wealth is great.

Romantic figure though he may be, he is almost wholly destructive, and a subsidiary cause of the existence and spread of the Sahara, for his flocks destroy the young trees and scrub so that deforestation sets in; he lights fires which sweep over wide areas, destroying valuable gum and preventing regeneration of vegetation, thus enabling the periodical storms to erode the top-soil and leave it prey to the dune-creating wind; and when his animals enter that strip where the desert meets the sown, and impinge upon cultivation, great can be the damage - and little the redress obtainable from a master who has no permanent stake in the locality and in a month may be two hundred miles away.

The only method of redressing grievances and restoring good relations is by holding periodical and advertised meetings at known centres, where it is the duty of the leaders to have their own men in their corners for the next round. Cases are seen, justice given, broken compacts mended, new agreements made. To the District Commissioner these meetings of an inter-territorial nature were always attractive. There was the opportunity to encounter one's colleagues, and the venue would normally be a spot where duck-shooting, or fishing, or hill-climbing could be expected.

The success of the meeting, from the District Commissioner's point of view, would be in inverse ratio to the amount of work done, for the less there was for him to do, the more certain it was that the leaders were doing their duties effectively. Where possible, proceedings would be wound up with camel, horse or other races, wrestling or displays. Nor was the cuisine omitted as a potent factor in diplomacy. The claim of Talleyrand's chef, Monsieur Chavre, that the success of the Congress of Vienna was mainly due to the exquisiteness of his pastry, was not an idle one. The supply of meat at these meetings was always plentiful and could be fabulous. I have eaten more meat at a sitting on such a festive occasion than on any other – liver, kidney and lungs, raw and with chillies and hot pepper on them, a real knock-out; camel's hump; sheep's tail; mutton; chicken. It is fortunate that the picking of teeth is no social solecism, and that if nature prompts an eructation, it is no sign of ill-breeding but shows proper appreciation of good fare.

Misunderstanding of the niceties of table behaviour can indeed lead either European or Arab into embarrassment. I have, several decades of civilization ago, watched an admirable *omda* select a chocolate biscuit in silver paper from a proffered plate, stuff it into his mouth and manfully start to munch silver paper and all. He was rescued, or rather humiliated, by the worst *omda* in the neighbourhood, a sophisticated, semi-urban man in whose house a week previously I had counted among other properties two scent-bottles, a large grey gamp, a vulgar swagger-stick and a pink petticoat. Reaching out, he snatched the biscuit from the lips of his more lovable if rural colleague, peeled it and handed it back, with an air of superiority, ready for consumption.

But they are a great galaxy, these leaders of the Arab peoples. In the final political emergence of the Sudan they may have played only a subsidiary, and certainly an unobtrusive part; but in the administrative steps which made it possible and upon which stable independence is founded, their role has been a vital one, and to study them and associate with them is to gain a unique insight into the Arab polity.

To Elizabeth   24 February 1927

On trek, resthouses vary in their distance apart, from five to twelve miles or so, but the porters keep up a solid three miles an hour and never seem to flag, and when the next rest house appears in sight, they'll set up a chorus of joy and execute elated dances and jigs, all with a load of about 70 lbs on their heads, perhaps in the shape of a tin trunk, or perhaps it's a box full of our whisky and soda bottles, which is rather alarming, but they've never broken anything yet.

Our progress from village to village is a triumphant procession. Each chief comes out to meet you with a large following of his people, all dressed in their best, which seldom exceeds one strip of calico, and if they are superior persons a hat of some description, varying from red women's bonnets to bashed and decayed Homburgs. If the person is a great swell, he may have a hole-ridden pair of boots – boots incapacitate a native almost as much as the lack of them does a European – but they are the hallmark of the acme of gentility.

To his Father   October 1932
Sinkat

There has been a regular harvest of affrays and fights just recently in the Deindeib-Odi neighbourhood. Fuzzy's worst peccadillo is that he will draw his weapon on the very lightest provocation, and fall to. Every man goes armed – guns they won't touch, rather disliking and despising them (very unlike the Arab, who would sell his soul for a bit of brass tubing with a lump of wood stuck on one end and a sight on the other). But no young man is complete without a sword and a *khanjar,* a curved, kukri-like knife kept as sharp as a razor. The odd thing is that in all this constant scrapping they are as sober as judges, since the Hadendowa, and all the Beja tribes, live principally on milk and don't know what an intoxicant is.

CHAPTER FOUR

The Fuzzy-Wuzzies

I do not think the reader can get even a representative view of the Sudan without visiting the great eastern bloc – roughly speaking everything east of the Setit and Atbara rivers and northward to the Egyptian frontier, whose main component part is the Beja tribes, best known as the Fuzzy-Wuzzies. The area itself is immense – at least 100,000 square miles. Of that, the northern and north-western stretch, beyond the Port Sudan railway line, is either total or partial desert, with rainfall which varies from nothing in droughty years to a few inches in better seasons. South of the railway, rainfall increases from five or six to some ten inches at Kassala, and more further down the map. North of Kassala is a flat, alluvial area watered by the annual flood of the Gash river, which brings down the rains of Eritrea for several months each summer and services a big irrigated cotton scheme. North and south, from Suez to Kassala and beyond, stretches the great chain of the Red Sea Mountains, rising to over 9,000 feet in the Sudan and above 10,000 feet in Eritrea and Abyssinia.

This is the home of the Beja tribes, hill-men by nature, who have spilled themselves over on to the plains and are even now adapting to the conditions of modern life. Racially they are of Hamitic stock – that is to say, sharing distant origins with the Ethiopians, Somalis and some of the inhabitants of South and South-West Arabia, not with the Arabs and other Semitic races. Yet upon this stock has been grafted a prevailingly Arab culture, and the unifying bond of Islam has encircled it. Not a Beja tribe or clan but claims its ancestral founder from among the heroes or worthies of early Islam, embodying in that doubtful claim the historical fact of Arab civilisation over-running and absorbing a non-Arab people.

By far the biggest single unit of the Beja is the great tribe of the

43

Hadendowa, who form the southern block and who provided most of the fighting men during the Eastern Sudan campaigns of the 1880s and 1890s. Next in size come the Amarar tribe, to their north and west. Third, the Bishari, who gravitate between the river Atbara and the barren mountains of the Egyptian frontier and who own probably the finest breed of riding camels that the world has to show.

The late Nazirs of the Amarar and Bishari tribes were not on amicable terms. During a visit of notables to the capital, while they were being conducted round the excellent little Khartoum zoo, I saw the former, who combined administrative and diplomatic gifts with a malicious capacity for the soft remark which successfully elicits wrath, point to the mangy Asiatic camel with its two flaccid humps and suggest to his Bishari colleague that he should borrow it as a stallion for his famous herds. His sally nearly caused a breach of the peace.

Historical references to the Beja are few and almost wholly uncomplimentary. Diodorus Siculus in the first century BC remarked of them, 'They make a horrid noise as they go about, and resemble herds of cattle. They are interested in nothing.' In 1180 a Sicilian Arab, Ibn Jubeir, observed: 'The Beja live like animals. This is the country of Islam which more than any deserves extermination.' In 1400 the Arab historian El Makrisi recorded that 'The Beja country is always in commotion. They live like brutes and have no religion.' Leo Africanus in 1530 merely referred to the 'base and miserable Bujiha', and even Sir Samuel Baker in 1860 wrote that 'the Hadendowa are an extremely bad tribe.' And yet, after all these centuries of vilification, the Beja's administrators have found them a fascinating if exasperating problem. They have shown a dawning adaptation to civilisation greater than their reputation would warrant. Without having any illusions, I can testify to their qualities, and to having had more good friends among them than in almost any part of the Sudan. What is their secret?

In the political and economic emergence of these people it is the great Gash cotton scheme which has probably played the most decisive part. But since it is the raw material with which we are here concerned, I ask the reader to mount his camel – a fine Bishari animal with the Banagir firing-mark on the cheek which betokens the best of all breeds – and to accompany me, along with an *omda* and several sheikhs of the people among whom we are to go, east of the railway line into the heart of the Waribba hills, the central massif of the Hadendowa, where their most typical and least-touched life is to be found.

A Governor under whom I served used to say that there should be only two forms of travel in the Northern Sudan: the aeroplane and the camel – and there was deep truth in this. On the great distances from point to point as little time as possible should be wasted. Once among the people, all hurry should be dropped, and contact should be as leisurely as it can be made.

In our vast Beja area the Kassala–Port Sudan railway, extended by a coastal road 200 miles northward, forms the backbone and affords comparatively rapid movement north and south. From any vantage point on this we can plunge horizontally east or west into the hinterland, and we now start from the little market centre, court centre and police post of Derudeb.

Here we shall find the principal market in dom nuts, and one afternoon's ride will take us into Khor Arideb, as good a specimen as can be found of the dom-producing country. The dom palm, *Hyphaene thebaica,* stretches far down the map of Africa, at least to the Equator and beyond it. It is one of those ungrateful plants that prefer sandy soil and meagre rainfall. On richer and well-watered ground it grows rarely and scrubbily. Here, beside the sandy *khor* and from a rainfall of eight inches a year, grow such dense groves of the trees that one could ride through them for an hour under the midday sun without wearing a hat.

The dom's nut is nearly as big as one's fist, and consists of a glossy skin, a hard, fibrous and sweetish pericarp which can be eaten and is much loved by goats and camels, and a kernel the size of a walnut which provides some of the best vegetable ivory in the world. Just as, whenever you stick on a threepenny stamp you are licking gum from the Central Sudan, so many of the buttons on which your trousers depend came from the Eastern Sudan, whose main rival in the trade, apart from Eritrea, is Ecuador.

The dom nut has a big effect on the Hadendowa, bringing them wealth and that contact with the outside world which rising wealth engenders. Unlike cotton, it needs no inspectors, no engineering, next-to-no government interference. It does not plant civilisation with a heavy hand among the hills, but draws the troglodyte gently from his fastnesses to mix with others. Moreover, it is one of the few commodities in whose production primitive methods still prevail over those of industry, for nuts husked by hand in the forest command a higher price than those husked by machine at Atbara. No machine has been invented which does not slice and damage the kernel.

Now watch the first Hadendowa tribesman whom we have encountered. As he squats cross-legged, with the ends of his simple cloth robe thrown over his shoulders, the ringlets of his *tiffa* or fuzzy thatch of hair hanging over his neck, on one side of him a big pile of dom nuts. In front of him is a flat stone and in his hand is a piece of granite. Placing each nut on the slab, he gives it two judicious cracks with his granite hammer and tosses a perfect kernel on to a growing heap on the other side, throwing the rind to his expectant black goats which wait a few paces off. If skilful, he will husk nearly 1,000 nuts a day – 70 lbs weight and worth four shillings or five shillings even thirty years ago. Try his method of husking a nut, and it will cost you five minutes of thumping and a broken thumb.

The dom nut was an almost unmixed blessing. Its occasional problems were incidental. A case occurred of a somnolent Hadendowa sitting in the shade of a dom palm. A fellow-tribesman who wanted some nuts shouted 'Fore!' several times and buzzed a stone up among the clusters. One of the nuts from the resulting shower struck the sitter full on the head, and despite his *tiffa* and the thickness of the Beja skull, stretched him dead. The resulting claim for blood-money exercised the Nazir and his experts in Beja jurisprudence for a long time, and finally resulted in payment for *half* a man.

Pursuing our way down the Khor Arideb and up a tributary, we work into the ever-mounting hills. But where are the people? Gazelles are scattered up and down the *khor,* feeding on the coarse tussocks of grass, for the Beja like so many pastorals are not primarily hunters, and do not freely acquire firearms, as do the Arabs. Here and there we come on an encampment, but it is usually the tent of a single family, sometimes two, rarely three. Lack of grazing and lack of the gregarious instinct account for this sporadic development. The tent is usually made of matting woven from dom palm fronds, occasionally of blanket woven from goat and camel hair. The women will be minding the home. The children will be tending the black goats and a few sheep. The eldest son will be 100 miles away in the Gash, cultivating cotton and making money. The father will be away taking a camel-load or donkey-load of dom nuts to Derudeb.

If the father is at home, it is unlikely that he will be engaged in any very energetic pursuit. He may be sitting in the shade of a palm tree with a *basunkw*, or local banjo, in his hand, beguiling the hours with limited but somnolent and mellow cadences. He may be dressing his *tiffa*, which can vary from a mere thick thatch to a complicated coiffure, with neat plaits hanging down the neck beneath the crowning hay-rick, all lubricated (in prosperous times) and set off with one or two *hulals*, the sharp, curved, silver-headed, ibex-horn scratching-sticks with which he disturbs the denizens of his head.

Once when a party of Beja notables were paying a visit to Khartoum and were invited to a garden party at the Governor-General's palace, the feature which most captured their imagination was the pipe band of a Scottish regiment. Though the skirl of the pipes pleased them, what impressed them more were the bearskins, which they believed to be *tiffas*, superior to anything they could see at home among the hills, and which must take a king's ransom in mutton fat to keep in prime order.

The father will be armed with an ebony-shafted, brass-bound spear; he may or may not carry a round shield of elephant hide, but will certainly bear the curved knife which is a mark of the Beja, and the straight, double-edged sword which is their main weapon of offence. Their courage is a matter of course. When a man was brought into the District Office badly mauled by a leopard, I asked his story. He and his brother had found the leopardess, an uncommonly large and powerful one, on one of their young camels, which it had killed. Since he had no weapon of his own, he borrowed his brother's shield and with that alone made straight for the enemy. The leopardess had sprung at him, and, taking the shock on the shield, he had fallen, guarding his vitals with it. While the leopardess was trying to get at him round the corners and scoop him out, his brother was able to pierce it to the heart with his sword.

When tribal passions are roused – though not to the point of killing – the Beja's weapon is the stone. A line of tribesmen on one side will face a similar line on the other (ammunition is unlimited among the granite hills), and the contest may go on for hours. Women may act as *vivandières*, gathering stones and bringing refreshment; a man may throw only at his opposite numbers, not sideways down the line; and though deaths occur, they are rare, and only a few broken shins and black eyes are the usual result. A colleague of mine, mounted on camel-back, once came round the bend of a valley and found himself at the end of a double line of such fighters. The camel, taking fright, bolted, and, clinging like John Gilpin to the saddle, he careered the whole length of the combatants' ranks unhurt, and out the other end.

Even the scattered encampments we encounter are not all of one section or clan. That is what makes administration so difficult. Among the Hadendowa a sheikh with £10 of tribute to collect may have to collect £5 of that in the rich cotton area of the Gash, £2 in the heart of the Waribba hills a hundred miles northwards, from clansmen who gather dom nuts, £2 from a few parishioners who sell milk in Port Sudan a further hundred miles away, and the last £1 from a couple of individuals dotted along the river Atbara a hundred miles to the west.

Nevertheless, the sheikhs who accompany us take the opportunity to collect such sums of tribute as they can glean from their unwilling citizens. Nobody loves an income-tax collector; but whereas in Britain evasion is difficult and dangerous, and the odds are on the side of the collector, and whereas our ancestors took an axe to the man, the Beja tribesman will not use his sword, but will simply do his disappearing trick – and very difficult it will be to trace him in this tangle of *khor* and scree and cliff and palm forest. Our sheikhs therefore lose no opportunity. I have, on a big progress of this kind, accompanied by the Nazir, had to sleep on two iron chests containing as much as £3,000 of specie. Physically, it was not comfortable; but mentally there was no cause for insomnia, for I was far safer among barbarous, independent, lovable primitives than is a bank clerk who handles £3,000 worth of notes in an American or English city.

A further cause of difficulty in Beja administration is the lack of a sense of time. This is prevalent in much of Africa and the East, but nowhere so markedly as here. If a Beja man is given a time and place to be present, it must not be expected that he will arrive. He has no calendar, no diary, and usually reckons by moons. Procrastination is the essence of his nature. Management of affairs depends mainly on getting a sufficient number of necessary people to one place at one time. The only way of ensuring this is to announce a meeting long beforehand; go to the place, and wait there until rumours trickle out that the meeting has begun and the men concerned trickle in.

Even then victory, if that means permanent settlement of anything, is not assured. There may have been a lengthy, acrid and dangerous dispute between two sections, and at long last, after great effort, all the parties, along with sufficient judges, arbitrators and neutrals, have been gathered at one spot and the palaver is continued for days. When it is finished, the whole troupe is seen approaching you.

'Well,' you ask hopefully, 'is the matter settled?'

'Yes.'

'Are you all agreed?'

'Yes.'

'All absolutely. *Nem con?*'

'Yes, praise be to God.'

'And what is the decision?'

'That we will all meet here again this time next year and settle the matter.'

We encamp among the hills, and there will be entertainment, for the sheikhs with us are good raconteurs, whether in halting Arabic or in their own difficult but attainable Beja tongue. Or we may indulge in a game of *andot*. This is played with twelve little scoops in the sand, six of your own and six of your opponent's, and forty-eight pellets of dried camel droppings, four in each hole. The object is to play your pellets round so that the last one completes a four in one of your enemy's scoops. The possible combinations and moves are unlimited; the rules are intricate, and the foresight of a chess champion is needed, combined with the finesse and balanced judgment of a bridge expert. A couple of herdsmen will play the game for hours in the sparse shade of an acacia, and the usual rule is that the wilder and more benighted the tribesman, the more invincible he will be with the pellets. I once made a neat wooden board with twelve round cavities in it, substituted marbles for camel dung, and took it to Messrs Thomas de la Rue, leading maker of playing cards in the City of London. They were impressed and intrigued, and thought seriously about patenting the game, but eventually decided against it on the grounds that it required too much skill and concentration to attract the British public. And the yo-yo swept England!

Talk will turn from camels to ibex-hunting, from ibex to marriage-customs and from customs to Dervish days and the fighting at Suakin and Omdurman. The night grows colder and the fire blazes up as more branches of *mirikh,* the broom-like shrub which grows abundantly, are thrown on it. Osman Digna, the redoubtable Dervish emir who controlled the Eastern Sudan from 1882 to 1898, was betrayed and finally captured in 1900 on the mighty Jebel Sabidana, not far from where we sit, to live as an exile in Wadi Halfa until 1926. The influence of that man, famous in his day, upon the Hadendowa I have always found a mystery. No tribesman remembers him with affection, few with admiration. He was not physically brave, and frequently led the fight from his prayer-mat in the rear. He was not kindly or clement, and lacked the genius for procrastination which is the Beja's joy. He ruled by a mixture of fear and sagacity, and ruled to the end. By the time of Omdurman he well knew the force of modern firearms and the inevitable outcome, and had advised the Beja contingent to keep well clear of the fighting.

One of our accompanying sheikhs had been present at the battle, and had been with the massed Dervishes in the sunken *khor* which lay across the path of the 21st Lancers and occasioned their celebrated and costly charge, in which Winston Churchill took part. 'There we were,' our man told us, 'comfortably sitting in the *khor*, obeying Osman Digna's advice, listening to the *rut-tut-tut* of the musketry away to our left, and thanking our stars that we were well out of it. All we wanted was to be left alone. Suddenly there appeared this line of foolish British horsemen, and though we shouted and signalled at them to keep away, they insisted on charging into the midst of us. What could we do but fight?'

Those battles, to us almost a half-forgotten romance, for the Fuzzies who fought with their swords and their gallantry against rifle-fire are best forgotten. In 1932 the memorial on the battlefield of Tamai, near Suakin, was to be unveiled with an impressive ceremony and the speeches with which men comfort and congratulate themselves for the horrors of a previous generation. I was bidden to unearth some of the old Beja tribesmen who had been in the battle. But not a man could be traced. At last a greybeard blurted out the explanation: 'Do you mean to say that after fifty years the Government means to have us old men out and hang us *now?'* Points of view differ.

At sunrise, with a chill breeze singing a rustling song in the dry dom palm fronds, we take our line again. Surmounting a pass, we come on a number of ancient tombs. They are built of flat stones, solidly, in a circular mass, with a large fish-tail projecting. Their antiquity is uncertain, their builders a matter of conjecture or myth. Some say they were 'the Anag,' a race of giants known to the writers of *Genesis* as 'the children of Anak'. Others say they were 'the Rum', another giant race with a light skin who preceded the Beja and were driven out by their ancestors (so claimed) who came from Arabia. These tombs are widely found, but one of the biggest groups lies further west, in a forlorn and desiccated ravine, a veritable Sheol, or place of the dead, a Valley of Bones, said to be haunted, to which most locals are reluctant to go, as it was there, by tradition, that the aboriginal Rum met their destruction.

Long ago this spot, Nubt (the story goes), was the capital of the King of the Rum, Shakaital, after whom a neighbouring mountain is still called. He had three remarkable possessions: a sword that could cut anything in twain, a grindstone that could grind anything to powder, and a daughter who was the most beautiful in the world. At that time the Beni Hilal came from Arabia to live on the coastal plains around Suakin. The son of their sheikh, hearing of the beauty of the daughter of the King of the Rum, decided to woo and win her. So he went to the Rum and served them, looking after their flocks and herds. The lady encouraged his advances, but the Rum did not and eventually accused him of misconduct, which he denied. They therefore decided on trial by ordeal, took him to the wells at sunset, gave him a bucket and told him to prove his innocence by filling all the troughs by morning.

Now the Rum were very big men, and their buckets were so large and heavy that no ordinary mortal could draw water with them; so the young suitor soon found himself defeated. He therefore ran to his lady love, the King's daughter, and asked her to help him. Being as lusty as her brethren, she easily handled the bucket, and when the Rum came in the morning, they were chagrined to find the troughs full. However, they suspected what might have happened, and on examining the lady, sure enough they found a spot of mud still wet on her breast. So they killed the young man

– and when the sheikh of the Beni Hilal heard of his son's death, he came up to take vengeance.

The battle took place near Nubt, and the combatants suffered the fate of the Kilkenny cats, which fought each other to death – none survived. The King of the Rum, seeing that all was lost, and determined that no other should have his three matchless possessions, took the sword that could cut anything in twain, went to the grindstone that could grind anything to powder and smote it in two halves, which can be seen to this day. He then went to the most beautiful daughter in the world and cut off her head – but still she walks. He then stuck the sword point-down into the ground, which swallowed it up – but if a camel kneels on the spot, the sword will pierce him.

A colleague and I visited this spot, and though the ghost of the beautiful daughter did not materialise, it was an eerie and unpleasant enough place. Besides other relics there were numerous gravestones with Arabic inscriptions, some of them decipherable and dating from 841 to 890 AD – probably a reminder of the early incursions of Arab communities who, by establishing suzerainty and mixing with the locals, gave rise to the legends of the Beja origin.

The track grows more precipitous, and it seems marvellous that a beast like a camel, even unloaded, can successfully tackle it. Yet tackle it the camel does, in his own time, up and down the steep and jagged declivities. For the camels of the Red Sea littoral are no mere creatures of the sandy plains. When let out to graze they may occasionally be seen right up on the heights frequented by ibex, and, loaded, they will negotiate rocks and passes which none other but a mule would face, and, at the other extreme, deep mud in which even a mule would be bogged up to the hocks.

Down some of the *khors* run rocky streams which might almost be in a Welsh valley, and the illusion is fostered by the glimpse of a grey wagtail or a sandpiper. Finally, as we top a fresh pass, the bulk of Sabidana and the whole welter of the tangled Waribba mountains confront us. There are many ranges bigger in the world, many more beautiful; yet these Red Sea hills are unique in their austerity, their grotesque friezes, their ferocity, their mystery, in the very fascination which they cast and the affection which they instil. The colours alone are matchless, and in a westering sun the vast pinnacles and slabs and cliffs of granite may show pink, purple or deep red. The drier the atmosphere and the more barren the surroundings, the more variegated and compelling the colours become.

Should we attempt to scale the Sabidana, it will need a whole day, and even then we shall not succeed, for the summit is a 200-foot pillar of sublime and unconquerable granite. Only once in my life have I known thirst. I do not mean the honest thirst born of hard exercise and long endurance, with an assured drink at the end of it, but parching and frightening thirst, with the horror of desiccation and collapse in its train; and that was on Sabidana, and all in a matter of hours. What had appeared from below to be large boulders proved to be stupendous blocks and gobbets of rock, tumbled one on top of another, so that progress was a matter of scrambles and leaps, where a slip might land one in a twenty-foot crevice with a broken ankle or worse.

Starting soon after 4 am, together with a Beja policeman, I had scaled the highest point attainable in five-and-a-half tremendous hours. We had also consumed the skin of water carried with us. The effort, however, had been notably rewarded by the views, the surveying work made possible, and the sight of a herd of fourteen ibex moving like wraiths across the dimpled lights and shadows of the hill-face, their white socks, black face-marks and the two sweeping scimitars of the old sultan at the rear of his harem all showing up plainly.

It was on the way down that disaster threatened, for we lost our direction in a maze of gullies and kept working into positions whence further descent over precipitous edges was impossible, and retracing our steps nearly as dangerous. Dehydration and arduous exercise in a temperature of 108 in the shade can cause collapse and death within hours, and the very anticipation of it can cause panic. It was by luck, and no skill, that when within measureable distance of such exhaustion we stumbled into a little gully which held a pool of water – stagnant and scum-laden salvation – and led us by a series of hazardous descents to safety and to camp at sunset.

But it is time to leave the Waribba and make for our agreed destination. Northward lie further ranges of yet higher and even more barren hills. Westward and north-west into Bishari territory lies the sand-hill country, where the fine, red sand rises in swelling dunes covered with scarps and curves and facets and convexes, till they look like the work of some deranged Cubist architect. But our route lies southward, through lessening hills, until we debouch onto the desolate plain lying north of the irrigation scheme watered by the Gash flood.

In years of good rains such as this one, excess water reaches as far as this point, Erbab, before losing itself in the plain, and so irrigates some fine and seldom-cultivated land; and it is here, in this unattractive yet wealth-producing spot, that the Nazir is now sojourning and dividing up the cultivable land among applicants – his own Hadendowa, other Beja neighbours and visitors, townsmen from Kassala, and West African elements from the many Hausa and Bornu settlements.

After the fine country we have come through, the prospect is not agreeable: flat but rich loamy soil; rank grass; little shade, and flies innumerable – the big, biting gadflies which come with heavy rains and a dank, moist atmosphere. They carry no infection like the tsetse of more southern latitudes, yet I have seen three donkeys die in a morning from shock, sheer exhaustion and loss of blood caused by their innumerable bites.

We leave our camels at a distance, on gravelly, fly-free ground, and our little cavalcade arrives on foot. We have picked up and brought along with us a number of men, mostly 'wanted' individuals whom a dozen summonses would never have dislodged, but during our journey the sheikhs have ferreted them out. The principal Hadendowa section through which we have been passing is that of the Gemilab. As Macaulay once said of Samuel Johnson's poems, 'all were bad but some were worse than others.' Anyone ill-disposed to the Beja might have said the same of the Hadendowa, with an eye on the Gemilab as the 'some'. But whatever the misdeeds of the Fuzzy, they are the misdeeds of an independent, country-bred outlaw, not those of urban sophistication.

Over most of the country wine and women cause more than half the disturbances, but among the Beja water must be substituted for wine. I have known communities of whom Herodotus could almost have recorded – as he did of the Scythians – that 'when they have any matter of weight to decide, they discuss it twice, once sober and once drunk; and only if the same policy appears good to them both drunk and sober do they adopt it.' Not so the Beja, for they normally touch no strong liquor, and it is over wells and watering rights that their big, straight swords are so frequently drawn, keeping the courts ever busy.

Our several days at this meeting with the Nazir and the tribe end with camel-racing, sports, feasting and dancing. Among sports it is in jumping that these hill men excel. Annual sports days used to be held between the local tribesmen and any British regiment stationed at Gebeit, the old military post above Port Sudan. Any visitor might have expected that the British would win the jumps and sprints, but that the tribesmen, with their stamina and familiarity with the climate, would defeat them at any long distance. The opposite was the case. The Hadendowas' forte is *élan*. A Hadendowa would usually win the sprints, always the jumps; yet in any event demanding endurance and judgment the British soldier would outlast him.

As to dancing, care will be needed. These people are not given to dancing as a pastime, neither men nor women, as are some Arabs and most Africans. Yet when the drums beat, anything may happen – and no bystanders should be permitted to carry arms. I was present when the Hadendowa were presented with a new set of *nahas,* the great copper drums which were formerly a treasured possession of any large tribe and a symbol of prestige and leadership in the hands of the tribe's ruler. They were placed in position – the small calf drum, the fair-sized cow drum and the great, deep-voiced bull, nine feet in circumference – and the ceremonial beating began. As the profound, rhythmic double-bass note of the bull sounded, a few young men began to jig up and down in the open space; others joined them, and the curved camel sticks which all Beja carry, and a few swords safely ensconced in their sheaths, began to wave joyously in the air above handsome, mutton-fatted heads.

Yet more warriors joined, and the proportion of sheathed swords went up; the jigging became more athletic, and cries and exclamations broke out. As the tempo increased, the jumps became leaps and the cries swelled to shouts of exhilarated triumph. Next moment somebody had waved a knife, and in an instant pandemonium reigned. Scores of warriors were leaping, pirouetting and gesticulating like maenads, drunk with rhythm, drugged with sound and movement, their blades whirling like Catherine wheels in the air. Had blood started to flow, almost anything might have happened,

The *nahas* were instantly silenced, and a number of elders and leaders, bold men, were in among the youths in a flash, seizing the more frantic of them round the waist and hauling them away, mercifully before anybody had been carved up. I have a vision still of a young man, caught in mid-leap by an elder, his legs kicking wildly, his torso stretched poker-stiff, his arm extended holding a sword, like a marble statue, his eyes protruding from his head with the fixed glaze you may see in the eyes of a hashish smoker.

So we take our leave of the meeting, board a lorry instead of mounting a camel and push southwards for the Gash scheme and the civilising blessings of agricultural development. Far away, 300 miles northwards in the hills of the Bisharin, are gold mines, worked on the same sites as those exploited millennia ago by the Pharaohs, whose narrow but skilfully-executed shafts can still be descended, and who, thousands of years before any scientific method of diagnosing gold-fields, had a nose for the metal which the modern miner respects.

Here further south it is the soil which is the people's gold. Cotton was grown on the Gash flood as long ago as the middle of the last century by an enterprising Governor of Kassala, but was not seriously developed until the early 1920s. It is now a rich crop produced on a large irrigated area. The history of the scheme, political and agricultural, has been chequered, but its most remarkable feature has been the manner in which the Beja tribesman has acclimatised himself to the new regime.

Much unthinking aphorism has been uttered about the unchanging East and the inability of the Ethiopian to change his skin. If anybody demands proof of the falsity of such proverbial wisdom, let him turn to the Gash and see for himself. The Beja has not become an expert agriculturalist; but instead of standing apart, aloof and resentful, as many of his friends feared and his critics prophesied, he has exchanged the sword for the ploughshare, or at least for the hoe, to a degree which any intelligent onlooker might have doubted possible. Of the tenancies in this great scheme, 75 per cent were in Beja hands, up to and after the war, and I have no reason to believe that the proportion is much different now.

To a coming generation, the main historical interest of the Beja tribes will be a social phenomenon of unexpected adaptability in an apparently barbarous race. Under virile leaders, they are one of those units who, instead of either resisting or succumbing to a swift onset of civilisation, have risen to meet it and taken their little place in the modern world.

To his Aunt Nora Hornby   15 November 1928
Geteina

Trekking is all by camel, except in the case of emergency, and it is a delight to be comparatively free from the curse of the car. A camel is not a very rapid mode of progress – five or six miles an hour average – but it is contemplative and comfortable (given a decent animal) and it makes all the difference to go among these people, who are still living much as Abraham did, mounted as they are and not in modern machines. You meet with the true Arab hospitality, which generally takes the form of sweet drinks – honey and water or tea and coffee stewed black and mixed into a syrup with sugar – or seething milk (the best thing there is and better than a bottle of Bass in this climate!), and always a plate of tripes – gobbets of raw liver and lights, considered the very pick of the carcase! Unpleasant as it sounds, one seems to thrive on it.

To his father   22 May 1933.
In the Gash

Murders are the chief activity in the Gash. There seems to have been an unusual crop of them in the last month, and one particularly serious one where two men got killed. Had they been one on either side, it wouldn't have mattered twopence: they'd have cancelled out. But unfortunately they were both on the same side, and brothers. The result is that I have got not only their slayers in gaol, but also their father and several brothers or cousins, who cannot be let out because, if they were, they would promptly take the law into their own hands and exact reprisals by killing one or two of the other side – not necessarily the killers themselves (who in any case are in jug), but any of their relations would do.

It is a pity that our notions in these matters are so wholly at variance with their own. The idea of criminal responsibility – that one man deserves to be hanged for an inexcusable murder, while another does not deserve to be hanged for killing an equal in a fair fight – doesn't strike them in the least. They regard it purely as a civil affair, and the tribe – not the individual – as the unit. 'One tribe is two down? Right – things must be evened out by killing two from the other tribe.'

Trekking in the Gash, there are no settled villages. The various *omda*s and principal sheikhs of the area one is trekking in accompany one on trek, and one can bug down together in a small encampment or in the wilderness if it's an uninhabited neighbourhood, and get to know them very well indeed. The Nazir is with us as well, and the finest Arab I've yet met. The Fuzzy is a feckless man as a rule, but they have a few men of real outstanding ability, like the Nazir, and the *omda* O'haj of Deindeb, whom I may have mentioned – a young *omda* and extremely progressive, without being de-Arabised – a rare combination.

Generally, if an Arab catches on to European ideas at all, he takes to wearing laced boots and sock suspenders and riding in a motor car: it is a rare thing to find one who continues to prefer his sandals and his camel, and can yet appreciate the moral desirability of native administration, the necessity for combating locusts and diseases and so on, and the other features of *real* progress.

CHAPTER FIVE

The Nilotic South

The Dinka

The Dinka is an idle cuss;
He argues, scowls and makes a fuss
If he is made to work.
His long suit is a graceful pose,
One heel against a tree, his toes
Along his calf.

Leaning against his polished spears
He neither knows nor sees nor fears
Authority among his peers,
Lounging in statuesque repose,
Looking disdainful down his nose.
By courtesy of Dr J. Bryant

I am trying to picture, in this chapter, a large chunk of the southern provinces, as it was in the earlier post-war years, rapidly developing politically, economically, socially; yet still, thanks to geography and a primitive past, a long way behind the other half of the country. The northern provinces of the Sudan comprise a host of differing tribes and races, united by a common Islamic civilization and a wide and growing prevalence of the Arabic tongue. The southern provinces comprise a similar or maybe even more variegated haggis of tribal elements, but without the unifying bond of language, or of religion.

A grisly Arabic patois has been current coin among the Bantu peoples,

59

but even that is lacking among the Nilotics. English had a unifying effect among those who had passed through the schools. Whether this will be partly or wholly superseded by Arabic remains to be seen, but if that happens it will still be a long way from providing a *lingua franca* for the man in the bush. There are Muslim individuals and a few small Muslim communities; there are large and important Christian elements, both Protestant and Roman Catholic, the more important because they comprise the bulk of the educated class and have survived persecution and chaos. But the great bulk of the population is pagan, and paganism holds neither creed nor code to provide a rallying point and become the foundation of a nation.

Yet there is a certain broad unity about these diverse ingredients, a vague unity but none the less real for its vagueness, the unity of the African outlook on life which stretches, with modifications and variety, from the Sudan to the Cape and from Ethopia to Ghana. It is an outlook which struggles, against odds, for recognition and for human dignity.

Some British practitioners have found administration of an African people simpler than that of an Arab one, merely because their conditions were more backward and less complex. It has also been found more difficult, because of the greater gulf between administrator and administered and the lack, in early years, of the human material and human reactions which are a *sine qua non* for progress.

Asia has been civilised as long as Europe and longer; and many as are the divergences in outlook and habit and mentality between the two civilisations, I doubt if there is any so great that it cannot be bridged by imagination and sympathy. But with the African this is less so, for there has been in bygone centuries scarcely such a culture as to warrant the name of civilisation, though there may be an African attitude to life; and any modern North Sudanese administrator might find it as difficult to bridge the gulf as did his British predecessor. We had discovered empirically how to gain the confidence of Africans; gained empirically some ability to predict how the African will react; introduced some of their abler and progressive members to Western civilisation – admirable men on whom the emergence of the Southern Provinces will greatly depend. But I have never met a colleague, British or Sudanese, who claimed to be able to think himself into an African mind and to comprehend and share the innermost soul of the African.

My object, therefore, is to open one little window upon it by paying a visit to some centre where we can see as much typical life as can be found in one spot. Since more than two thirds of the population of the three provinces are Nilotics, and since the Nilotic culture and manner of life have a broad similarity everywhere, we cannot do better than imagine ourselves on the way to a big meeting of Dinka, Chiefs and populace alike, with their neighbours the Nuer of the next Province, at a Dinka dry-weather resort.

With small exceptions the Nilotic is a pastoral. Your Dinka cultivates in the rainy season, and sometimes practises a rough kind of mixed farming. But Nilotic culture is founded upon, centred upon, and unthinkable without – cattle. We are so steeped in our view of man as an economic animal that we find it very difficult to conceive the Nilotic's attitude to his cattle. To us a cow is a form of wealth, something to produce milk and beef or to be exchanged for cash or equivalent goods. To the Arab it is much the same, with the added factor that his beast may be a useful form of transport for him and his women and goods. To the Dinka, his beast is an inalienable part of his life, and not far removed from being a brother.

We assume that a man who sees something to his financial advantage will jump at it. Applied to the Dinka, that assumption is false, and many an administrative mistake has been made by adopting it. The Dinka's cattle are not for sale, and high prices and a big demand for meat will not necessarily extract them from him. They are even of inferior quality as beasts. Milk is not drunk universally and in quantity, and it is always advisable to have a stock of tinned milk when travelling among the Dinka, for fresh milk is not always procurable, and it is liable to have been spiced with a dose of cow's urine, whose acrid flavour appeals to them.

As to using his bull as a beast of burden, it would be unthinkable to a Dinka, and the man who first takes a load of grain to market on his bull will have initiated a change in Dinka society as significant as that wrought among us by Stephenson's steam-engine. The Dinka's cattle are a symbol of his prestige rather than his economic prosperity, and the only normal cause of exchange is as bride-price, between clan and clan, when a marriage takes place.

Now, in the dry season, the rains are not due until mid-May, two months hence. The populace is centred round a great shallow lake, four miles long and up to a mile across, and at this time of year only five feet deep in the centre and far less than that over most of its area. We are travelling towards it by lorry along a fairly well made-up track. The country is as flat as a chessboard, but tracts of it are covered with thickish bush, for here there is a forty-inch rainfall. There are equally flat vistas in the north where, as a raw young man on an uncomfortable camel, I once wearily asked my companion where lay the village for which we were heading. His reply was: 'You see that horizon? Well, it's the third b----y horizon beyond that.'

We meet a young Dinka on the track. He carries a spear and is stark naked apart from a smart trilby hat which he raises to us with the utmost politeness as we wave to him. There is only one thing nakeder than a man dressed in a hat, and that is a nude man riding a bicycle. The traditional Dinka coiffure is a thick but short fuzz, bleached with cow's urine to an ochreous colour. Nowadays hair is often tied up in an unbecoming bag of blue calico, and the trilby hat is not unpopular.

I recollect a hot and sticky March day, with the thermometer at 107 F, when a colleague and I arrived at a centre situated on a meandering river. We asked the local chief whether there were crocodiles and whether bathing was advisable. He replied courteously that there was a safe pool some half a mile distant, deep but much frequented and where no crocodile ever ventured; he himself would show us the way and join our aquatics (nearly all Dinka swim, though most of them clumsily.)

We set out, clothed in shirts and shorts, accompanied by the chief, who was Adam-naked, though he carried the usual spear with a little bundle attached close to the head. Within half a mile we came to the pool, which was deep and attractive. We doffed our clothes and dived in, and came up refreshed but wondering what our companion was doing. Looking shorewards, we saw his spear stuck upright in the sand, the bundle removed from it, and he was just stepping into a Jansen bathing-dress.

To return to the road. We next meet a middle-aged Dinka who is limping dot-and-go-one. We stop to ask him about himself and learn that he was herding his cattle four days ago and was bitten by a snake. Indeed his leg is immensely swollen and he can scarcely hobble, but when asked what he intends to do, his impassive reply is, 'Walk to the hospital,' which we know to be a mere seventy miles away. We take him on board and head for the meeting, knowing that the doctor is going to attend it in person.

We stop, a mile further on, to pick up a Chief, by agreement. In addition to himself and a retainer, his favourite wife, with an assortment of utensils, proceeds to climb on to the back of the long-suffering lorry. We raise our eyebrows at this, for the vehicle is already loaded to capacity (but in Africa no vehicle has a weight capacity, only a capacity of cubic space, and as long as a passenger can find a handhold or foot-room, there will be no mercy for the vehicle). We question the Chief. His reply is, 'Well, when you go on trek, would you go without a cook?' To this there is no answer, and we can only proceed with an extra wife and circumspection.

In a mile or two we come to a court-centre, where there is also a dispensary and a school, and which is in fact the focus of this part of the district. A new local government is being inaugurated here, for the democratic Nilotic nature is in some ways well suited to local government institutions, and a network of them is now springing up over Dinkadom as a foundation for administrative progress and eventual political adequacy. The organisation is already completed, but the buildings, simple yet sufficient, have to be opened with a small ceremony to mark the event.

This ceremony has to be gone through, involving an inaugural speech and the cutting of the tape, the symbolism of which is by now well enough understood, with the usual accompaniment of a large crowd, beef, beer, drums and dancing. The chosen head of the local government and some of his most honourable aldermen tuck up their gowns and join gravely and without self-consciousness in the terpsichorean exercise. Somehow it all seems perfectly appropriate, natural and dignified, where the Lord Mayor of London, dancing to a barrel-organ at his own show, with his robes tucked up, would not.

The ceremony has taken some time, and we now hasten onwards the last dozen miles to the meeting. As we approach the lake, the bush thins out, encampments and cattle herds increase, and here and there are boggy patches on the track. In one of these we stick, and there is nothing for it but to un-bog the lorry by manpower – apparently no difficult task, for there are willing hands within easy hail on every side.

The operation, however, takes rather longer than might have been expected for, unlike the squat, strongly-built Bantu man, the Nilotic, bred to a pastoral life with little manual labour and built accordingly – tall, thin, reasonably strong as far as the chest but petering out lankily from the loins downward – is not capable of great muscular output. His contribution to extricating our vehicle is to place a languid hand on the back of it and sing a song of victory.

With sufficient hands, sufficient time, and sufficient chanting in melodious voices, our lorry is extricated, and in the late afternoon sunlight we arrive at the meeting-place and can take stock of our surroundings. We are on the highest point in the landscape, a mound covering half an acre, bearing sizeable trees, rising ten feet above the plain, and probably the result at least in part of untold generations of human occupation and debris accumulating year after year. In front of us stretches the lake, and around it lies a vast area of flat land, intersected with meandering channels of bog and reed-choked water, with huge vistas of close-cropped green turf between, all leading back to the ant-hills and thickening bush which hide the horizon and mark the edge of the forest.

A frieze of tall Borassus palms stands out against the sunset across a broad waterway. Northwards, beyond a wide bight of the lake, there is no population and only the odd herdsman, and there I know that we can find herds of the rare Nile Lechwe, the fine swamp antelope which affords good sport to the energetic photographer (for it is protected) and lives in close proximity to the Dinka who, though without sentiment about animals, and as ready as any African to eat meat and occasionally to pursue it, like many pastorals are not primarily interested in hunting and are prepared to live peaceably with the wild life around them.

The remainder of the near landscape, however, is one mass of settlements. There is no shade and no timber: fires are made from cattle-dung. The shelters which house the population during the dry and dusty months are built of huge, plumed reeds sixteen or seventeen feet high, roughly arranged in the form of a candle-extinguisher, with a space of six feet diameter inside and meeting at the top, so that from a distance a village appears to be a cluster of lofty tufts on the horizon.

The cattle are tethered among the houses by night, for protection by human proximity from lions and by dung-fire from mosquitoes, and if you arrive at midday when they have been taken out to graze, you will find the ground studded with innumerable tethering pegs. At evening and morning the reed houses stick up over a sea of long horns and grey, pied and fawn backs covered in a mist of smoke from the dung fires. When camping near a village it is as well to pitch to windward, for though the scent is farmyardy and agreeable at a distance, at close range, with the pungent addition of Dinka tobacco, it is not aromatic.

Any such minor drawbacks of scent are blanketed, at this time of year, by the smell of dried, drying or semi-putrid fish, which is all pervasive: a hazard which has got to be accepted. For this is the low-water period, when fishing forms a major occupation and industry. A few young men and more women may stay in the camps, dressed becomingly in waistbands and necklaces of beads, an occasional ivory armlet and a grey covering of ash which can give a rather ghoulish appearance. But the bulk of the people will be either on or in the lake.

This is a remarkable sight. A couple of months ago in January, before the marshes and bogs had run off their surplus, the expanse of shallow water would have been two or three feet deeper and covered in large areas with a thick lace of water-lily, the seeds of which are eaten in hungry years and are far from unpalatable. In the early morning the flowers, which are the pinky-mauve of an autumn crocus, are fully out; the thickets of *ambatch,* a cork-like shrub growing in the water and used for canoes, carry their copious quota of yellow tassels, and the lake has positive beauty.

Now the water, muddy enough when looked into but silver in the low sun, is alive with figures, and half of them are black and half are snow-white. The white are pelicans. If it is a good year for fish there may be ten thousand of them. They are in droves on the surface, where they often fish is an organised manner. They will encompass an area of water with a cordon, which gradually closes, driving the fish into the centre as if the manoeuvre were directed by a mastermind. Only at the last moment, when the circle is small enough and the prey crowded and moidered enough, does some unknown authority give the word, and the fish are seized and swallowed in a free-for-all.

The birds form snowy ranks along the muddy shores. They float in skeins across the sky in wide and kinky Vs. For the pelican, which arises from the water and alights upon it with the movements and poise of an old-fashioned flying-boat, once in the sky has a power of soaring with motionless wings upon the air-currents as superb as any buzzard or eagle.

The quantity of fish eaten by them must be prodigious, but they are looked on as a token of good fishing, not as economic rivals.

The same applies to the hippos, even more strongly and with even better reason. In the centre of the lake, where the water is over five feet deep, lies a herd of maybe 150 hippos. The Dinka have known, empirically, for centuries what science has only realised in recent decades – that what some valuable species of fish live on is algae; that a potent producer of algae is manure, and that what produces manure is the hippo. Hence, the thicker the pachyderms, the thicker the fish.

On any normal day there will be thirty canoes assembled round the herd and only a few yards from them. Each canoe has two men, one to paddle, and one armed with a thin spear attached to his wrist by a long cord. When the beasts rise for a snort and a gulp of air, then submerge, the water around them seethes with fish. Into this cauldron the spear-man casts his weapon, hauls it back, casts again. At every tenth or twelfth cast, maybe, he will spike a fish, draw it in, bonk it on the head, and carry on his repeated casts.

The noise and commotion are tremendous, yet there is perfect understanding between man and animal; each knows just how far he can go, and nobody gets hurt – except when he disobeys orders. One day two men were bitten in half by getting between a baby and its mother – otherwise no rancour, no casualties: the hippos are protected, and the Dinka gets his richest fishing assured.

Of the Dinka themselves, there may be a thousand in the water, some in canoes, some alone or in pairs, some wading in long, extended lines of several hundred, which advance slowly though the shallow water and deeper mud beneath it, each man prodding as he goes with his light, barb-tipped weapon, or casting it in front of him before he steps forward. When a fish is skewered, it is tied to a string around the waist with other victims, and if you watch the line as it eventually emerges on the lake side, you may see up to forty or fifty pounds of fish round the waists of the more successful fishermen. Every camp has cords suspended and strips of fish drying or decomposing in the sun, and during this 'duffers' fortnight' – or rather two or three months – there is no lack of protein in the diet.

Fishing extends beyond the confines of the lake. As you travel across the flat, naked turf surrounding it you may occasionally see a solitary

Dinka mooching rather aimlessly around and stopping every few paces to stand and stamp. If you watch long enough you will see him go on his knees and begin grubbing. Asked what he is doing, he uninterestedly replies, 'Fishing'. He is neither barmy nor being facetious. There is a species of lung-fish which, when the water recedes from the flats in the dry weather, imbibes a quantity of oxygen and buries itself in the mud, its tail tucked into its mouth like a whiting, to remain entombed until the passage of months beings the next flood and it can regain its element. When the earth above is stamped upon, the fish, presumably thinking that it hears rain on the surface, responds with some kind of movement or sound which trained senses can detect, and it is disinterred.

There is other life around. Regiments of the big, dark-green spur-wing geese stand on the grazing grounds. Duck – the whistling-teal, knob-bill and garganey, with maybe a few pintail – are in profusion, and though they are not easy to approach with such lack of cover, we should have no difficulty in securing supper. White egrets there are, and saddlebill storks, and if lucky we might get a glimpse of the rare and prehistoric shoebill stork, morose, solitary and bog-loving, whose image is the province's crest.

Crocodiles are in the water, but they are seldom large; and though the district hospital is sure to contain a few cases of crocodile bite, and men with amputated feet or legs are not a rare sight, the damage is usually inflicted in defence, not offence, even a crocodile being permitted to turn and snap if trodden on by a heavy-footed, wading biped. Another minor hazard to the wader is the electric fish, a creature which has the power to emit a shock when touched. Though I do not credit current tales of people being stunned by the shock and thereafter drowned, I know from two or three encounters that it can be unpleasant and rather frightening.

Above all there is the sanitary squad. Vultures form only a small proportion, and the big majority consists of great marabou storks, loafing round the edge of every encampment with their pickaxe beaks, looking like scabby-headed, dirty-necked, dissolute old men with their hands under their coat-tails. If the ladies of a past generation who wore boas of soft marabou feathers could have seen the source of their neck-gear, the fashion would have disappeared the sooner.

Long ago, the species nearly caused a serious loss to the political service by almost cutting short the career of the late Sir Douglas Newbold, who later became Civil Secretary and one of the strongest and most beneficent influences on the twentieth-century Sudan. In his earliest months in the country he was not finding life easy. His Governor was not congenial; he had not acquired the language; the work was strange; he was on trek; the temperature was 112 F in the shade; he had succumbed to his first dose of malaria. Coming round after hours of semi-delirium, lying upon a bug-ridden bedspread in a stifling hut on a sand-dune, he peered through the low doorway and saw, only a few paces away, a great marabou perched on a scraggy acacia bush, regarding him with a baleful and anticipatory leer. Reaching a shaky hand for a pencil, he scrawled to the Khartoum Government an official letter of resignation from the service, on the ground that the birds were too big for the trees.

There is, however, one reputed inhabitant of some Dinka waterways which is, fortunately, not found in our present lake, though it is believed to exist in some of the deeper and mysterious stagnant channels which wind through northern Dinka territory. This is the *Jak anywong*, or more scientifically the *Jabberwockius niloticus*, a mythical riverain monster which is a mile long, has whiskers a quarter that length, and which will rise from the depth to snatch a man from his canoe and suck him dry of blood, so that the drained corpse floats to the surface.

There are stretches of water where no Dinka will swim, for fear of this kelpie, which sceptics have sought to identify with a monster river-turtle, with man-eating crocodiles or with water-lilies which entwine the swimmer and drag him to his death. I should like to be able to tell a good ghost story concerning the *Jak*, but the facts are just short of convincing. In 1947, at a meeting held on the bank of a haunted stretch, which from the top falls rapidly to a depth of fifteen feet, we were sitting at breakfast when a flight of duck flew past and settled. I suggested to a colleague that he should try for one with my small .22 rifle. He successfully shot one, but it flew to the centre of the river before collapsing dead on the surface. We asked a small Dinka boy to swim out, for a reward, and retrieve it, but he merely ejaculated '*Arioic*' – 'I'm scared.'

I said I would go for it, but my colleague courteously claimed that, being the younger and being the slayer, he should fetch it himself, and duly swam to the centre and grasped the duck. He had come more than halfway back when he slowed up, ceased to move forward and called, 'There's something there.' A moment later he shouted, 'My God! I'm going!' and sank under the surface. I jumped in, fully dressed, reached him, and together we made the bank and helped each other out. The small Dinka boy had run away. Half an hour later the Chiefs came to the senior District Commissioner and said, 'That was very lucky. We have never known the *Jak* touch an Arab or a European before. He had one of our men from a canoe three days ago, and there on the bank are the stomach contents of the bull which we had to slaughter to appease him.' Water-weeds? A touch of panic? Perhaps, but some scientific minds are thinking in terms of a fresh-water octopus – and there the matter rests.

Back on our mound we greet the two or three colleagues who have preceded us and also the assembled chiefs. The latter are dignified, impressive men, dressed in shorts and stockings and very clean shirts, or else in gowns of a simple local pattern, which always looks well. It is only when off their own ground, on a visit or on an occasion, that they are tempted into sartorial exuberance. Two Dinka Chiefs were once late for a sitting of the Province Council, and I rebuked them mildly for the misdemeanour. For the tea-party that afternoon they turned up more than half an hour early, announcing with a disarming smile that they had come early specially in order to atone for being late in the morning. One wore a seedy tarboush, a flame-coloured shirt and a pair of white duck trousers with all the fly-buttons undone. The other was clad in a khaki cap from the 1914 war, a huge, mustard-yellow nightgown with a mauve zephyr showing underneath it, striped woollen socks and arty-crafty sandals. (Incidentally, you must always cut up a cake before sending it round at a tea-party; if a mere piece is cut, the intended recipient will normally take the cake and leave the piece.)

On the present occasion, however, the only exception to restrained and seemly fashions is the Chief of a neighbouring tribe. Old Unguich is a fine character and figure, ugly as a heathen idol yet stout in limb and spirit, a loyal, dependable, wise man. His broad chest is covered with such an array of putty medals, possible and impossible, real or manufactured, as few field-marshals could show. His face beams, and a retainer behind him carries his fowling-piece.

On one occasion when a lion was infesting his neighbourhood and taking a regular toll of cattle and goats, I spent a night at his village and we carried out a hunt at dawn hoping to pick up the miscreant's tracks, for there had been rain on the previous afternoon. Once I thought I heard the enemy give a deep growl some way away, but when I turned sharply round at the sound it proved to be only Unguich's stomach rumbling just behind me. I then examined the weapon which he carried.

In its heyday it had been a Remington rifle, but the stock was parting from the barrel, to which it was secured by strips of an old puttee. The sights had been removed to avoid the tiresome formality of aiming; and the hammer, which was at full cock, was restrained by a bootlace whose other end was attached to the trigger-guard. I asked, with some trepidation, whether if we met the lion it would go off. The reply was in dog-Arabic difficult to translate, but literally interpreted ran, 'If the bullet is happy, it will, please God, go off.'

It is too late tonight for business, but that will begin tomorrow; and while the district commissioners and departmental officers discuss mutual problems, the Chiefs will get down to the hearing of inter-district cases, for the court system is sensibly elastic, and where Chiefs from more than one district are gathered together they can, united, form a court with jurisdiction over all the areas and peoples involved.

The Dinka are in a sense a litigious folk – but not in a disagreeable manner, for they are not a quarrelsome or cantankerous people. Yet in a society founded upon cattle, where every calf is traceable back to the third and fourth generation of its ancestors and where every cow, transferred from one owner to another, by calving multiplies and complicates its own problem, there cannot be a citizen who has not got at least one current cattle-case, and some have many. In these cases, and in cattle-law as well as cattle-lore, they are as intensely interested as a legal student may be in leading cases.

If there is no suitable one to hand, they will invent a hypothetical one. A leading Chief with a high judicial reputation was awoken in the small hours by a party who wanted a decision on the following legal conundrum. 'The lion lost his seal and offered a reward for it. The rat found it in a hole. The kite offered to carry it to the lion, but on the way dropped it in the water. The frog recovered it and gave it to the lion on the bank.

Which has done most and how should the reward be distributed?' (The kite was adjudged to have merited the greater share. Dinka jurisprudence is unfathomable.)

Proceedings are orderly, unhurried and efficient. Indeed Dinka courts are of high quality, and seldom wrong in their decisions. Their weakness, as with Arab courts but to an even greater degree, lies in the execution of those decisions. For among Nilotics there is little tradition of executive chiefship; but in their natural and pre-government condition it involved principally magical and sacerdotal functions, and passed from the holder to his successor, normally a man of his own family or clan, with possession of the sacred fish-spear of the clan concerned.

Whatever the sweets of power, the role of the Chief of the fish-spear carried with it the prospect of a (to us) grisly end, though no Chief himself would have it otherwise. The inspiring spirit must not be allowed to be snuffed out by an ordinary death. When clearly at death's door, the Chief would be placed in state and a ceremonial dance held around him of such vigour and intensity that, in his enfeebled state, the dust would bring on suffocation. He would then be laid in his grave, possibly with life still not extinct, and buried, his spirit thus passing legitimately to his successor.

Such an end to a noted Chief was prevented in the winter of 1943-44 only by the chance presence of a District Commissioner, and the presence of a Government anthropologist avoided a similar euthanasia some five or six years later. Nevertheless, during such a Chief's lifetime his prestige and his wealth are great, the best thermometer of them being the number of his wives. The former of the two eminent men just mentioned complained to me that he was not the man he once was. His fleet of wives had sunk to twenty-nine sail.

At the time when the Chief of the fish-spear held the pre-eminence, leadership for purposes of defence and aggression might be established by any great figure who showed prowess in the field; but this would be temporary and a matter of personality; no tradition existed, as it does among Arabs, of the duties, privileges and powers of rulers. Government has therefore had a hard task in establishing a system of Chiefs who could at once serve Government itself and take executive responsibility, while commanding the acceptance of their people. This lack of natural rulers is one of the reasons for the Nilotic areas being a generation behind much of the rest of the country in political and economic advance, and the remarkable feature is that a cadre of responsible men has been found and formed in so short a segment of history.

Two figures frequently seen in Dinka proceedings catch the eye. One is the village idiot. The Chiefs sit on chairs or stools, and the populace squat on the ground. But the village idiot is perched on a kind of pedestal in the middle, a big ostrich feather sticking out of his hair, a large football boot on his left foot and a pink sock on his right, interpolating wise remarks from time to time or pretending to lead the discussion. He is accepted as part of the picture, and nobody pays much attention. The purpose he serves is not thought-out but is presumably much the same as that served by the jester in past centuries – to prevent pomposity and to emphasise the common humanity which underlies all social distinctions, from king to beggar.

The other figure is more important and has a more conscious and official place in the proceedings. This is the *gamloon*. There is no equivalent term in other languages, for he is neither interpreter nor loud-speaker. If a member of the court or a litigant or a witness is speaking, and he pauses for an instant at the close of the sentence, the *gamloon* in a loud and ringing voice repeats the last few words of the sentence, practically like an echo, though occasionally gathering up in a word or two the significance of a longer phrase. His function is not without value. He guards against orators who drop their voices at the end of a sentence; he gives the speaker himself that fraction of respite which helps in collecting thought and maintaining sequence; and by the insistence of repetition, like rhyme in poetry, he tends to bear in upon the audience the meaning of the utterance.

The majority of cases dealt with concern cattle, varying from involved questions of personal law and custom to straightforward instances of inter-tribal cattle raiding, for the Nuer have always been militarily the more aggressive, and inclined, but for Government control, to dominate their more pacific Dinka neighbours. There is, however, one inter-section fight to be dealt with, for the powers of the biggest courts extend even to cases of causing death, provided it is done in tribal fights and not in an individual quarrel or as a deliberate killing

The problem of Nilotic fights is not a simple one for the administrator.

No government worthy of the name can tolerate large inter-sectional imbroglios involving wounds and death. Yet such fights have a certain purpose in a primitive society. They exercise the virile instincts on which a tribe's emergence depends. They have surprisingly little effect on the general public security of the neighbourhood. As a rule, the casualties are astonishingly small, partly because of the Dinka's trained skill in avoidance and partly because certain rough rules of the game are generally followed. Indeed, the last really serious and abnormal battle had occurred a dozen years ago and more, when one section started before dawn (an irregular manoeuvre) and by a pincer movement caught their opponents unprepared and between two fires. The result was a Glencoe, with forty-one dead on the losing side against a mere handful on that of the attackers, leaving a legacy of ill-feeling and potential revenge which is not dead yet.

But that was not usual. The more customary procedure was witnessed by a veterinary colleague, who was informed that a fight was getting under weigh and, very commendably, drove straight to the spot in an effort to restore the peace. The conflagration had, as usual, been started by a small spark among suitable tinder. Two sections were mutually hostile, and the ill manners of a boy to an elder of the other section, an ill-advised assault by the latter, and the summoning of help by both sides, had set light to the train.

The combatants numbered possibly five hundred on either side, and were drawn up some forty yards apart. Spears were being thrown across the intervening space. Flanking fire – *i.e.* sideways at men further down the line and engaged with their opposite numbers – was not indulged in; but the supporters of the hundred-odd men in each front line would throw their heavy sticks high in the air at the opposition's heads, thus engaging their attention while their No. 1 could hurl his spear direct and with better chance of scoring a bull. There was no concerted movement of attack or endeavour to come to close quarters.

When the veterinary inspector boldly attempted to separate the opposing lines by driving down the lane between them, he was baffled by the combatants politely pausing to allow the truck to pass before continuing with their own game of Aunt Sally. Even when two policemen attempted to walk between the lines, firing shots over the fighters' heads, the combatants good-naturedly let them pass – and then carried on as before. Women were on the spot, making a show of dissuading their menfolk from combat, but a few were not above picking up a club and having a throw themselves. This had been going on for two hours when the officer arrived, and it continued for three more, until sundown, when bad light stopped play.

In the intervals of hearing cases among the Chiefs and conducting business between neighbouring District Commissioners, a good deal of departmental business has also been done. The Inspector of Education has visited us and in consultation with the Chiefs has selected some of the next year's intake for 'Dinkchester,' the big Government boys' school situated in the neighbouring district. For it is essential to ensure that a quota of boys comes from all the main sections in the province and not from one or two only. Education is like manure; it wants to be well spread. It is also important to secure that those boys selected are of the right kind and drawn from houses which are likely to produce the rulers of the next generation.

The province medical inspector has visited us, to get across propaganda about the new drug for cerebro-spinal meningitis, and in the course of inspecting his hospital and dispensaries. The province veterinary inspector has been running a rinderpest-inoculation campaign, such a concentration of cattle-camps giving a good opportunity. In the earlier stages there was suspicion of all inoculation, but once it became apparent that inoculated herds escaped the full blast of disease which is always endemic and from time to time devastatingly epidemic, the Chiefs' confidence was won; and confidence, together with the increase of cattle numbers which will give a surplus, is a first necessary step towards inducing the Dinka to use their wealth economically.

All this has taken several days, and the meeting is about to break up. No meeting would be complete without dancing, and more than one dance there will be, spontaneous and unsolicited, among the camps. Dinka voices are more musical to our ears than those of the Bantu races. They are vigorous, less nasal and tolerably melodious, though their singing is based on the same type of pentatonic scale, and Western types of music must be hard for them to understand. Once long ago I played a number of gramophone records to a party of Dinkas. The music was various, both vocal and instrumental, but included a duet, sung by Caruso and Tetrazzini, from one of the fruitiest Italian operas. This aroused immense enthusiasm, and when the records were finished and I asked whether there was any particular one which they wished to hear again, there was an universal appeal for an encore of 'the one where the man was beating his wife.' Instrumental music there is none among Nilotics, and the dancing is done to vocal accompaniment and to two bass and two tenor drums, which give unusually melodious and varied results for percussion.

The attitudes, like their songs, are concerned with cattle; this particularly applies to the gestures of the arms which, uplifted above the head or thrust backwards from the shoulders in a distorted and double-jointed posture impossible to anybody but a Dinka, are indicative of the great perpendicular horns of the Nilotic bull. The dancing itself I rank above that of the Bantu races. The blue beads of the men and the kid-skin aprons of the women are becoming; the long, lithe figures, capering and leaping, carry a wonderful animal gracefulness and seem able to pause in mid-air for a split second as if defying the laws of gravity. It is a display worth going far to see and a fitting close to our gathering before we take our farewell and reluctantly leave for duties elsewhere.

To Aunt Nora   15 September 1927
Wau

This is the slack season, when business in the office isn't particularly heavy, though as the grass is twelve feet high and many of the roads are impassable, trekking is also a difficulty. Nevertheless, I've been out for a couple of short rounds inspecting cotton, which is – or ought to be – sown about August. The dilatory and improvidential habits of the tribes make it very necessary for someone to go round and stir them up at the critical time.

One gets plenty of walking exercise, trekking perhaps fourteen or fifteen miles in the early dawn from one village to another and then spending the day perlustrating all the cotton fields in the vicinity and hauling the good-tempered but lackadaisical tribesmen on to their cultivations, and delivering impressive Arabic homilies to the chiefs on the subject of seizing the golden hour – though as their Arabic is generally as bad as one's own, and all have different dialects, one's finest forensic gems are usually lost upon them.

CHAPTER SIX

The Nuba Hill-men

The richness and immense variety of the peoples of the Sudan make it impossible for us to visit all, or even half, the communities which go to form the whole. We can only select important parts of the jigsaw and by piecing them together get some idea of what the whole picture must look like. From those parts the Nuba cannot be omitted. They are too individual and distinctive, and at the same time too typical an example of the diversity of elements which, in the Sudan, have to be fused into a nation.

The Blue Mountains cover an area which may amount to 15,000 square miles, and they lie west of the White Nile in the province of Kordofan, mostly between latitudes 10.30 and 12.30. They vary from small, conical *jebels* to huge masses and jumbles of granite mountain. The texture of the hills shifts from vast cliffs, blocks and slabs, with whole systems of caves inside them, to smallish stones which Beelzebub has so placed that they slip away under every step, with a nice admixture of coarse sand and gravel at intervals to get into the shoes, so that negotiating them in a shade temperature of over 100 degrees is not for the dilettante. But the beauty, the diversity of the vegetation and the interest of the people themselves make the effort worthwhile.

The Nuba groups number between 300,000 and 400,000 souls, and what makes them remarkable is that they form a great geographical and racial island. Into the bays and creeks and inlets of this island flow the tides and cultures of other races. In the north the settled Arab life of the Northern Sudan impinges upon them. From both west and north the cattle-owning Baggara tribes seep into their territory. To the east are other Arab and quasi-Arab elements. To the south are the Nilotic Dinka. Yet the island in the main retains its integrity.

The Nuba are a black and African race, probably of great antiquity, with their origins further north and west. While Arab civilisation has pushed slowly southward to its present limit, they have maintained themselves in their hill fastnesses. So wedded are they to their hills, to whose inaccessibility they once owed their survival, that even now, when they can mix freely and fearlessly with their neighbours, they still mostly prefer to cling limpet-like to their hillsides and are very slow to drift downhill to live on easier ground and cultivate more remunerable soil. What further distinguishes them is that although mainly one race and with one common problem of survival, yet they are split into innumerable communities, each independent of the others, each with its own customs and culture, and each with its own tongue. In this block of people are found eleven totally different language groups, mutually unintelligible, and 121 distinct dialects.

This is the despair of the administrator and the joy of the anthropologist. The Nuba have been the victims, though rather insouciant ones, of several professional anthropologists, who have collected truck-loads of beads, bones, pots, utensils, throwing-knives, bangles, hoes, spears and other evidence, studied their system of inheritance, ceremonial customs, burial methods, daily habits and (in some cases) their languages, and have written up their findings in anything from magazine articles to long and cumbrous tomes. I have always held an open mind upon the practical value of anthropology. It is one of those twilight studies which come between the vulgar glare of purely utilitarian inquiries and the decent obscurity of the incomprehensible which clothes higher mathematics. On the whole I gravely doubt whether much knowledge is acquired which can ever be of humdrum service to administration.

No one hill in the Nuba mountains is typical of all, and to do a Baedeker tour of the area would be tedious and take far too long. There is nothing for it but to look at different aspects in different places and try to build up a complete picture.

Before we get into the core of the unassimilated Nuba, if we come from the north or north-eastern approaches, we shall go through a wide fringe of what used to be called 'arabicised Nuba'. These are people whose origins are Nuba of Fung (from the Abyssinian border) who were assimilated by the tide of Arab civilisation three and four centuries ago and are now sucked into the big local government amalgam which forms the Kingdom of Tegali.

At one time the Nuba tended to exercise a fascination over their administrators similar to that exercised by the romantic Arab nomad and the statuesque Nilotic African. The term 'Nuba renaissance' occurs not infrequently in official correspondence, and the underlying assumption has been that, preserved from corroding external influences, this African civilisation has a great future before it. But, at the risk of being burned in effigy by Nuba enthusiasts, I state my firm belief that it is a fallacy: that a primitive, pagan African culture has very little future at all, and does not possess those elements of adaptability and creative innovation which are of survival value; and that its fate must be either slow supersession by, or absorption into, a higher culture, or equally slow but equally certain extinction.

The 'arabicised Nuba', at one time slightly cold-shouldered by administrators as being neither one thing nor the other, I believe to be an interesting example of successful amalgamation. These peoples had retained much of their ancient way of life; they clung to mountain homes as their ancestors had done. Yet Islam had laid upon them a unifying and a civilising hand. They were quiet, law-abiding, sensible, hard-working folk who, except when impelled to excess by insobriety, produced very little crime of either violence or dishonesty, and who seemed a living embodiment of the philosopher's contention that poverty is the path to happiness. Their worldly wealth in cash or in animals was small, yet they always appeared contented, useful citizens and capable of taking a part in the advancing civilisation around them.

Much of their procedure showed how a new and superior faith lays its hold only gradually as it is grafted on to a people's customs. Those who had been within the pale of Islam for two or three centuries were tolerably orthodox. Another community, who had been in that state for only half a century, were more pious and earnest than many Arabs who had been in the fold for a millennium, and had dropped all pagan rituals and ceremonies – with the exception of one annual beano held at some hot springs during the early rains and intended to produce a good harvest.

A black kid would be taken, its face turned towards the springs, and it would be let loose. If it swithered and went out of the way, ill fortune could be expected. Did it lead to the springs (and if it had been kept suitably thirsty, it generally did), a good year was assured. On arrival it would be slaughtered and ceremonially eaten, with texts from the Koran and appropriate prayers in lieu of pagan invocations; and anyone who spat or let his stomach rumble would incur a year's bad luck.

This kind of half-way stage is found elsewhere, particularly on the western fringe of the hill, where live small communities who are circumcised and who would be most offended if any imputations were thrown on their adherence to Islam, while at the same time they will keep the abhorrent pig, eat wart-hog (as will many Arabs, maintaining that it is not a true pig, and therefore not under the Koranic ban), indulge in frequent and prolonged alcoholic excess, and, when a man dies, desert the Sharia law for their own ancestral, matrilinear habits. The process of assimilation into a superior faith and culture is therefore a very gradual one, as doubtless the early missionaries found with our barbarian Saxon ancestors. But it is a sure one, and in my opinion a beneficial one, and necessary to the forging of a sound civilisation.

In the critical days of 1940 and 1941 these hills provided the stoutest and most copious material for recruits to the army, and at all times produced many of the best police. Training the recruits was a most interesting job. The military authorities at Headquarters, having their hands full and being wise men, preferred recruits to be given their preliminary training and drill in their own districts, and this quasi-military duty fell to the District Commissioner and the N.C.O.s of the Sudanese police.

Admirably the latter did their job. The recruits went to Headquarters with a knowledge of elementary drill and of handling and firing a rifle, and with certain other skills which army training might not have included. One of these was handling camels (which proved essential transport for the campaign in Abyssinia). The technique of the camel – second nature to the Arab who lives with the species – is the Waterloo of many an otherwise excellent soldier: it is with difficulty acquired by the cattle-owning Arab, and quite baffling to most Africans. A man who would cheerfully face a lion when armed with only a spear will scuttle apprehensively out of range when a kneeling camel begins its usual grumbling roar of protest at being loaded; and I shall not readily forget the expression of horror on the face of a young man (soon to win distinction at the battle of Keren) when a sour-faced camel bolted with him like Beelzebub in that ungainly, lolloping gallop which nothing can stop.

Another art in which we trained them, subsequently of value in Abyssinian warfare, was stalking. I would stand on a hillock in moderately thick cover, armed with a magazine of stones and small rocks. The recruits would then be made to scatter into the bush, and, on the blowing of a whistle, to stalk me, each in his own way and by his own route. As soon as a man was descried I would throw the heaviest brickbat available, aiming at his head – and whether it hit him or not, he became theoretically dead. This made them very careful. At the end the one who had approached nearest without being detected received a prize of one shilling. Only one man went into hospital with a broken skull, and the skill developed by the best of them was uncanny.

Now we must assume that we have passed through the fringe and reached the core of the true Nubas. From hill to block of hills we shall find differences. This extends notably to physiognomy. In the Kowalib, to the north, we shall see people with dark brown skins, the women much pleasanter to look at than the men, with tight, curly hair usually coloured with ochreous clay, and with fine eyes, fine though somewhat steatopygous figures – that is, with large bottoms – and becoming brass ornaments. In Fungor and Kau at the south-west corner we shall find people almost black, the men muscular, magnificent specimens, while the women are weedy and ugly as sin. In the Moro hills we shall find a race which is physically of an A1 standard, broad and tall and strong, while a stone's throw away across the valley on the hills of Tira Limon are a C3 people of smaller stature and punier muscle.

The babel of languages is matched by a diversity in moral standards almost as marked. A glance at any court's records will reveal this. The book of the court of the Tira Hills shows that out of ninety-five criminal cases tried in the last eight months, fifty-nine were cases of theft. The Kowalib book shows eighty-five cases, of which fifty-seven were cases of adultery. Those figures accurately reflect the character and tendencies of the people. I think I am right in saying that the Kowalib language has no word with which to translate 'chastity'. On the other hand, among Tira theft is not regarded as a crime at all, but as a normal activity in which a young man is expected to be trained; and a youth would find marriage difficult until he has persuaded his potential in-laws that he has accomplished one or more worthy thefts, preferably of a cock from the hen-house attached to a dwelling. Whereas there is little virtue in driving off a cow or a few goats wandering unguarded in the bush, the abstraction of a fowl involves the highest degree of skill, cat-like quiet and adroitness, since one clumsy movement may occasion an untimely squawk and lead to discovery.

As the moral values alter from hill to hill, so do the subtler qualities of character and make-up. From among the Otoro or the Moro we may expect to elicit some response, to meet with a glimmering of intelligent appreciation and the comprehension from which spring social and political process. Among the Korongo, a mere day's walk away, we must look for no response; cheerful enough they may be, perhaps no more troublesome than any other hill tribe if left to their own devices, but with an animal unresponsiveness to new ideas and a disinterest in the outside world which makes them impervious to civilisation.

It is no policy of their rulers and no fault of their neighbours; it is this self-sufficiency, this lack of interest in the world outside which has preserved large blocks of the Nuba as an intriguing human zoo into the middle of the 20th century and made them almost unique in Africa. The Protestant missions which worked among them for thirty-five years made extremely little headway. More remarkable, Islam, though it has engulfed certain outlying parts, has lapped at the main cliffs of Nuba-land for centuries without causing noticeable erosion.

As with physique and character, so with architecture. There is no uniformity. Among the Kowalib the huts are ill-built, of flimsy mud-and-wattle walls a mere inch thick which may disintegrate under a season's rains. Seventy miles southward among the Masakin we are in a different architectural world. A homestead is a complicated affair, with many rooms built on a system, peaked and turreted like a fairy castle and constructed of thick, solid mud compacted into a firm cement which will stand against gale and tempest for many years. Jump the valley into the Moro hills, and around us is yet another superior style – houses built of stones carefully selected and laid together on foundations piled up against the sharp slope of the mountainside, in such guise as to last for a century. The rooms are well spaced and ample, and have almost the appearance of a Cotswold stone farm. All centre round the pig-pit, which lies in the middle, the hub of family life, with a flat, flagged floor and chambers for its porcine tenants to shelter from the weather.

In all these villages the houses are well scattered, with good intervals between them. Travel eastwards to Kau and Fungor, and a village is so tightly packed, house against house, granary touching granary, that it is difficult to thread a way along the labyrinthine tracks which permeate the rabbit-warren. No epidemic of cerebro-spinal meningitis (which thrives in cramped and crowded conditions), no conflagration (a fire will whisk through the roofs of the entire village) will persuade the people to alter their immemorial habits: considerations neither of hygiene nor of safety can impinge on tradition.

In the Nuba's sports and pastimes there is variety. All Nuba are, or were, hunters; but the bigger species of game have long been exterminated within easy radius of the hills. A few small gazelle and duiker are all that survive of the once-rich animal life, along with guinea fowl, some baboons and the hyrax – the rock-rabbit or coney of the Bible; and even these remnants of fauna have a hard time against the hosts of old muzzle-loader and Remington rifles with which the Nuba are armed.

These firearms vary from the fairly efficient to the grotesque. I was once staying at a hill village, and the *mek* (the chief) confessed over a cup of tea that he possessed a firearm which was not registered. What about it? I drew a long face and told him that the first thing was to produce it, and then we would decide. Half an hour later there came the sound of heavy breathing, and slowly into the lamplight staggered three myrmidons carrying the fowling piece. The barrel was hexagonal, five feet long and about a third of an inch thick. The stock looked like the stump of a tree (probably it was – a replacement of the original). In rusty letters on the barrel was the word Stuttgart, and a date which looked like 1486. Probably this was 1686, but I am fairly sure that Cromwell had something more effective at Marston Moor.[3]

I asked whether the weapon had ever been used. The answer was

---

3   The Battle of Marston Moor, in Yorkshire, fought on 2 July 1644, was the largest of the English Civil War, and ended in a resounding victory for Oliver Cromwell and the Parliamentarians.

'Once only. We were much troubled by hyenas. We therefore used this weapon of my grandfather's as a trap. We collected many rusty nails, buttons, pebbles and screws, poked them down the barrel on top of a triple charge of powder, tied a big lump of putrid meat on to the muzzle and attached that by a wire to the trigger. This engine of destruction we placed in a suitable open space, close to where we now sit, and we retired to rest. At midnight we were awakened by a splendid detonation. At dawn we went in great expectancy to the spot, but were at first disappointed to find no sign of a victim – until, hunting around behind that bush you see in the lamplight, we found the sole remains: the hyena's tail.'

Hunting went on by every method possible, including what was known as a *dare,* an organised band armed with clubs and spears and accompanied by dogs, who would surround a patch of country with a cordon and then gradually close in, killing anything that could be cornered inside it. I once met such a party returning. There were forty-one men, and they had been hunting for two days. The total bag was two young duiker, three guinea fowl, two francolin (partridges), two hares, one hawk, one wild cat, one mongoose, one hedgehog and one lizard.

I never discovered anything that walks or crawls which Nuba would not eat. Cobras were on the menu, though I think the black mamba may have been off. Most revolting of all to our way of thinking were the huge, black-spined, yellow-bellied caterpillars, four inches long, which appeared in profusion in acacia forest at the height of the rains. They could be pounded to a mush in a gourd, but I have seen one dropped, wriggling, into the mouth and swallowed with relish.

Of the definite sports the most widespread was wrestling, which was indulged in by nearly all hills; and at the proper season, usually after the harvest about early December, villages – and occasionally hills – would visit rivals at some distance to play away matches. The wrestling specialists were the Korongo, probably the burliest of all Nuba, among whom the contests were accompanied by no small ceremonial, ritual and musical effort. Several pairs of contestants could operate at the same time in the ring. Every man, woman and child on the hill turned out to watch the event. The neophytes – young men being admitted to the honours of full manhood through the wrestling ceremony – were lined up, paired off and sent into the ring smeared all over a ghastly grey with wood-ash, while the Master of Ceremonies conducted the proper ritual, beating the ground with a palm-frond flap and stirring up a thick pall of dust, and the musicians blew deep, sonorous, bellicose brays upon kudu-horns fitted with a huge prolongation of wooden tube to act as an amplifier. No refreshment was allowed until close of play, when a troupe of ladies would appear on the ground, each with her gourd holding about two gallons of beer for the warriors' refection.

A morning's walk away, on the Masakin hills, were the stick-fighting specialists. The contestant is protected by layers of sheepskins, rags and clouts around his thighs and waist, his trunk guarded by a giraffe-hide shield and his head fortified with a matted wig of cow-dung and rancid cheese compressed into a dense thatch. The weapons are stout singlesticks, and the vigour of the mutual onset is terrific, yet I have never heard of a death being caused by the weapons. There was an occasional fatality, or an eye put out, by a player getting tired of whacking away at an absorbent mass of stuff, running in with his shield uplifted and giving a downwards jab with its sharp corner. There might also be a danger to spectators. I was once watching a series of contests when one stick broke against another: the severed end hurtled through the air and removed my helmet, leaving a gash on my forehead.

Perhaps the most impressive of these gladiatorial sports was the bracelet fighting, restricted to three little hills on the eastern side. Each fight began with some brisk quarter-staff work, but this was only a preliminary to quicken the blood. On his wrist the combatant wore a bronze bracelet with a double flange to it, an inch deep, on the inner side of the wrist. While guarding his own head with his left hand, his object, after staves had been discarded, was to get his right hand above his opponent's head and bring down the cutting flanges of the bracelet upon his crown. The moment blood was drawn, the contest was over. Great skill was shown by the competitors, but the most remarkable features were the vigilance and speed of the referees. There were two of these, and they watched their men like cats. If any competitor broke the rules in a single important particular, such as by letting out an uppercut (which might be dangerous) or by losing his temper, they would seize him by the waist and eject him from the ring, to be laughed at by the women. Nuba skulls are solid, and I never heard of a death being caused, though blood-letting was copious enough.

Nuba life was governed largely by rites, ceremonies and magical practices – although I do not think the Nuba was so tightly controlled by these practices as is the Bantu tribesman of Central and East Africa. The latter can live in a perpetual state of semi-fear of the occult, attributing nearly all that happens, whether good or ill, to numinous influences. I always had the impression that the Nuba's sense of natural religion was small (which may account for their resistance both to Islam and to Christianity), and that it was the outward and ceremonial side which mattered most to them. Certainly every important event in the cycle of the year or in the course of private life was preceded or accompanied by the appropriate *sibir,* a name which covered any ceremony or celebration, The variety of these was immense, and the role of *kujur* an important one.

The stock translation of *kujur* as 'witch doctor' has a malevolent and Rider Haggard nuance and is not satisfactory. A *kujur* was not, properly speaking, a priest, but rather any man in whom the public recognised the effective power, hereditary or otherwise, to carry out the occult practices inseparable from their social life. He might wield great influence or slight. He might be an all-round wizard or specialise in a particular branch. He might be dangerous, or benevolent and useful. The practice of the *kujur*'s art by individuals without the proper credentials was normally frowned-upon, and could lead to serious trouble.

L'apprenti sorcier has always been a stock figure, demonstrating the danger of dabbling in what is beyond our proper province – and of this there was a typical example in 1939. One of the *kujur*'s most important functions was that of rain-maker – a post which could carry great prestige, not without some risk to the holder. At the end of July the court of the Otoro and Tira hills sentenced a Tira man rejoicing in a name which sounded like 'O'randy O'murray' to one-and-a-half years' imprisonment, ostensibly for causing hurt by witchcraft and stopping the rain. It was also reported that he had been nearly killed by an angry mob. O'randy's sister's daughter had married a man of the Noli clan, one of the two clans among the Tira associated with rain-storms and thunderbolts. O'Randy himself had no hereditary connection with such things, but he sometimes played with roots and cures and curses, often obtained from West Africans and suchlike disreputable non-Nuba sources.

He did not like his niece's marriage, and put a spell upon her by administering some root medicines to her food, to make her barren and cause her to hate her husband and fall in love with another man. The spell worked admirably: no heir appeared, the woman could not abide her husband, and began to receive the advances of a rival. Her Noli husband, suspecting what had happened, accused O'randy of putting a spell on the girl. O'randy denied it and said he would take an oath. A meeting of elders decided to administer it. The Noli clan keep special spears for such oaths. These weapons are in the charge of particular members of the clans, and are hung up in the smoke from the house fires, where they get blackened and stained. Anyone swearing falsely on these spears of the rain clans is sure to find himself in the path of the next thunderbolt.

On one of the spears, in full assembly, O'randy swore that he had not bewitched the girl. A day or two later he appeared with a black goat before the girl's husband. He was deeply distressed and said that, as a matter of fact, he *had* perjured himself, and would his adversary please 'sprinkle' him. When you have taken a false oath, there is only one way of avoiding the consequences. You must sacrifice a black animal or bird – a cock, goat or sheep – and the person offended by the oath must take a bowl of water and with his hand sprinkle it over your head, and so release you from your guilt.

The Noli man, justly incensed and having lost the affection of his wife, refused to do anything of the kind, and said the culprit must incur his punishment. O'randy was terrified. It was July; storms were about daily, and the next lightning flash might find him out. He was not of a rain clan, and had no hereditary influence on approaching troughs of low pressure. However, other methods might prevail, so he went to an Arab *fiki* of the less reputable kind on the borders of Tira and bought from him for four shillings (which he did not pay) a suitable recipe for averting storms.

A day or two later a healthy and much-needed storm was approaching the Tira hills, and O'randy was seen by six witnesses standing with upraised spear in front of his house. Tied to the spear below the head were some fowl's feathers, some grass from the roof of a house, a roll of blackish paper with texts on it, and two pig's feet. This mixed bag he waved slowly backwards and forwards, repeating an abracadabra which witnesses could not hear and which he refused to divulge. The storm obediently passed by, and Tira was left dry.

This happened several times. O'randy was not a popular figure at the best of times, and now what need was there of further witnesses? Rain was badly needed, and if rain was to come, he must be killed. The Tira had killed a similar rain-stopper ten or twelve years previously, forcibly restraining the Government police while they did so, and Government had only made them pay a number of cows as blood money. When they killed another man in about 1914, all Government had done was take one or two of the offenders and put them into the army. Was it not better to pay a few cows or provide a few recruits than to lose all their crops? Accordingly a large party set out to deal with O'randy.

Fortunately they found him absent from his house, which they pulled down. Meanwhile Loicho, the excellent *mek* of Tira, hearing what was afoot, set out to search for him, discovered him and had him put under arrest. The vengeance party, arriving soon afterwards, demanded blood. The *mek* said he wanted to hold an inquiry into the case; it was already evening, and he would hand him over for death in the morning. This partly pacified the avengers, but what pacified them more was the fact that at the moment O'randy had been taken into custody, there began a rainstorm which lasted into the small hours of the following morning.

During the night the *mek* sent his prisoner up to the Court-house, ten miles away, where the main court under the big *mek*, Keppe, was going to hold its monthly sitting next day. Thither the mob repaired, now swollen to considerable numbers and armed with spears, sticks and guns. When they demanded their victim, the weapons were laid down – for when you kill a rain-stopper, it must be done only one way: he must be beaten to death with blows on the body. The head must not be struck, and anyone hitting it is liable to fall victim to the next thunderbolt.

The court had considerable difficulty in keeping the mob from rushing the court-house. Eventually, however, it succeeded in hearing the witnesses, extracted the whole story, and informed the multitude that it had decided to hand the accused over to the Government to be put to death – while actually recording a sentence of eighteen months' imprisonment on O'randy for putting harmful spells on a woman and for deliberately trying to prevent the rain. Whether the mob would have accepted this is uncertain, but the decision had scarcely been announced when clouds burst in a rainstorm, which left no doubt that the judgement

was approved by the Highest Court. The crowd dispersed, and a day later
O'randy found himself lodged in gaol and safe, and there he had to remain
in protective custody until feeling had died down.

What of the *meks*, the Chiefs who rule these hill communities? Without
good leaders no community can hope to cope with modern life, and no
government can hope to maintain a progressive administration. As usual,
variety of practice and tradition marks the Nuba. I do not think there
is any strong tradition of secular kingship among them; there is neither
the tradition of responsible if autocratic leadership which so marks the
Arab civilisation, nor the irresponsible but accepted tyranny found by the
explorers of the nineteenth century in a Mutesa of Buganda and other
Bantu potentates.

In some hills there had been secular leaders with greater or lesser
powers according to personality and custom. In others there appears
never to have been more than the influence wielded by more or less
puissant *kujurs* through their semi-magical functions. Any question
of headship was further complicated by the customs of inheritance,
which in some hills were patrilinear, like those of Asiatic and European
civilisation, while in others they were matrilinear – *i.e.* when a man dies,
the normal successor to his property and position would be not his own
son but the son of his sister, all rights of inheritance accruing through
the mother.

On a *mek*-ship falling vacant, the right personality could usually be
found in some ex-N.C.O. from the army or the police. Some Nuba hills
provided a large percentage of the recruits to the Sudan Defence Force,
and army life seemed to instil those elementary qualities which are the
bedrock of administration – sense of discipline and power of command.
Many of the more trusted *meks* were former sergeants. Occasionally an
individual could be found with some traditional claims to greatness,
though they were seldom rooted in the distant past. Such were *Mek*
Keppe of Otoro and one or two others, men of character and substance on
whom a local government could rest. True, that substance might run out,
for no *mek* can act as the dispenser of the wealth of his tribe as can an Arab
sheikh. In *Mek* Keppe's top jaw were two fine gold teeth. Beneath them
were two conspicuous gaps, due to his having had four teeth extracted in

order to build up a gold reserve in his head, and his money having run out with the operation only half completed.

Here and there were institutions which argued a sense of initiative and responsibility in the public, on which democracy might hope to flourish. Such institutions were not common, but one which I witnessed on an insignificant little hill called Shifr was the sitting of youth court, which proved to be a kind of mixture between a dining club and a people's summary court. There must have been over seventy young men squatting on the ground, and perhaps thirty older ones allowed to sit round the edges and watch, but no elders (beyond my aged self) were tolerated at the proceedings. Dress varied from feathers, a few seedy, incongruous garments and small masonic aprons of leather strips, to stark nakedness set off by black and white stripes up and down the legs, and woad and ochre over the body.

The master of ceremonies was clad in a yachting-cap, a tie, a pair of footless khaki stockings and an extra layer of ochre, and carried an old, wire-stringed tennis racquet as a badge of office. The hierarchy consisted of a 'District Commissioner', four *meks,* a 'Clerk' who could string together a few of the letters in the Arabic alphabet, a *hakeem* (doctor), who distributed kohl, senna pods and other local simples, and two chuckers-out. All sorts of minor cases of misbehaviour against the social code and complaints between young men were dealt with, mainly by small fines, and proceedings were orderly and formal until court work was over and the beer and mutton were laid on. The 'court' had no official sanction whatever, but was a spontaneous, natural institution which showed no sign of competing with the local *mek* – a simian edition of the emperor Nero – and was probably healthy, as it taught the young bucks discipline and respect.

With the right personalities at the head of individual communities, it was possible gradually, by persuasion, diplomacy and jockeying, to combine smaller bodies into larger amalgams, and so to work towards big, financially viable local government units. Slowly a tradition of responsible authority, new to the Nuba mind, was nurtured. As elsewhere, the younger generation, particularly of the rulers, was offered education. What the future will hold for this remarkable congeries of peoples, it is difficult to guess, and depends principally on themselves and their latent powers of adaptability; but at least they have been given the basic organisation and machinery which should enable them to cope with the problems of advancing civilisation, and so to survive.

To his sister Elizabeth
Rashad

I've just been on a trek over the Moro hills, west of Talodi – a climb of something getting on for 2,000 feet above the plain, up craggy hillocks. Once up on the rocky plateau on top you find an immense population, for the Nuba far prefer scraping a living from stony terraces and living in cool, healthy, undisturbed surroundings, to cultivating richer soil down in the hotter valley where they are easily got at and worried.

Men and women alike are completely starko, except for beads, bracelets and other ornaments. I happened to come in for a dance in one village, and the effect of the full moon shining on those rounded limbs, the eerie braying of the horn, the waving of plumes, the swaying of the bodies, the noise of the stamping and above all the rhythm – all this was stimulating to a degree that leaves small wonder that the Nuba's morals are not of the best!

CHAPTER SEVEN

Tuleshi

On the south-western fringe of the Nuba Mountains lay a particular hill called Tuleshi. Its social and economic importance was small, but it is worth discussing because it illustrates better than any other unit the problems which the administrator found himself up against, and the extreme difficulty of equipping a people against their will with the wherewithal to ensure their political emergence.

Tuleshi hill covered an area only three or four miles each way at most. It lay separated from other Nuba and Daju hills by valleys which could be walked in an hour or two; and up to and under its slopes in dry weather came sections of the Baggara Arabs. Its population was between three and four thousand souls.

The Mek of Tuleshi was called Tia, and his functions were supposed to be part temporal, part spiritual. He held the traditional powers of magic needed to ensure the harvest, and had the pre-eminence as leader and representative of the hill. He was in fact king and priest in one, head of church and state.

But he was no Melchizedek. He was not even a Henry VIII except in his tally of wives. He was a gibbering, beady-eyed little bantam of a buffoon, more of a mascot than a monarch, who had done his best for twenty years with an impossible command. Nobody listened to him – not even his wives. He appealed to me once to interview one of his harem who had refused to cook his food or do the household chores – 'and it would never do if I, a king, lost my temper and broke her head, would it?' I did have an interview with the woman, or rather she gave me an interview – a shocking old hag who sat smoking her pipe of villainous, acrid Nuba tobacco with a smirk on her face like a supercilious gargoyle off Nôtre

Dame. It was difficult to be solemn while the pathetic little man ranted on about her unwifely ways; and although I was told afterwards that my lecture to her on a wife's duty and the obligations of marriage, particularly in the kitchen, was worthy of an archbishop, I doubt if it secured Tia a single well-cooked meal.

But the real reason for the ineffectiveness of the Mek was not his lack of personality; rather, it was the ancestral Tuleshi constitution, or lack of one. Although Mek of the hill, Tia's duties and privileges applied directly over only half of his territory. In the other half he was expected to function through a representative, another grain-priest called Kurky, an anthropoidal old man who could only sit in unutterable squalor, spit constantly and mumble. Further to facilitate administration, by immemorial custom Mek and his vice-regent must never under any circumstances meet, and if they were ill-advised enough or ill-starred enough to do so, both would infallibly be smitten by the *aro,* or spirit that presided over the ill, and would die.

Thus in Tuleshi it was not an exaggeration to say that no authority existed. Among every other African community that I have met, authority is to be found somewhere if you look for it long enough. It may lie openly in the autocratic figure of a single man. It may be found in a democratic council of elders. It may be hidden in a vague but none-the-less effective public opinion which the individual fears to flout. In Tuleshi none of these was traceable. Government had no agency through which to work upon the people, no channel through which to convey its policy or enforce its demands. The populace greeted you with smiles and friendly waves. Taxes were paid promptly. But after that each young man did what was right in his own eyes. A cow might be driven off and slaughtered, but no compensation could be extracted. A fellow Nuba might be set upon and severely hurt, but no miscreant would ever be brought to court. Several killers were living on the hill, 'wanted' for months or even years, but no authority would arrest them, and if Government personnel were out looking for them, they would retire into the labyrinthine caves among the huge boulders of the hillside, carrying their muzzle-loaders with them, assured of receiving food from their female relatives at night. It would be a bold man who sought them in their fastness.

The very process of identifying a wanted Tuleshi man was difficult. In most Nuba communities the first six sons of a man are known automatically by six place-names: Kuku for the first-born, Kodi for the second, Koicho or Kurky, Tia, Tiso and Tutu. If there are more than six, you begin at Kuku again. Every man of course has other, more particular names; but on Tuleshi these were never divulged or spoken of to any outsider – and in a community where old-fashioned families were common, the number of Kuku Tias and Kurky Tutus was fabulous. When you asked for 'first son-son-of-third-son,' it was not surprising if the person approached looked uncertain.

The first time I visited Tuleshi, I took a list of fifteen men who were wanted for various crimes, from murder downwards. Inquiry elicited that thirteen of them had decamped or were unidentifiable or had made for the caves or had gone away to see a man about a dog. Two, however, were reported to be sitting in their houses, and to have been there for months. Several Chiefs of Police were sent to arrest them, but returned looking sheepish and saying the two men didn't want to be arrested. As there seemed to be a complete stalemate, the only thing was to arrest them oneself.

We went to the first man's hut, in which he was reputed to be sitting and waiting with his gun on his knees. The Chiefs' policeman who led the way walked cheerily enough in front at first, but as we approached, the thermometer of his courage dropped towards zero, and when the hut came into sight he pointed eagerly at it to make sure I had got the right one. He then disappeared behind a boulder, accompanied by the Mek and most of his retinue. His colleague was bolder, kept within sight, and just as I was approaching the door, with a sudden burst of manliness ejaculated: 'We might as well die together' – whereupon he advanced two paces as a gesture of good intent, before diving precipitately into a pig-pen.

This was depressing. But when I poked an apprehensive nose round the corner of the doorway, the hut was empty; our bird had already flown. We then turned aside to the other criminal's house. He was in residence, sitting outside the door with a shillelagh, two spears, a kind of cutlass, a snicker-snee and barbed fish-spear lying across his knees. Once again, the retainers pointed hopefully, said in an encouraging tone, 'That's him! See him?' and evaporated.

I advanced, feeling more lonely than one did in one's corner of the ring at school when the bell went and the seconds retired, and wishing that I had my .275 Mauser instead of a walking-stick. A nervous smile played round the man's lips, and his shifting eyes kept me guessing. I suddenly realised that since he spoke no word of Arabic nor of any tongue save Tuleshite, we had no means of communication. However, when I doffed my hat and smiled, and said in English that I had come to offer him a lift home, he also broke into a smile and handed over his ironmongery. This I hung about, feeling like a pirate in a charade; and the Mek and his entourage, seeing the cutlery gone, came up to within speaking distance.

Our friend then asked if he might go inside his house to collect some food. Too complacently, I gave assent; and, having gone inside, he announced loudly that he had his gun with him and was not coming out. If we wanted his nearer acquaintance, we could come and fetch him. To this there could be only one answer – through the Mek, who shouted interpretations from a distance – that if he did not come out at once, we would set light to his roof. That fetched him out in rapid time, and by evening he had been put on a lorry and lodged in the nearest gaol, where he learned a little Arabic and became a potentially useful citizen.

I did not try again this mixture of heroic melodrama and *opera bouffe*. Once was quite enough. The next time a murderer was wanted, and the same bankruptcy of local authorities had become apparent, we adopted two different methods. Two sisters, an aunt, three brothers, two uncles and his father were interviewed as to his whereabouts; but none of them had seen him, nor could imagine where he could possibly be. When people begin playing the idiot boy, it is best to call their bluff, and all were put under arrest and removed to the rest-house, to be sent to Lagowa gaol, twelve miles away. Twenty minutes later, just as they were going to start, the murderer arrived to hand himself over, announcing cheerfully that he had been in the hut closest to us all the time, listening to our conversation. He was a genial criminal, and mercifully the case was not a capital one.[To his mother Owen wrote: 'He is rather a nice chap, and I hope it won't be necessary to hang him,']

One cannot go on for ever arresting aunts, even when they are fairly clearly accomplices after the fact. It was growing more and more plain that Tuleshi, if left to itself, would become like Conan Doyle's Lost World, a little plateau which the tides of the world passed by, a human zoo, causing no major upheaval but a perpetual series of small injustices and denials of authority, which in the aggregate amounted to an assumption that the Government's writ did not run on that hill. Even with this one might be patient, were there any hope that time and the attrition of surrounding civilisation would work a change. But there was little such hope so long as Tuleshi remained perched a thousand feet up its hillside, inaccessible save by mountaineering, its people speaking no other tongue, mixing with no neighbours, controlled by no indigenous authority. The verdict expressed to me by the Warrant Officer of the local police post was a sound one: '*Wallahi,* Your Honour, the head of this people is a hard one. Oil is of no use. A hammer is necessary.'

It was agreed eventually that a bloodless military operation would be needed. At least one patrol had been occasioned by Tuleshi lawlessness in the past, and there had not long previously been a request for an air demonstration and the dropping of a bomb or two to impress – a request which had been rightly refused, since the effect might possibly have been sanguinary and would certainly have been ephemeral. Tuleshi, it was now decided, were to be given instructions, at the right time of the year (after a good harvest) to descend and build new villages at the base of the hill, and to construct certain small roads of access, thus ensuring that they would rub shoulders with all and sundry.

Regular sessions of the Court system to which they nominally belonged would be held under their hill. A weekly market would be established. A school would be instituted at the Court centre, where boys could learn Arabic. Various offenders and wanted men were to be handed over. A recruiting drive would be held to obtain a few specimens of Tuleshi manhood for the army, thus providing future rulers for the kingdom (after all, several of the more successful Roman emperors began in the ranks.) Only thus could their feet be placed on the lowest rung of the ladder of Progress. In the short term, when the time-limit for their descent had expired, a battalion of the Sudan Defence Force would hold their annual field-firing exercises on Tuleshi, and would destroy the old 'upstairs' villages.

All this was duly carried out, and with fair success. To do Tuleshi justice, the populace had mostly completed, or half-completed, their new 'downstairs' homes by the appointed day, and at the appointed time we climbed the mountain to witness the culmination of the field firing – the destruction of the old clusters of houses. The whole population of Tuleshi, from Mek Tia downwards, sat on the heights surrounding the doomed habitations, and a large crowd of visitors had come to view the spectacle, including neighbouring Nuba and a substantial quota of Arabs. The latter did not include the Nazir himself, who, not being clipper-built, had essayed to scale the mountain but had not succeeded in passing a certain tall and umbrageous acacia a hundred feet up the slope. Its shade proved the furthest limit of his effort, and it became 'Nazir's Tree' from that day.

The old villages were thoroughly combed by police to make sure that not a soul remained, for a few of the more thick-headed had left grain or effects stored in them, and we feared that some suicidal idiot might try to enter them after the shooting had begun. The all-clear was given, the police withdrew and the mortars opened up. As the first bomb burst, a couple of Arabs stepped out from behind a hut. They had come as onlookers, and had mistaken both the time and the route. For a moment they stood irresolute. Then one removed his shirt, the other his pants, and, tying them to their spears they began to wave them in token that they were on the side of the angels and had no intention of resisting. Machine-gun bursts were already going over their heads. At that moment the second mortar bomb, fired as a sighter, fell a hundred yards behind their tails, and I never saw men ascend a mountain-side more like chamois, shirtless and pantless.

The nearer clusters of houses went up at once in an impressive inferno. The further clusters, some of them eight and nine hundred yards distant and hidden from the gunners, caused more trouble. At the top end was the house of the *aro*, the tribal spirit and genius of the hill. It was uncanny to see how the spirit appeared to fox the mortars. They put bombs behind it, short of it and on either side, but could not strike it, and the audience was getting restive and drawing conclusions. In the nick of time a bomb fell *plunk* through the roof; the infantry then went in to the attack, the demonstration was over, and a chastened Tuleshi descended to the edge of the Great World.

We explored some of the caves – a system of galleries and halls beneath vast boulders which would have rewarded any speleologist. The only hostility experienced was from a black mamba, encountered, and rapidly avoided, by the A.D.C. Possibly it was the *aro* in material and vengeful form.

Meanwhile most of the wanted men had been procured, and a session of the Nuba court was dealing with the cases. Three of the remaining 'wanted's, who had broken prison at Lagowa Police Post year previously, had been happily harbouring at home. Two of them had sent word that they wanted to see the District Commissioner. They were promised safe conduct and presently arrived for a chat, saying they thought it would perhaps be as well to come back and to do the rest of their sentence – but what would it involve? The Warrant Officer of Police – a real character – began reeling off the things they would have to endure in gaol: no beer, reduced meat, no female company. These produced no signs of alarm, but when the officer came to 'no tobacco', with its ring of a papally-imposed penance rather than a prison regulation, they exploded. It was eventually agreed that they should be permitted a weekly pittance of tobacco in reward for good conduct, and with this compromise they came like lambs.

Recruiting had its setbacks but was not unsuccessful. The first canvassings were received without enthusiasm. The following day, however, a number of fine young men presented themselves. But the possessive mother is not a product of Western psychology, and is a prominent social feature among the Nuba. By the afternoon the lads' relations, particularly the mothers, had assembled and dissuaded the volunteers, and again it looked as if we should draw blank. After dark, however, many of the lads slipped down and said they wanted to join after all. Twice we were woken up by shrill, angry female voices pleading and scolding, but in the morning twenty young men were still there. We selected the ten best, stout specimens, all starko, and they went off in good spirits. Most of them later deserted and bolted home, but a few stuck it, and dividends may be coming in now.

The market began; the school started; an Arabic-speaking and less simian henchman was found to act as Grand Vizier to the Mek. That was the story of Tuleshi. There was only a single unfortunate casualty, and that was a fortnight after the operation. Men went hunting the battle-zone for dropped ammunition and empties, and one of them found an unexploded mortar bomb. Everyone had been meticulously and repeatedly warned, but warnings did not easily penetrate the Nuba skull on any hill, least of all on Tuleshi. The finder tried throwing his trophy several times, but, getting no satisfaction, he took a heavy, iron-headed club and put all his strength into the bonk. That was too much even for a Sudan Defence Force mortar bomb.

If I returned to the Sudan today, I think Tuleshi would be the first community I should inquire about and visit. Nothing would surprise me. Probably they are all living happily upstairs again, a score of malefactors sojourning with the mambas in the caves, the *aro* once more presiding over the hill, impregnable against the forces of progress. Possibly they are mixing and inter-marrying with other Nuba, chatting in Arabic, upholding the law, forming a Temperance Society, churning out boys for the secondary schools and sending a regular quota of young men of military bearing to the Sudan Defence Force: *Sic itur ad castra.*

To his father   25 Feb 33
Sinkat

Quoting an entry in his diary:

I took a little detour with a few of the sheikhs on the eastern border, right up among the hills. We pushed up a little rocky dingle, left our camels and took to the heights. Up and among barren slopes, with little but leafless thorny trees, and over the Italian border ... Over and down into Khor Oral, which becomes rapidly steeper, dom palms and a kind of mimosa decorating the sides, while its floor is all of great white marble slabs and boulders. It soon becomes a fierce gorge. We found pools of water beginning, stiff with leopard tracks all round their sandy edges, then came on actual running water in deep crevasses and stone runnels, and finally a succession of whacking great pools with cascades falling over sheer rock face into them – a veritable paradise.

Decided on a bathe, so dropped clothes and slid over a ten-foot wall of rock into a basin of water ten feet deep, and had a gorgeous swim. Tried to induce El Amin Hamid (*omda* of the Gemilab section, a very good companion) to come in, but he can't swim and preferred to watch. On trying to come out, I found there was no hope of getting up the rock face whence I'd plunged in; thought to clamber up the side, but that too defeated me, and finally had to scale some 200 feet of craggy hillside, still mother-naked, before it was possible to get across and down to El Amin and my clothes.

CHAPTER EIGHT

Crime and the Law

In an advanced civilisation litigiousness is not very common: the expense and the time-wasting of resort to law are alone enough to confine such resort to rare occasions and major stakes. Among a peasant population this is not so. All communities have their own rules to govern relations with neighbours, and when left to themselves can usually secure tolerably just settlement of disputes. But when an alien procedure is forced upon them, or is made available at very little cost, it appears to encourage the meaner and more anti-civic qualities – litigiousness, contentiousness, quarrelsomeness, petty over-reaching. There is an irresistible temptation to forsake tradition, eschew compromise and hie to the alien code which, if impeccably just in the abstract, cuts with the razor-blade of Law instead of healing with the salve of Custom, and seldom produces neighbourly love and cooperation.

This was especially so when interests in land were concerned, and the litigiousness of the Central Sudan Arab was proverbial. In distant and tribal areas this was not so, and in the deep South it was unthinkable. Both the bulk of litigation and its acidity had a direct ratio to the nearness, and consequent ease of access, to the central legal authority of Khartoum. The coming of local and tribal courts in the 1920s was as great a step to social progress as it was a relief to the District Commissioner prevented by a clutter of barren civil litigation from more constructive and vital duties; and latterly most of what civil work remained was undertaken by professional District Judges on circuit.

If one wished to see the corroding effects of the law, they were mirrored in the faces of the petitioners and litigants who haunted the law courts in Khartoum – grasping, anxious, self-centred, Scrooge-like faces. In fact 'haunted' is the word, for there were cases of Jarndyce v. Jarndyce[4] which had continued down the years, and whose protagonists had become like familiar ghosts, if unwelcome ones. I recollect one elderly Copt whose hopeless case had continued for seventeen years: his file ran to 1,374 pages, and his wits were going the way his money had already gone.

But while the District Commissioner progressively and thankfully left the burden of the Civil Law to professional hands, the criminal law remained very much his province to the end. In some provincial capitals and big cities there would be magistrates of the Legal Department, and a Judge of the High Court would travel on circuit and conduct a certain proportion of the Major Courts; but over the bulk of the country the exercise of the criminal law was in amateur hands.

There were two parallel legal systems working simultaneously: the State Courts which administered the penal code, and the Native Courts, established under ordinances originating only in the 1920s. These administered no written code, but went by the custom of the locality or tribe, provided that it was not 'contrary to equity and good science' – an elastic and yet perfectly reasonable and practical conception.

Law is not, like Higher Mathematics, an absolute science whose justification lies in its own perfection. It is an intensely practical science affecting the lives of human beings, and its success, and indeed its very validity, must ultimately be judged by its results. By this criterion, I believe, after seeing something of the law in operation elsewhere, that the standard of justice in the Sudan was extremely high. Stickling for the niceties of legal procedure can be an actual impediment to justice in a still-primitive populace, and it is not understood or appreciated by the people. The Sudan Penal Code and Code of Criminal Procedure were based upon the Indian, a wholly admirable code which gives full power to authority while in no way prejudicing the individual's chances of fair play, and which is above all comprehensible by any person of normal intelligence.

The penal law, and all important ordinances, had to be thoroughly grasped, and a testing examination in them passed, by every District Commissioner who hoped to become a First-class Magistrate. But

---

4   The lawsuit in Dickens's novel *Bleak House.*

knowledge of Law, with a capital L, was not obligatory; and it is to the eternal credit of the Legal Department that, while by advice and criticism they strove to keep amateurs on the right lines, and were quick to pounce upon anything which upset the interests of true Justice, they scarcely ever interfered with a judgement on purely procedural and technical grounds, or allowed mere legalism to pervert equity. They appeared to remember the dictum of Lord Mansfield when he was seeing off a man appointed to a high judicial post in the Far East. This man, though able and fair-minded, lacked all legal training, and the great Chief Justice's parting words were, 'Remember, dear fellow. Listen very carefully to the evidence, sleep on it, and then give your decision. But please do *not* record your reasons. Your decision will undoubtedly be right, but *since you know no law,* your reasons will unquestionably be wrong.'

The weightiest item of a District Commissioner's legal work lay in presiding over Major Courts for the trial of bigger crimes, especially murder. Advocates were unknown, save when a member of the intelligentsia was accused, and the Court had to facilitate, and sometimes (with a simple accused) virtually conduct the defence as well as the prosecution. This was not difficult, and the very fact that the accused was not represented by counsel made the court doubly considerate of his interests.

As President of the court one was supported by two members, nearly always Sudanese and very often sheikhs or chiefs, whose penetrating examination, shrewd perception of points which might have escaped a European, and level-headed judgment were of the highest value. From long practice one came to have a nose for evidence which seldom let one down, and knowledge of custom helped that intuition. There was the witness who was sullenly lying – easy to distinguish by his eye and tone. There was the witness who was perverting the truth out of loyalty to one side – as for instance a woman who had been the wife of the accused and sister of the complainant or the deceased; her evidence would in all probability be in favour of the latter, because in tribal communities blood-ties are more binding than those of marriage.

There was the weak-minded witness who meant no harm, but was saying what his 'party' had told him to say. There was the perfectly honest witness who said what he thought he had seen, or anyway what he knew he *ought* to have seen, though he never could have seen it. There was the witness whose evidence was concocted – and if two or more witnesses gave identical, word-for-word accounts, one could be nearly certain that they were pre-concerted, since two honest men never get identical impressions of the same series of events. There was also the witness who was telling the honest truth.

One's trained perception was apt to break down only over that rare phenomenon, the Professional Liar. The real art of mendacity lies not in dull denials or plain perversions, but in the combination of frank and honest demeanour with subtle doses of *suggestio falsi*, a judicious and surreptitious *soupçon* of *suppressio veri*, and a criss-cross of superficial confidences proving on examination to be mutually exclusive. All this leaves the investigator in such a swither of uncertainty as renders him too demoralised to come to any conclusion at all, right or wrong. Fortunately for justices, these artists are rare.

In England the population is over 600 to the square mile; the nation has a thousand years of civic tradition, and police are numerous and well-trained. Of murders and crimes of serious violence, more than fifty per cent eventually come to court. In the Sudan, with a population of ten to the square mile and slightly-trained Government police, who might number 140 in a district of 40,000 square miles, the proportion, at least among murders, was much better than that. This is not as odd as it seems, for it is easier to be lost in a crowd than in a desert. Nobody notices a man among a thousand in a street, but a solitary figure crossing the wilderness, or a stranger appearing in a small and unfrequented village, is an object of curiosity to anyone who sees him, and it is not easy to cover one's tracks. Moreover, Sudanese police are of high and estimable calibre, and most local authorities are conscientious where major crime is concerned.

Really ingenious criminals were rare, and their offences were not usually those of violence. One was the turkey-thief who operated in Khartoum. Certain Greek and other foreign merchants used to keep a stock of turkeys, which would be fattened up and profitably disposed of at Christmas time. This thief specialised in their abduction. He would go to the tripe-sellers and purchase a long piece of bullock's gut – as many yards long as he could find. One end of it he sewed up, leaving the other end open.

Armed with this curious weapon he would repair in the small hours to the pen where the turkeys were kept. Standing outside, he would select a gobbler and throw the closed end of the gut over the fence to a point close in front of his victim. The gobbler, seeing a tasty piece of tripe offered under his very beak, would take it up and begin to swallow. The thief, holding the open end of the gut to his mouth, would blow down it with all his might. The consequence was that the closed end in the unfortunate turkey's gullet swelled up like a balloon, with the two desirable results, (a) that the bird could not gobble or squawk, and (b) that it was safely if somewhat chokingly attached to a long hawser, of which the thief held the other end. Rapidly drawing in the flapping but silent victim to within his grasp, he would make off with it before the light came and interference was likely. He was popularly credited with twenty-seven turkeys thus secured before he was caught, by sheer ill chance, in the middle of his act.

To return to crimes of violence: good medical evidence was rare, since owing to climate and distance what Mark Twain called 'a nice fresh corpse' was not often available. Nonetheless, the police, under training, became very competent at getting the best evidence procurable, and small local dispensers and dressers often produced valuable medico-legal reports.

Tracking is possible only where the soil is suitable, Moreover, good African trackers are rare; but some are remarkable, and at their best can be uncanny. Most nomads can track well, and know the imprints of half the camels and many of the persons in their own and their neighbours' areas; but the trackers retained to aid the police were far more professional.

'Tracker's evidence' was sometimes sniffed-at by the more legally-minded, but the term was too loose to have any meaning without further definition. If a tracker saw the imprint of the criminal, and said, 'Yes, I know that track: it is Ahmed's', he might very well be right, but no court would accept his evidence as conclusive. Take, on the other hand, the following instance. The tracker had been escorted to the corpse, and had seen the prints of the killer leading away from it. Subsequently a man was arrested to whom suspicion pointed but against whom there was next-to-no direct evidence. The man was wholly unknown to the tracker. An area of sand was then cleared, and twenty men were made to walk across it. The tracker was summoned and bidden to pick out the imprint which he had seen by the corpse. Having examined closely, he shook his head and said, 'It isn't there.' He was then removed afar, the sand was swept smooth, and twenty more men, among them the suspect, walked across it. The tracker was recalled. He moved nonchalantly across all twenty, then returned slowly, stopped over a print and said simply, 'This is the one.' It was the suspect's, and, as in most other cases where such exposures occurred, a confession of guilt followed.

The Sudan has steadily become a civilised and law-abiding country. Yet the clash between the standards of a primitive barbarism and civilised society set one problems of equity, though not of law. There was the case of a Beja tribesman, from the wildest clan of the mountain-haunting Hadendowa in the Red Sea Hills, who found his sister in child by an unknown man, and speared her instantly. Had she divulged the name of her lover, he could have sought out the man to avenge her honour; but since she refused, he was bound by his traditions to take her life, for the primitive moral code is often Puritan and sometimes mercilessly mosaic. Nothing, in such a case, could avoid a death-sentence, but in the event it was commuted to ten years' imprisonment.

Then there was the case of a West African family of sorcerers. The man was reputed to have, and to use, the evil eye; and nobody who looked into that piercing and malevolent optic would have seen reason to doubt it. He was believed to have caused several deaths, and when the young daughter of another neighbour fell ill under his supposed spell, he was accused, admitted his responsibility, and was induced to take the spell off. This he did by gargling water, spitting it out and sending it to the victim to drink, following this up with a visit and jumping four times across her. As, however, these infallible remedies had been enacted under compulsion, and without intent to heal, they failed and the child died.

The public set out to deal with him, but found him absent, and so apprehended his mother, who was by repute a worse witch, whose looks would have sent her to the stake 300 years ago. The dead girl's brother dragged her around and beat her, as a result of which she eventually died. A brutal assault on an unoffending old lady? Possibly. Yet there was not one person, from the accused downwards, who was not convinced that he had rid the neighbourhood of dangerous vermin. If memory serves aright, his eventual punishment was four years' imprisonment.

Even superstitious beliefs cannot be dismissed. The belief in ba'atis is fairly widespread. A ba'ati is a kind of revenant which comes back from the tomb, frequently in the guise of a tall and black human shape, and devours human flesh. Some tribes are well known to produce *ba'atis*. A Mesellimi (a member of one of these tribes) had died and been buried, but there was a strong rumour in the town that he was back again and had been seen prowling in a certain quarter by several sober citizens. Public apprehension was considerable. One man, after refreshing himself liberally, was finding his way home down the twisting lanes when, coming round a corner, he found himself confronted by a tall, black figure looming ominously over him. With a howl of 'THE BA'ATI!' he brought his heavy club down on the apparition's skull and fled to the *merkaz* to report his combat with the supernatural. There was, alas, no case for the Society for Psychical Research to investigate. The police found an innocent citizen stretched out. Law held that, since the accused went armed, and since by drinking he had rendered himself liable to absurd hallucinations, he could not avoid responsibility and was technically guilty of murder; but his sentence was ten years.

Kipling, in his verses anent the female of the species, points out that some extraneous emotion often turns a man away from facing the logical conclusions of his own justice:

Mirth obscene diverts his anger; doubt or pity oft perplex
Him in dealing with an issue ...

This was certainly true. When going to an inter-Province meeting, on the Province boundary, I found myself taking up, under guard, a young Dinka who had been accused of attempted parricide just over the border and was wanted by our neighbours for trial. His father had divided the cattle among his sons, and this young man considered that he had been wronged. So much did he brood and so deeply did he feel his wrongs that he decided to terminate his father's existence. But if he speared him, the Government might hang him, which would be unpleasant. He therefore went to the local veterinary dresser (an Arab), told him he was much bothered by hyenas, and asked for the loan of a little strychnine. The dresser correctly refused. The young man, however, returned a day or two later and repeated his plea, stressed the losses which were occurring among his calves, and offered the dresser a *douceur* if he would but help him in his predicament.

The dresser, having sized his man up, accepted the gift, went to his cupboard and produced the necessary bottle full of evil-looking white crystals. The accused took it home, and, not believing in doing things by halves, administered a full tablespoon-full of it to his father's porridge in the evening. What was his horror when the sole result was that Pa had to get up six times in the night? In the morning the disgusted young man returned to the dresser and complained that his strychnine was useless, and would not kill the hyenas. The dresser inquired how he had administered it, and whether an adequate quantity had been given. His suspicions now confirmed, he called up a nearby policeman and handed the young Dinka over. Being an honest man, and having a shrewd idea of what was afoot, he had given his applicant a bottle of Epsom salts. The rabelaisian aspect did not alter the fact that murder had been attempted; but I believe the simple young man received a comparatively lenient sentence.

A similar Rabelaisian element did not help the accused in a certain case of theft of cash. At the centre of a big cotton scheme north of Kassala, I chanced to be present at the station early one morning when the train from Port Sudan came in. An Arab leaped off the train and came up in a flutter of consternation to report that he had been robbed of twenty-one pound notes during the night. He had been to Port Sudan to sell sheep and was returning. His money had been in a wallet which had been at his side in the carriage. The train had stopped for some time at a station, where, being sleepy, he dozed off. Before dozing he had noticed that a certain West African – a Borgu, the most notoriously criminal tribe – who had also boarded the train at Port Sudan, was eyeing him. When he awoke in the small hours, his wallet was still there, but it was empty.

The Borgu man was singled out as the presumed thief. Various fellow travellers confirmed the robbed man's tale, and I eventually ordered the accused to be searched. Nothing was found, and the man was full of injured innocence. He was just a little too sure of himself, and I ordered his detention. A further search, both of his person and of the train, revealed nothing. The train went on, but the Borgu stayed. He stayed for three days, under observation, which showed that he was suffering from complete costiveness. He was asked whether he did not think that a mild dose might be of advantage, but he did not seem to think so. When, however, it was insisted on, he was forced some hours later to 'go outside', watched by two police officers. The twenty-one pound notes were recovered, to the Arab's joyous comment that 'Patience is from God, and prevaileth.'

Another case of murder, in which the court was moved to pity, was that of a Baggara Arab who had tried to slay his wife. The pair reminded one of some old *Punch* cartoon of the hen-pecked husband and the powerful wife. He was a puny and meagre little specimen, while his spouse was a fine figure, robust and tall and maybe thirty years old. There had been disagreement for a long time, and it had been decided that divorce was unavoidable, but there was dispute over retention of a particular property which led to extreme rancour.

Having lured his wife into a deserted spot, the accused had set about her with a *shelegai* (the ten-foot Baggara spear), a knife and a barbed fish-spear. When he stabbed at her stomach, she swivelled sideways so that the blade penetrated only obliquely, not piercing her vitals, whereupon she seized the spear and wrenched it from his hands. He drew the knife and, aiming at her kidneys, gave her a deep gash on the hip, whereupon she wrested the second weapon from him. He then picked up the fish-spear, but she grabbed the *shelegai* and knocked it out of his hands. The amazon then passed over to the offensive and chased him half way to the encampment before stopping for loss of blood. She was then carried forty miles by donkey to the nearest hospital, where she duly recovered.

The court was moved to a slight measure of pity for the accused by his abject shame, which brought him a ten-year instead of a life sentence. He was not afraid of the gallows, but after defeat by his wife he would never again be free from the gibes of his companions. Whether the lady, after such a demonstration of physical prowess, ever again obtained a husband, I never heard.

The causes of most killings were the same as everywhere in the world – wine and women. There were of course other causes, and in some areas the occasion was not wine but water, especially among the Beja of the Eastern Sudan who seldom touch liquor but in whose arid country water is the means of prosperity and often of life, and many a fatal dispute occurred over wells. Some deaths were caused in the course of robbery, particularly among nomad Arabs, many of whom owned firearms of precision.

Only once did I hear of death being caused by a favourite device of some robbers, the use of datura. This plant, *Solanum incanum,* grows profusely over much of the country. The method used by the runner is to insert some of its seeds into the tea or other drink of the intended victim. This causes dilation of the pupils, palpitations, intense thirst and delirium, during which the miscreant can do his work at leisure and make his getaway. The one case that came before me was typical of this type of crime. A practised West African, with five convictions, had come to the animal market and there spent some hours carefully prospecting for a victim. He selected three rather simple-looking Arabs, watched them sell several sheep and pocket a sum of over £20, and trailed them back to the environs of the town where they intended to spend the night. He then donned a red sash – a badge of authority – walked up to them and truculently informed them that he was a *ghafir*, or watchman. He told them that Government had a petrol store nearby, and allowed no camping here. In the morning he would have to take them before the *mamur*. In the meantime, since it was late, they might as well settle down for the night.

The bluff worked with the simple tribesmen. The villain presently lit a fire and made some tea. After a while he thawed further and suggested his captives might like a drink. He brewed another pot of tea, taking the leaves out of a different pocket – his actions half-hidden in the dusk – and offered cups to all three. One, who was elderly and relatively shrewd, was uneasy and took only a few sips; the younger two gulped their drinks and had seconds. When the old man began to feel the effects of the drug coming on, he seized the bag containing most of their cash and by an effort of will staggered into town and to the *omda*'s house, where he collapsed and was picked up still clasping the bag.

The police were instantly informed, and followed his tracks back. But darkness had set in, and it was not until morning that the other two victims were traced, wandering among the sand-dunes semi-conscious and in extremities of thirst, and were taken to hospital for treatment. Meanwhile at dawn a camel-policeman took up the criminal's tracks, followed him for eighteen miles without a check, ran him down and collared him – a fine piece of work. There was no reason for the court to feel compunction in giving him seven years.

In matters of public security the assistance received from the populace, and certainly from local authorities, was praiseworthy. If a given community was jointly engaged in thwarting public security, the weapon of communal punishment was occasionally used, normally in the form of a fine. Such punishment had no basis in law: it was an administrative measure, and provided that it was scrupulously reserved for suitable instances, it was entirely justified. Typical offenders were villages which habitually harboured and encouraged animal thieves, and against which a number of cases had been proved beyond doubt. In a highly-developed community criminal responsibility is rightly a purely individual matter. Under conditions of tribal life this is much less so; and when a given community, man, woman and child, is actively or tacitly abetting a series of crimes, there is nothing inequitable in enforcing communal responsibility. It is the only feasible method of guarding public interests.

Among a fine people like the Sudanese civic sense has developed rapidly, and by the 1950s punitive methods outside the law had become almost obsolete. But in matters such as black-market offences, the drug trade and traffic in illicit arms, the public conscience is still untrained and far too easy – a deficiency which only prolonged civic tradition and experience will improve.

Nothing achieved more in establishing a tradition of justice and law-abidingness than the steady growth, from the 1920s, of the native courts. When these were started, many doubts were expressed about the advisability of granting criminal powers to authorities who were not only untrained in law but in a great many cases illiterate. There were fears of bribery and corruption. There were misgivings that barbarous practices might spring up and flourish surreptitiously under the cloak of the law.

These fears were, with very few exceptions, belied. The experience was in fact a humbling one, which showed that impartiality is not the perquisite of one race, and that our own methods are not the only ones for arriving at truth in fact or equity in decision. As to barbarous practices – there was no recrudescence of them. Responsibility drove them out. Trial by ordeal certainly survived well into the 1930s in some Arab areas, the usual method being to drop a large darning needle into a bowl of boiling fat (or, for women, cow's urine, as being a degree less severe). The accused was expected to extract the needle, and this he or she never failed to do: the test arose only afterwards, in the victim's capacity to heal within three days. But any such method was a hole-and-corner practice rigidly excluded by the courts.

The methods of these native courts were not legally orthodox by European standards; the procedure soon became traditional and was not codified beyond certain instructions issued to all courts embracing the basic principles of justice. Yet the substantive justice given was of a remarkably high standard, was understood by the populace, and among other virtues ensured a promptitude which would have been impossible in Government courts. To a simple people, in a country where distances are big and communications slow, speed of justice is next only to impartiality of justice – a point which excessive legalism is apt to obscure, until 'the law's delays' become a proverbial affliction from which the Western citizen scarcely expects to be free.

If cases of injustice did occur, they were nearly always among the small local courts, where pettiness, spite and tin-pot autocracy were more likely to be found and had fewer restraints than in the big and really responsible courts. But never, either among Arabs or Africans, have I known a proved or even a strongly-rumoured case of a bribe taken by a judicial authority. That is not to say that it may not have occurred; but since little that happens in a tribal society remains unknown, since tongues wag and the 'candid friend' and the informer are seldom far away, bribery could at worst have been exceedingly rare – and that, in a society where administrative and judicial integrity is not a tradition, is a wonderful tribute.

At Provincial Headquarters I had an excellent little gardener called Rihan. He was an industrious and honest man, and, for an African, had fairly green fingers. But we all have our weak moments. One morning in the early rains, while I was in the office, the head servant had laid out drinks in the house in expectation of a guest who was coming to lunch. The second servant, coming by chance into the room, found Rihan, who ought to have been outside in the garden, standing in the middle of the floor with my best cut-glass decanter of gin up-ended and glued to his lips. Had he poured himself a drink like a gentleman, I should have been inclined to take a lenient view; but 'kissing the monkey' with one's best cut-glass was too much of a good thing, and I sent him to the town panel of the native court, expecting a fine of ten shillings, which I could pay and then deduct from his wages. In loyal horror at such an act of *lèse majesté* as drinking the Governor's gin, the court sentenced him to six months' imprisonment. This was not only an injustice to Rihan: it was also a great injustice to me, depriving me of a gardener at the most critical time of year. The District Commissioner was requested to use his power and drastically reduce the sentence. Rihan emerged smiling, the garden smiled, and we were all happy again.

The methods of native courts differ from ours, and have both their advantages and their disadvantages. There is no word in Arabic which really translates 'verdict': the word used only means 'decision', and does not distinguish it plainly from the judgment. This reveals the traditional attitude, by which the scale of punishment tended to be in ratio to the certainty or otherwise of the charge. If you were sure a man had *not* stolen a donkey, you acquitted him; if you were sure he *had* stolen it, you gave him six months; but if you thought he had, but were not quite certain, you gave him *two* months. That is of course a crude example, but it was the principle worked on at first, and it had to be sublimated into a more correct and orthodox attitude – a sublimation which the years and experience largely accomplished.

Presidents and members of courts more often than not knew the men they were trying, and all their family history and records. To the purist this has obvious and grave objections, yet I cannot but think that in practice it made for common sense and equity. It could certainly cut down unnecessary proceedings – for instance in a rather woolly case of alleged animal theft in which the complainant claimed one direct eye-witness called Ali. Alis being as common as Johns, the President asked the complainant, 'Which Ali? Was it the elderly Ali who lived at Um Roka?' 'Yes.' 'Was it the Ali who has a scar on his left cheek?' 'Yes.' 'Are you *sure* it was *that* Ali – the one who possesses the large white donkey, and whose son married the niece of the *omda* of Shigeig?' 'Yes – it was.' There was a slight pause, and then the President gave a grunt. 'That man is blind. He has seen nothing for seven years. Next case.'

Both the conduct and the recording of cases improved greatly as the results of education spread far and wide among the ruling families. Only latterly and in a few courts were records of actual evidence taken in detail. But all courts kept full records of the charges, main facts, parties, witnesses and judgments. In the Northern provinces these were in Arabic, and were often model summaries. In the south they were mostly in English and were less competent. Whichever they were, to study the records of a court was to gain a deep insight into the customs, tendencies, failings and values

111

of the community concerned, and to place a finger on the pulse of public conduct and social principle.

It also revealed occasional remarks outside the normal powers of a court – as for instance the fearsome rider to a Dinka court's judgment, sounding more like a papally-imposed penance than a legal doom: 'He never to drink beer again.' The palm, however, must go to an entry anent a young man who had committed an indiscretion with an unmarried girl: 'Found guilty of virginity and sentenced to six months.'

Diary 1936

January 3. Had chest pains all day, early till late, and it turns enjoyment to gall. Must stick it… *11th.* Nearly all morning felt as if I might just subside and die, but I don't think anyone saw. God pull me through another month or so, till Salmon [a successor] knows the district properly, then *nunc dimittis* - and yet by God I'm going to stick it through if there's the smallest chance of winning…

18th. Feel dizzy to a degree, but must stick it…

30th. Heart irregular … had to face all over again the withering prospect of dying. I know now that I do not fear *death* one little bit, but that the process of *dying* is appalling: and day after day, month after month, one has to be prepared to 'go', and under marching orders for a march that doesn't come. That is what has brought grey hairs.

One has to wrestle over and over again with what one believes and what one doesn't. These moments of approaching death are desolating. The certainty that one's ego is being dissolved is terrifying; and there is no comfort to find and no rock to cling to; till one backs onto Jesus, knowing that he did rise for us, and realising that despite the dissolution of *this* ego, the 'parts' will be 'reassembled', as it were, to go on with the work of God on another plane.

March 1st. God give me strength not to panic… *March 10th.* If only God would hasten it: 'to cease upon the midnight with no pain.' Oh, Margaret, I've struggled so hard to carry on and overcome this.

CHAPTER NINE

Prisons

During the second quarter of the 20th century the population of Sudan prisons steadily increased; but let no one imagine that this showed a growing tendency to crime. On the contrary, public security was excellent, and dishonesty and violence no more general than in most parts of Africa or the Middle East, and a great deal less general than in some. The reasons are those inseparable from, and indicative of, social progress.

As problems become more numerous and complicated in a rapidly advancing country, so the Government through no fault of its own is pressed into a process of what we might call 'legiferation'. Legislation on all kinds of subjects comes tumbling out, and the simple citizen finds that all sorts of acts which would previously have seemed to him innocuous are now offences against Old Father Antic, the Law. Second, the very improvement in public security paradoxically adds to the prison population, since the thief or killer who a few decades ago would have been untraceable or would have defied arrest now finds himself apprehended and haled to the bar. But probably the most important factor is the slow change in the climate of public opinion – the dying-out of the primitive view of all offences as 'torts' or civil wrongs against the individual or tribe, and the substitution of a proper appreciation of crime as an offence against the whole community and its reasonable laws.

By up-to-date Western standards, the Sudan prison administration was probably slightly primitive. In view of the state of civilisation of the populace – and by the standards of neighbouring countries – I believe that the prisons were in essentials well run and adequate. Scandals of maltreatment by warders were few. Riots and disturbances, though known, were rare. Discipline was according to schedule and was neither arbitrary nor unnecessarily harsh. Records were meticulously checked, and detention for more than the allotted span scarcely ever occurred. As to feeding – it was rare to find a prisoner whose weight was not greater when he left gaol than when he entered it; and from the number of circulars and schedules on the subject which pullulated from the headquarters of the Prison Service, one would have thought that a staff of experts in nutrition and one or two distinguished chefs were specially retained to ensure the gastronomic content and physical improvement of the criminal classes.

The contentment of the inmates of a prison is not a guarantee that the establishment is being properly run. Yet it is surely a relevant factor. Judged by this criterion, Sudan prisons must rank high, for there is no doubt of the comparative content of most inmates. I remember them as cheerful and forthcoming. Once, returning from leave, on my first weekly inspection of the Province prison I found inscribed in large, sprawling chalked letters over the entrance, the legend 'WELCOME FROM LEAVE'. Considering the comparative ease of escape, when working in the bush and guarded by a somnolent warder armed with a Martini which was outdated in 1895, escapes were not many, and sometimes not pushed home.

At weekly inspection I once found a Dinka prisoner stark naked. This was highly irregular and required explanation. Inquiry revealed that he had bolted from a working-party three days previously, and had made a clean getaway. Feeling thirsty, however, and needing to prime himself for his long cross-country journey home, he had pawned his prison pants in order to repair with the proceeds to a pub, whence he was shortly afterwards recovered.

There was a celebrated occasion when five prisoners were working as a gang on road repair under the care of a warder. The warder nosed out an *araki* still in a village, and after consuming a sufficient dram threw away his rifle and collapsed into glorious coma under a tree. The gang completed their task and bound their warder hand and foot; four of them then carried him shoulder-high while the fifth bore his rifle, and the cavalcade arrived back at the prison safely in the evening and deposited him in a cell. Their action was, I am happy to say, rewarded with a remission of sentence.

Paradoxically, human nature was more lovable among the major, long-term criminals than among short-term ones. These latter included pick-pockets, sneak-thieves, hashish-smokers and pimps – all those in whom petty depravity is combined with a lack of those honest qualities which may make a great rogue. Such an one was an elderly prisoner who complained to me during an inspection. He had been sentenced to six months for hashish peddling, and was most indignant at finding himself inside. He did not for a moment deny the charge on which he had been convicted: on the contrary, he had been convicted six times before. But the last sentence had been passed in Port Sudan, where he had been subsequently boarded and released on medical grounds. That, of course, was the equivalent of a Papal indulgence, and he considered that, with a doctor's certificate in his pocket, he had a perfect right to continue his illegal trade, he himself being, as lawyers say, *ultra leges.*

As for long-term prisoners – to make out that men who have committed serious crimes in the eyes of the law are a galaxy of heroes or philanthropists would be a gross overstatement. There were habitual offenders among them – thugs, men of ugly temper or constitutional dishonesty. Yet from a simple, tribal population, the proportion of such rogues was surprisingly small. The Arab peasant who has had a bowl of *merissa* too many and has hit another over the head in a hot quarrel; a Dinka tribesman who has joined a hundred others in the immemorial diversion of an inter-clan spear fight and had the ill luck and the straight eye to throw a fatal spear; the nomadic and lawless rogue who has lifted two camels off a neighbouring tribe, as his ancestors have done for generations, and tried to run them across 300 miles of desert to French territory: these men have broken the code and must pay the penalty, but they may yet turn out to be lovable personalities and even useful citizens.

The most habitual criminal I knew was named Mohammed Ali Talatin. The sobriquet means 'Thirty,' and referred to his thirty-odd convictions for theft. He was a kleptomaniac, who would doubtless in some countries have been treated as a subject for the doctor rather than the judge. If anybody in the village had lost a blanket or a bowl or a piece of soap, the first thing to do was to go or send to Mohammed Ali's house, where the article would probably be found, itself unconcealed, and the theft undenied.

In the absence of a psychiatrist we cured him, at least temporarily, by making him a postal runner during the rains, when the roads were closed to transport. Once created a Government servant and given responsibility and a badge of office, he rose in his own estimation and had a trust to perform. On one occasion he even saw off two robbers who tried to steal the mail-bags. When the dry weather deprived him of his position he returned to his old ways and his old home – the prison – but for a time, at least, amateur psychotherapy had prevailed.

The fundamental decency of most long-term offenders was one of the reasons for the success of the guarantee-system in the Sudan. The other cogent reason was the sheer necessity of relieving pressure on accommodation. When a long-term prisoner had served a part of his sentence under the full rigours, such as they were, of prison discipline, it was open to him to produce a guarantor, in the form of his sheikh, chief, or any substantial citizen, who would go bail that he would not run away. He was then allowed to work without a guard all day, and return to prison under his own steam at night.

This system was liable to abuse, yet it was of the very essence of the country, and had great virtues. Regulations forbade an inmate receiving food other than prison rations; yet a guaranteed man could, and did, receive supplies from friends and relatives who would visit him more as if he were a hospital case than a guest of the Government. Regulations forbade him receiving remuneration, but he could, and did, often make small pocket-money in devious ways.

Above all, regulations forbade a prisoner sleeping out of the gaol; but many guaranteed prisoners, I fear with official connivance, were attached to the houses of officials or to other permanent jobs, slept on the verandah or in a hen-house or stable, and gradually became trusted old retainers with a stake in the estate. Unusual talent could thus be made use of instead of being wasted on unintelligent routine labour. The keeper of the little collecting zoo at Province Headquarters was a murderer, but his St Francis-like capacity for handling and dealing with birds and young animals was superb. It brought hundreds of pounds to Government from the young creatures which he successfully reared, and later sold to foreign zoos.

Cattle thieves were the best choice for looking after a herd of dairy cows, but for tending one's garden one normally chose a murderer. What the connection is between killing and gardening I have never asked a professional psychologist – perchance an atonement complex, or a reversion to type, through Cain, to the prototype of all gardeners. But it was an observable fact, and a seven-year recruit from a tribal fight was the surest man to water one's young petunias tenderly, and even to grow successful lettuces. They seemed to be crisper and to have better hearts when tended by a hand which had shed blood.

Guaranteed prisoners often became most trusted and valuable men. There was a particular camel thief in whose hands my wife and I could unreservedly leave our small son if we had to go out for the afternoon. It gave him the greatest joy to carry the child round shoulder-high while his little rider tried ineffectually to belabour him with a camel whip. At a different station I was once awoken in the small hours by a series of shouts. I thought for a moment that it was only a drunken Dinka; but the calls came nearer and passed along the river's edge in front of the house.

Presently they were joined by other voices, perhaps a quarter of a mile further on, and as they continued I rose and walked along to inquire the cause. A burglar had attempted to break into the house of the Education Officer, who was absent on duty, but the murderer-in-charge, who was sleeping there, wakeful as the Roman geese, had detected the intruder, made a bee-line for him and given chase with loud view-halloos in the moonlight, bringing others out on the scent. The burglar had made his point for the marsh beyond my house, and had saved his brush by plunging into the river – whether to escape or perish, we never discovered.

The grim business of executions was mercifully rare. The extreme penalty was carried out only for the worst murders in which either exceptional brutality or deliberate resistance to authority accompanied the deed. My records show that of seventy-seven major courts over which I presided, more than forty involved capital charges; yet in a number of those sentence of death was never passed, and in only six extreme cases was it finally confirmed.

Improbable as it sounds, I have met a man who had been hanged more than thirty years before. His case was well attested by local knowledge. He had slain a man during the *mahdia,* and had been sentenced to death by the Khalifa's *kadi,* Wad Marioum, and had been duly hanged. It was an unpleasant and long hanging, but eventually he had been cut down and handed to his relatives to bury. As they came to lay him out, they noticed a tiny vein still pulsing in his throat. They kept him laid out on a bedstead in a hut, and for fifteen days he remained in a state of suspended animation, after which he recovered his full powers and vitality. The people of his victim were furious and appealed to the *kadi* for him to be hanged again; but the answer was that the sentence had been given and carried out, and that if God had decided that the result should be unusual, it would be impious to question His decision. The man prudently migrated until local feeling died down, and was alive and well in 1931. He even tried to sell me a horse.

The spiritual welfare of prisoners was not neglected. At a small sub-*merkaz* where a little prison was maintained I was once wakened just after going to sleep by a most doleful caterwauling. Sitting up and listening, I recognised, lugubrious and *andante maestissimo* but unmistakeable, the strains of 'Art thou weary, art thou languid?' In no good mood I asked who was indulging in Hymns Ancient & Modern at that time of night, and learned it was a band of Nuba girls from the neighbouring Protestant mission, who were in the habit of serenading the prisoners with a nightly hymn before Lights Out sounded. The inmates were said to appreciate the attention, and occasionally to answer from within the walls, like Richard to Blondel.[5]

At the weekly services held in the Governor's house at Province Headquarters any mission boy who happened to be locked up at the time was allowed to come. In fact these services were remarkable for their polyglot character. The congregation included members of at least four different language groups, in addition to British staff, and a hymn or psalm had to be granted to each group, to be sung in their own tongue, lest they should feel neglected.

From the prison we had a constant quota of faithful criminals. There was Amos, a storekeeper who had pawned the keys of the Government grain store in order to procure refreshment; Nikemia, a Dinka, had abstracted several cattle from a neighbour's herd; and Micaiah, a dresser, had been ill-advised enough to water yellow-fever serum and use the spare quantity gained for giving injections, on payment, which purported

---

5   Legend has it that in 1192 the itinerant minstrel Blondel de Nesle identified the
     catle in which King Richard of England was incarcerated, when he and the king
     recognized each other's voices as they sang.

to cure syphilis. All three were excellent singers, and St Peter himself would have been hard put to it not to unlock the gates at the sound of their alleluias.

In the ordinary gaols there were four permanent headaches: criminal lunatics, juveniles, women, and educated or highly-civilised prisoners. Lunatics who might be susceptible to treatment could in some instances be sent to the central asylum in Khartoum. As many as possible were released, to be cared for by their friends, if necessary under guarantee and with the loan of a chain to secure them when violent. But any Province prison was forced to maintain a few dangerous madmen, and their cases were usually pathetic and sometimes distressing. Juveniles were few. Offending boys were put under probation, or might be beaten, or their fathers might be fined, but every effort was made to keep them out of gaol, where they would mix with criminal types.

The few whom the prisons were forced to admit were usually kept in a separate encampment outside the town, and not the least service done by the Roman Catholic mission was to accept such boys into their workshops, and there teach them discipline and a trade. Results varied, but with some they were definitely successful. But even lads can be surprisingly precocious. At a weekly inspection I saw one newcomer whose angel face bespoke an unsullied nature and suggested a boy of thirteen. On my asking the Prison Officer somewhat testily what on earth could have landed an innocent like that in trouble, the reply came straight: 'Adultery for the third time, Sir.'

A visit to the women's wards was always uncomfortable. Here were weak young girls who had fallen into matrimonial trouble (for adultery is punishable by most tribal custom), mixed with old harridans who had battered their neighbours in drunken brawls, and hags who had lived by illicit distillation of *araki* and would do so again when released. Occasionally there were witches who had been proved to be dabbling in the black arts – an offence taken seriously by native courts. Just as the claw-wounds of a lion are believed to be more septic than those of a leopard, so it was the opinion of our Head Warder, Sergeant Major Allagabo, that bites inflicted by a woman in the course of an affray were more dangerous than those of a man and certain to become infected. He had reason to know.

There was one particularly gruesome old catamaran in the Province prison. She was tall, coal-black, pock-marked and had a cast in her eye. She had bitten several warders, and her influence on the other ladies was pernicious. Her name was Juno. At weekly inspection Allagabo – who combined old-world loyalty and Dinka dignity, was never prouder than when he was allowed to sit a horse (provided that it was stationary), and was equally proud of his few words of English – drew himself up to his full height of 6' 3" and said disapprovingly, 'Juno had one black fairy, Sir.'

The ordinary Province prison, *a fortiori* the District prison, had little accommodation for the gentlemanly inmate. In the rare event of a man of prestige and high education being incarcerated, he could usually be sent to the capital. Other educated and more civilised men were so far as possible segregated together.

When Sheikh Ibrahim el Meleih, the Chief Merchant of our Province headquarter town, was convicted of a black-market offence, everybody knew he had been framed. Everyone also knew that all the merchants in the market were guilty of similar offences, and probably on a larger scale; but that could not be officially taken into the reckoning. Of the charge itself, there could be no doubt. Sheikh Ibrahim was tried by the District Commissioner, as was proper, and was sentenced to a considerable fine, and one week's imprisonment. The latter was a mere token, to show that there was neither fear nor favouritism, and that, however august you are, and whatever your prestige, offences against the law cannot be winked-at and forgiven.

It was agreed that his status deserved the privilege of a separate cell, and this was granted. We all had a very soft spot for the offender, who played a wild but stout game of polo and was generous to a fault. When returning homewards from the office I encountered a gang of prisoners and learned that they were carrying the wardrobe and other moveables of Sheikh Ibrahim el Meleih to furnish his quarters. When, on weekly inspection, I arrived at his cell, I found it a most comfortable apartment – and there was the inmate himself smiling and welcoming at the door. The floor was carpeted, and with one courtly movement he swept me on to a divan, and, turning to the sergeant of warders, ordered coffee to be brought. Had I remained, I know it would have appeared, though polite conversation might have been difficult. One can forgive a man most things for panache. It is so rare.

To Elizabeth   20 March 1946
Wau

The variety of this job, and of the other Europeans one meets, makes up for the lack of social dealings with the people themselves. With Arabs you can be neither lonely nor dull, for you can exchange rational ideas on every kind of topic – which is the essence of human intercourse. But with blacks you can't really interchange ideas, their ideas seldom extending beyond meat, beer and women. At least, that applies to the potbellies, or haggis of tribes of negroid stock which inhabit the west of this area. The Dinka, however, who number some 600,000 and lie east and south of Wau, are Nilotics, and a better type altogether, with greater susceptibilities, and less plebeian and obtuse, in spite of the fact that they are plebeian and mostly naked.

To Elizabeth   26 November 1946
Wau

My cook came a fortnight ago, as screwed as an owl, and wanted to give notice, and as he has scarcely recovered sobriety yet, I don't know what conclusion he will finally come to. It will be a nuisance if he does go, just as the really heavy visitors' season is beginning, for good northern Arab cooks are hard to obtain down here, and the local black potbelly is not of the most cleanly habits. Some of the currants in the cake are liable to be flies, and though you may compliment him on the beautiful tenderness of the meat, you would find on investigation that he had made it tender by chewing it.

CHAPTER TEN

Police and Police Drivers

Nowhere else have I met, at first hand or by hearsay, any body of men of quite the same nature and calibre as the Sudan police – and it would be difficult for anyone to comprehend the workings of the country and the administration during the first half of the 20th century without hearing some brief mention of them. They were, of course, an armed and disciplined force, organised on a semi-military basis, with non-commissioned ranks from warrant-officer through sergeant-major and corporal down to *askari*, or private. They lived in regular lines; they comprised foot, camel and horse police, and also included drivers of the Administration's vehicles in their ranks. The bulk of a District's force was normally concentrated at the *merkaz,* with the remainder distributed over police posts of varying strength at widely-spread focal points.

Numbers varied according to the population's density, the state and needs of public security, and the square mileage of the area. A large District west of the Nile, with an area of 43,000 square miles and a population of 400,000, was not untypical, and had a total police force of 130-140 men. No other public security force (short of military resources) existed, apart from the raw and semi-disciplined retainers of the local governments, most of whom were armed only with sticks. These figures speak for the law-abiding nature of the populace as a whole and the grip of the big men on their people.

What made the police unique was the multifarious nature of their duties. In our specialised society the policeman is the guardian of the law, the symbol of security, the director of traffic and the snooper who checks our driving licences or firearms certificates. In the Sudan he certainly had to carry out these duties, but he also had to carry out a host of others far less professional.

In smaller centres with lock-ups or minor prisons, it was the police who did duty as warders. Was the District Commissioner going on a camel trek? He would require a corporal to ride with him, and an *askari* to ride with the *hamla* or baggage camels and chivvy them. Was there an urgent message to be sent to a local authority beyond the reach of postal facilities? A policeman, by foot, bicycle or animal, took it post-haste. Was a bridge being constructed over a river which the experts denied could be professionally spanned under a cost of £10,000? A corporal with an engineering bent and a gift for managing labour would be given a gang of prisoners and, under a little supervision, would produce in three months a timber bridge, anchored with stones, which would last seven floods at least.

Was a man-eating crocodile reported in the river? The best marksman in the force was sent to sit up for the villain until he gave an opportunity. Was a surveyor launching into a waste area to trace a parallel of latitude in the interests of a geophysical year? A policeman was detailed to go with him and see he did not die of thirst. Was the *mamur*'s gun rattling ominously, with a quarter-inch gap between the stock and the barrels? The police armourer would hack and hammer and tinker until it closed securely once more (or blew the user's eyebrow off with the next discharge, and then went on the scrap-heap.) Had a quarantine to be established to prevent the spread of an epidemic? The police established and enforced it. Was a visiting *kadi* travelling to a local centre and afraid of being eaten by lions on the way? A policeman accompanied him to guard his sacred person.

The chosen policeman might not be above enjoying his errand, as occurred when a particularly nervous *kadi*, of Egyptian origins, visited a large but remote centre and displayed his nervousness by constantly inquiring of the Nazir whether there were any ravening beasts in the neighbourhood. The Nazir, who was a great man and had not passed beyond the age of indulging in a practical joke, suborned the accompanying policeman and agreed with him on a plan of action. When the *kadi* was returning towards headquarters at dusk in a lorry, along the eighty-five-mile stretch of lonely road, the policeman was to hammer on the roof and call on the driver to pull up, as there was a lion in the road.

The policeman performed with zeal and gusto. The driver braked hard, and the Arabs on the back shouted in mock-consternation. The policeman leaped down and began loading his .303. The *kadi*, forgetful of dignity, made a dive underneath the lorry, and was with difficulty, and after many minutes, persuaded to emerge from beneath the differential. The story was told me by the policeman when the party arrived back at base, and on meeting the *kadi* later I congratulated him on his escape, saying a rumour had reached me that he had met a dangerous lion. 'Yes,' he replied, 'it was an enormous one, as big as a bull, and its eyes were like green flames. But I took my beads and calmly recited the proper texts, and he passed on. He passed on.'

On occasions the police had to carry out diplomatic and semi-diplomatic functions. During the latter years of the war large numbers of Free French forces came through the Central Sudan. The epithet 'free' was not misplaced: selected policemen had to be stationed at one or two points on the route to forestall the occurrence of scandal or breaches of the peace. One of the best corporals reported to me in detail how a French officer had tried to obtain feminine and alcoholic satisfaction in the local village, and how he had kept one hop ahead of the visitor round the houses, to make sure that no *araki* stills were working, and that only the elder and more impregnable ladies were at home. The corporal's account of the incident was succinct: 'I then dissuaded him from further search by informing him officially that the Ingleez did not approve of his activities. He clenched his fists – like this – and raised them over his head, as if signalling. No, Sir. I did not understand what he said, for I do not know French. But I do not *think* he liked the Ingleez.'

It was probably on trek that most policemen showed at their very best. It might have been a gruelling, five-hour stretch by camel, in a temperature of 112F in the shade. It might have been a 200-mile journey, perched like St Lawrence on his grid[6] upon the hardest and most corner-some piece of kitchen gear on the back of a shaky tumbril bouncing over a shattering surface, with occasional spells off for pushing the vehicle through layers of blistering sand in the merciless heat. It might have been an afternoon's trekking by horse and pack-pony such as I once experienced at the south end of the Nuba Mountains.

---

6   Tradition relates that St Lawrence of Rome was martyred on a gridiron, with burning coals beneath it, in about 258 AD.

We had been cheerfully informed (a) that the path was plain, (b) that there was not much heavy cotton soil, and (c) that no rain had fallen; all of which statements proved mendacious. The *soi disant* guide lost his bearings and admitted he was flummoxed. We ploughed through mud up to our hocks and swam two water-courses, roaring in muddy spate, and two horses went part-lame from twisting a leg. We then entered a sea of the short, stubby *um sineina* or 'mother of teeth' thorn – aptly named, for every twig bears short, strong, curved talons which pull at your legs as if to say 'Not so fast', rend your long-suffering clothes and leave scratches on the flesh which too often turn septic.

From the sea of thorn we entered an ocean of high grass – 'elephant grass', eight feet tall. This was the worst of all, for visibility was limited to three yards, destroying our sense of direction and impelling a feeling of claustrophobia close to panic. Meagre rain fell the whole time, and dusk came on. It was not till after dark that we came to a small island of blessed, gravelly soil and short grass, on which we thankfully stopped.

The police corporal, who had only once before been through that area, had piloted us to safety by as straight a course as was possible. Within twelve minutes of dismounting he and his mate, with two assistants, had got our big tent up, by which time other minions had been marshalled and chivvied into fetching wood and clean water. In another quarter of an hour the horses had been tethered and fed, fires blazed, bivouacs of ground-sheets had gone up, and we could settle, exhausted, to a relatively comfortable night, It was a typical specimen of any good Northern Sudanese policeman's initiative and resource.

Some tribes or localities produced more and better police than others; but it was important, in recruiting and managing a District force, to see that it was a motley one, with representatives from as many parts of the area as possible, and a few outsiders for choice. This was partly in order to have a man or two who could act as guide or diplomat in every quarter; but a further reason was that tribal loyalties, cliquery and secretiveness can penetrate even a police force, especially where such clannish people as Nilotics are concerned, and the presence of other elements prevented the focusing of such excessive tribal solidarity in a manner prejudicial to loyalty and discipline.

The dependability of the District police force was wonderful. Probably police wives, in the lines, gave more trouble than the men, and they could be a difficult problem. Often it was one of their children that set off the powder-train. Because Fatma had smacked the head of Anna's infant, a bit of Billingsgate would ensue, and this might attract supporters on either side, working up to an Amazonian aggression. 'The female of the species is more deadly than the male,' wrote Kipling – and such fracas were never easy to deal with. One could not easily put the combatants in prison. A fine would merely fall on the long-suffering and under-paid head of the husband; and although in more distant days the Sudan Defence Force authorities were empowered to beat rowdy wives, both chivalry and the law forbade this otherwise admirable and effective system. All one could do was lecture them and send the ring-leaders under guard to grind the prisoners' grain for a few days: that hurt their pride more than their muscles.

In the first quarter of the 20th century literate policemen were rare. There were even District Commissioners who had an innate if twisted suspicion about such people, feeling that education saps a man's virility and virtue, that these damned fellows who wielded a pen must at best be pansies and at worst be crooks, and that the old, illiterate, unimaginative nugget was more reliable. This attitude was of course stupid *ab initio,* and experience proved it to be so. By 1950 there were Districts which would recruit only literate men, and everywhere, at least in the North, the proportion of literate police was rising fast. Very competent, too, were the investigations and criminal work done by the trained police, and there were county constabularies in England who would not have come well out of a comparison with them.

One minor disability shared by Sudanese police with those of other countries was heavy-footedness. A policeman's boots have always ranked with mothers-in-law, Wigan, kippers and Ford cars as a safe music-hall joke the world over. I can hear the song from my childhood now:

> *When Ah'm walking on me beat*
> *You can 'ear me plates of meat ...*

The solid, iron-heeled sandal of the Sudanese policeman could be heard across the District – and when a policeman meant business, he usually

The author's house at Wau

Author chatting up a Moro Nuba woman outside her house

Jebel Kassala in flood season

Margaret Owen on trek

Dinka man hoeing tobacco plot

Gemilab boy , Kassala

Nuba bracelet fighting, with referees

Dinka clearing sudd from steamer channel

Dinka spearing fish round hippo herd, Lake Nyubor, Upper Nile Province

Amarar man

*Dinka man wearing arm bracelets,
and covered in ash*

Author on his camel George, 1930

Alor Dinka dance, Bahr al-Ghazal

Wau police practise anti-riot drills

took those sandals off. Barefoot, he could go anywhere and was often as valuable as a plain-clothes man. Shod, he was seldom effective in the role of a sleuth.

I often wondered why the police's musketry was as good as it was. Rifle practice was held only once a year, and if the regulations were strictly observed, each man could fire only thirty rounds. Yet there were many marksmen, and the average standard was only a little below that of the Sudan Defence Force. What was remarkable was the improbability of the results. An *askari* might be made to lie down only 100 yards from a three-foot-square target, to fire five shots deliberately, using a rest. His score would probably be one magpie, two outers and two misses. Take him back to 200 yards, add a bayonet to his rifle, make him shoot rapid, without a rest – and the same man might achieve four bulls and an inner. A rifleman seldom ascribed consistently inaccurate shooting to his own poor marksmanship. Either the evil eye had been put upon him, or the rifle was inaccurate, or it was bewitched – or all three. Kipling's advice to his recruit – 'When 'arf of your bullets fly wide in the ditch/ Don't call your Martini a cross-eyed old bitch' – did not appeal to the Sudanese temperament.

In carrying out musketry training there could be hazards unconnected with stray bullets. On one occasion the target-markers were being most troublesome, delaying to record the result of the latest shot, and then recording doubtfully or inaccurately. I stopped the firing, cantered up to the butts to objurgate the markers, and dismounted. I began in a somewhat hectoring tone, but the next moment I had mounted again and was in ignominious flight. A colony of the huge black-and-yellow hornets of the Red Sea Hills had taken up residence in the butts and had become umbrageous at the markers' jerky movements. One of them stung me on the forehead, beneath the rim of my helmet, and musketry had to be suspended until the enemy could be dealt with by smoke and sulphur.

A man's performance in the field did not necessarily match his score on the range. This applied more to the African than to the Arab, for the excitement and irresponsibility of Africans in charge of firearms in the field is legendary. At the battle of Omdurman, when the Dervish attack seriously threatened the isolated Sudanese battalion, eye-witnesses recorded how the men, cheering and longing to get to grips with an overwhelming enemy, fired their rifles repeatedly into the air, instead of reducing their foes' superiority by shooting at them.

In 1952 an African policeman killed a prisoner. His first shot was a perfectly legitimate one, as the man was attempting to escape; but, having knocked him down, he fired four more rounds into him – and was duly tried for murder. Knowing from first-hand experience what had happened, in my Governor's covering letter to the Chief Justice I felt bound to recommend a reduction of sentence, which was granted.

Three times, on trek, I had been obliged to shoot a buffalo when not armed with a satisfactorily heavy rifle, and had taken policemen in support. On each occasion my first shot had (very luckily) anchored the bull. Before I could stop them, my supporters had fired respectively seven, nine and ten shots, mostly from behind me, one nearly removing my ear and two others almost severing my femoral artery. The bonds of restraint are quite broken by the exuberance of action.

Only once did I return the compliment by nearly killing a policeman, and that was with a goose. The art of shooting birds on the wing does not commend itself to the Arab temperament. It is incomprehensible that anybody should deliberately do something which is difficult and unremunerative. It would be so much easier to shoot several creatures sitting and together, with a single cartridge. Consequently, few Arabs really follow what is going on during scatter-gun shooting. Certainly my police driver, Beida, did not. Seeing some knob-nosed geese flighting near a marsh, and needing something for the kitchen, I took Beida and went down with a gun to a likely spot. Soon a skein of geese came straight over, about forty yards up, and, taking a good lead, I dropped the leading gander dead in the air. Beida stood goggling round with his eyes on the marsh, instead of lifted goose-wards. The ten-pound victim fell like a meteor, and for a split second I thought it was going to strike him full on the head – which would have broken his neck. Fortunately it just grazed the rim of his wicker helmet and his shoulder, knocking the hat off and causing him to leap like an impala, apparently six feet from a standing take-off.

With few exceptions the drivers of Administration vehicles were police, and they formed a special cadre within the force. This at first sight seems anomalous, for a man in charge of a vehicle clearly cannot engage in the full-time duties of an ordinary policeman. Yet it was one of those measures which work, and justify themselves by results. It ensured that the drivers were a disciplined force, without the right to paralyse the executive by striking, and with their own *esprit de corps* and prospects of promotion. Since a driver was frequently on trek with an officer, and since it was seldom possible to carry all the personnel one wanted, it also ensured the presence of an extra person with the powers and training (and arms) to carry out police duties if called upon.

Police drivers varied from men scarcely capable of riding a bicycle up to first-rate mechanics; and as the former were weeded out, there soon came to be, in most districts, a reliable cadre of drivers who became very much the District Commissioner's personal men, who commanded one's affection and respect. They were a wonderfully resourceful lot. Odd pieces of wire, bicycle spokes, elastoplast and string helped many a vehicle complete a journey, and when a piece of jagged rock in what should have been a smooth, all-weather road tore a hole in the radiator of the Governor's Ford tourer, the perforations were bunged up with the driver's monthly allowance of soap from the police store.

The most powerful man I ever knew was a police driver, Murr el Gawab. The simile of a benign gorilla is permissible in his case, for his arms were long, his chest like a beer-barrel, and when he broke into a smile (which was frequently) it looked as if a great slit had been cut in a huge, black pumpkin. I have seen him take a one-and-a-half ton lorry by the bumper and with a sudden effort lift it from the ground and shift its position. His father was unknown, his mother of irreproachable slave ancestry. The name itself denotes 'prompt reply' or 'pat answer'. The local legend was that his mother, being childless, had made a pilgrimage to the tomb of a celebrated *fiki* near Berber, on the Nile, and had there spent the night in petition, prayer and fasting. Lo and behold, not nine months later but on the very next morning she was delivered of a beautiful little boy. The only blemish on a loyal and valuable character was his own strength – for a cold chisel in his hands gave him an unrestrainable sense of power and illustrated the truth of Lord Acton's dictum 'Absolute power corrupts absolutely.' His dubious ancestry – for slave-blood was then seen as a defect in any Arab community – made him sensitive, and after his elevation to the rank of corporal there were all-too-frequent cases of privates being wheeled into the office on a charge of 'Insolence to Corporal Murr el Gawab, Sir.'

Even when they were not efficient, one formed an attachment to most drivers. I was always on the point of sacking Beida, but never could quite take the step. The nearest approach occurred when he appeared looking even more hang-dog than his wont, bringing a ramshackle truck far below one's dignity and admitting that he could not produce the Governor's saloon because he had lost the keys. Asked where and how he had mislaid them, he looked uneasy and repeated that they were *lost*. Pressed further, he at last blurted out the truth: that he had gone to the police pit-latrine and had been ill-starred enough to let them drop from his pocket. When I pronounced the Mikado-like doom that his punishment would be – to go down into the pit and fetch them – his countenance of dejection was so intense that it was impossible to discharge him. Actually, I think he went to a well-known professional burglar and lock-picker, for he reappeared holding a piece of metal with notches in it which was certainly not supplied by Mr Ford but which switched on the engine.

A fortnight later we arrived at an inter-district meeting on a tributary of the Nile, and found that the oars were missing from the boat in which we were to do our fishing. Beida was sent back to fetch some personnel a hundred miles away, and without prompting stopped at an Egyptian irrigation station on the river, purloined the oars from a dinghy, and brought them triumphantly back. After that he was safe.

Drink was the end of some drivers, even in Arab Provinces, but men with a weakness for alcohol did not as a rule survive long, and the general standard of sobriety – low among civil and commercial drivers – was tolerably high in the police cadre. I can recollect only one bibulous driver who lasted. Lance-corporal Kabbushoor's sole defect was a predilection for what Dick Swiveller (in *The Old Curiosity Shop*) termed 'the rosy'. But he was one of those rare men who, instead of losing quickness of reaction and sureness of judgment from a drink, appear to draw inspiration from it. After a potation, he could very nearly make a lorry swim, and I have seen him pilot his truck through conditions from which any sober and wise driver would have drawn back.

He knew his own failing, and feared it. Once I left him with his lorry while an Arab friend and I went on a hunt. On return we found Kabushoor looking worried. He was taciturn; but on being pumped recounted how, an hour earlier, five immense black creatures with horns had approached to within twenty yards of where he lay, quaking and quite sober, and had waggled their great hairy ears at him. Tracks revealed that five curious buffalo had walked up to inspect him – and since he had never come across one before, and did not know what they were, he was afraid that we would draw the obvious conclusion when he told us what he had seen.

Drivers were often literate, for even if they could write only a few sentences, it paid. Once on an expedition the driver, left with the car, discovered that the battery was not charging. After a forced march to the nearest road, he managed to send Headquarters the pathetic message: 'The Governor is in the woods. Send battery and save us.' It was good enough, and elicited a relief car and a new battery. As to the language of the garage – mechanical Arabic is a technical haggis compounded from at least five different tongues – Arabic, English, Turkish, Italian and French. The words *katawit* and *kwail* are easily translated as 'cut-out' and 'coil'; the steering-wheel was *direksion* (from French) and the distributor *bobina* (from Italian). Whenever a driver was foxed by a breakdown and asked its cause, his inevitable answer was a doubtful '*Yimkin bobina*' – 'Possibly the distributor.' I once visited a very nice driver who was lying in hospital with grave internal troubles, and after a short conversation I asked what he thought was wrong with him. He paused for a moment, and a wan smile flickered round his lips before he answered, '*Yimkin bobina.*'

To his father   March 1940
Rashad

A man came back from his cultivation and heard a squealing, so went to his house and found his wife striking their small son, aged six, in the face till his nose bled. They had had words before over her ill-treatment of the child, and he lost his temper and snatching up the wooden haft of an axe that lay nearby gave her a crack on the left side; whereupon she subsided, and, like the gentleman in the legend,
When sobered by fright to assist her he ran
Mrs Winifred Price was as dead as Queen Anne.

Or at least, she died within a few minutes.

131

There have been so many nice letters of congratulation on Robert's arrival ... Also a delightful letter from Douglas Newbold in Khartoum. He gave a most amusing description of the recent visit of the Egyptian Prime Minister and Cabinet Ministers. 'I met them at eight successive parties, and they must have taken me for an aged spy of the Cromer period ... The Minister for War ate his asparagus the wrong way up and struck a Gyppy soldier who hadn't shaved properly in the face with his stick.' Our gallant allies!

To his mother   April 1940
Rashad 19 April 1940

I'm afraid this brings bitter news, in that it is most unlikely I shall be able to get back ... A wire arrove saying that owing to the possibility of developments in the Mediterranean all key-men are debarred from leave in Europe, and as head of a district I count as a key man.. . It is all very sickening and more depressing than I can say. I had been looking forward with such longing to seeing Margaret and all of you and to beholding my son. Hatred doesn't come easy, but I think I am beginning to develop a hatred, of almost German intensity, for dictators.

To his mother   7 May 1940
Rashad

The Nazir, Zubeir, had taken a new wife, and during the accompanying beano his enclosure had been packed with a crowd of guests, many of them Nubas, who were all dancing and firing *feus de joie* with their rifles. One Nuba fired a shot, and in reloading, the cartridge (they are all home-made and very dicey) exploded in the breach and gave him a cut over the eye. Being already excited and a bit drunk, he thought somebody had shot him, and that the bullet had lodged in the back of his head.

Going outside the compound, he fired straight through the grass fence into the crowd. The bullet went through one man's clothes, scraped another over the ribs, wounded a woman in the side and killed a Nuba dead. He then went off by himself, and, thinking that he was being pursued, shot himself. So that's that.

To his father   21 June 1940
Rashad

Well, nothing stands between the world and slavery now but the British Empire, and, whatever the outcome, I was never prouder of being an Englishman … The determination right throughout the Empire to see it through and come out on top gives one heart, and I've faith that we are going to succeed despite the appalling ordeal that must lie ahead… Events in the Sudan so far are mere child's play, but anything may have happened before this [letter] gets home … I fear the Wops can put far larger forces into the field than we can. I wish I were back with the Hadendowa, on the frontier.

To Elizabeth   October 1941
Rashad

I was glad of a spell in the Obeid last month. Companionship is always pleasant, but I don't think I've ever actually felt the lack of English company until these last four months under war conditions… Nothing big has happened on the eastern front yet, but there was a good scrap ten days ago. Several of our armoured cars were ambushed and had to fight their way out – without loss and without much damage – near Kassala. The next day the Sudanese sergeant in charge decided to go the same way and get the Wops to ambush him again; they duly fell for it, and at the last moment he left the track, nipped in behind their forces, held his fire to 100 yards (Sudanese are usually pretty wild) and mopped up 400 of them, largely Italians – not bad for a Sudanese sergeant.

CHAPTER ELEVEN

The Public Health

With the possible exception of Education, there was no department with which, as a District Commissioner, one was in closer touch than the Medical, and no department at all whose work was of greater moment to the whole country. Disease and health so affect every activity of the body politic that, in their broader aspects, all medical problems are also administrative problems. This was expressed in classic form by a certain admirable District Commissioner who was not a little worried at the undoubted spread of venereal disease among his simple but not notably puritanical parishioners. He wrote a long and cogent report on the subject to the Governor of the Province, pointing out the incalculable harm which might result if the evil remained unchecked, making certain constructive suggestions, and emphasising the duty of every single member of the administration to put his shoulder to the wheel. His report opened with the words: 'The spread of Venereal Disease among the Nuba is one of those things for which District Commissioners are primarily responsible.'

For the keen professional doctor, trained to expect and exact high standards, the Sudan must have had many drawbacks and exasperations, and I never ceased to admire the practitioners, Sudanese, British and others, who achieved such results under such difficult conditions. Communications were slow (especially until post-war air transport became available) and drugs and supplies often deficient. The up-to-date apparatus for which any true doctor's soul must long was seldom available. The staff always fought for it, but learned to do without. What little I know of gynaecology and obstetrics is mostly gleaned from the two never-to-be-forgotten sisters, purple characters, who founded and presided over the Midwifery School at Omdurman and who used to instruct and demonstrate to their pupils how to carry out a caesarian operation on an old inner-tube stuffed with straw.

The response of the people themselves was often disappointing. Even where support was to be looked for, it was not always forthcoming. I recollect a particular entertainment given by the mission boys at Province Headquarters. After the customary items of sweet little girls with posies of roses and singing through their noses, and some first-rate heavy-metal work by the band, came a sketch the moral of which was that, however civilised we may become, we must never abandon the traditions upon which we were reared.

This, in a community rapidly adopting the veneer of civilisation, was laudable and healthy, and I prepared to applaud. The sketch, however, portrayed a dying Zande man, whom the doctor failed to revive and abandoned with a professional shake of the head and a snapping-up of the stethoscope, as much as to say that Hippocrates, Pasteur and the whole boiling of them could not hope to prevail. The man, now in *articulo mortis*, was then restored by the local medicine-man. The latter was the head clerk of the Public Works Department, a magnificent figure of 6'2" with a torso like a Greek statue. He and his three assistants, clad in huge head-dresses of feathers, with skins, flaring torches, bells, rattles and all the other paraphernalia inseparable from voodoo, whirling round on one leg and leaping and shouting like the priests of Baal, were nearer to the traditional pictures of Darkest Africa imagined by Rider Haggard than anything I ever saw in the bush. Under the magic, the dead man revived, sat up, scratched his head and made some ribald jest about the Public Works Department. We all enjoyed it, but I was glad the Province Medical Inspector was not present. Even the stethoscope had been borrowed from his hospital.

In the long run, and under the surface the people came to appreciate, respect, trust, and even be grateful for the Medical Service. This was shown by the competition among local authorities for the establishment of dressing-stations and hospitals in their areas. But the immediate response of the populace must have disappointed many a doctor, especially when, as so often happened, a patient who was undergoing treatment or a course of injections would walk off as soon as he felt revived and with the course incomplete; or when a patient was bought in as a hopeless case, although earlier application for treatment might have availed. This naturally did not occur in towns and advanced areas, but it was common among the more primitive, and is the outcome of an age-long tradition of fatalism which accepts what comes, does not concern itself greatly with a chain of physical cause and effect, and takes but little account of future results. Moreover although the Arab has outgrown magic as long as the European or longer (though neither of us have outgrown superstition), the African has not; and his primary reaction to disease is to wonder not *what* has caused it but *who* has caused it. Thus if a doctor busies himself performing actions whose results are by no means obvious to the victim, he is not hailed as a benefactor but may even be suspect as a wizard.

When the annual flood comes down the Gash river which cuts off Kassala, the capital of the East, the only method of crossing it for three months each year used to be to sit on an *angareb*, or bedstead, and be borne over by four stout West Africans who held a monopoly of the hazardous traffic and were experts. After exceptional rains there were patches where they might all four be shoulder-deep in the roaring flood and one or more of them even submerged for a few moments. Only once in history did they deposit a passenger in the water, and that was the Medical Officer who had just been vaccinating their children in a smallpox epidemic and had probably saved scores of lives.

Even when cases were brought readily, they were not always the right ones. An Italian doctor, a most likeable personality with inaccurate but totally uninhibited English, was dining with me when he was urgently summoned by a dresser to attend a woman just brought in and reputed to be dangerously ill. He rushed to the hospital, but was back in five minutes, incensed and waving his fist - 'Dronk! DRRRONK! She tooter like ze fern in ze vind!'

Every province had its Province Medical Inspector and headquarters hospital, with a varying number of medical officers and hospitals in the districts, and a net-work of dispensaries and small dressing-stations in all centres of any importance. The dispute as to whether available funds were better spent on one new hospital or three new dispensaries was a perennial one, with most doctors inclining to the hospital and most administrative officers inclining to the dispensaries. The latter were the first line of defence in the medical field, both for intelligence and for treatment. They gave first aid, dealt with simple cases, sent serious ones to hospital, inspected the local schoolboys, and reported the first rumours of epidemic outbreaks.

In areas where there were seasonal movements of population for grazing, a dresser might have to spend months living a circumambulatory life among cattle-camps. I recollect taking out a dresser who emerged from his dispensary armed with a blanket, a syringe and one huge bottle full of an indeterminate-coloured liquid with an indescribable smell. We could only guess that he had taken all the various dopes from his shelves and mixed them into one glorious panacea for all troubles. When I inquired, he said that it was castor oil; but I am sceptical.

The responsibility taken by these medical assistants and dressers was often far greater than their education and professional training warranted. In this instance the Arab was superior to the African. For the average medical assistant in the Northern Provinces I conceived the highest respect. He was called on for many a difficult job and never shirked it, even when it was beyond his professional qualifications (which extended often only to a primary education and a little training in a hospital.) When a highly-placed official was visiting us and was smitten by a nasty sore throat, since by ill fortune all the medical officers chanced to be absent, a medical assistant was sent for from the Province hospital. He diagnosed the trouble instantly and pronounced it without hesitation. It was either diptheria or syphilis. It was, however, another medical assistant who first diagnosed correctly the grave and unexpected outbreak of yellow fever which occurred in 1940.

Even teeth, which are a bugbear any doctor hates being asked to cope with, the medical assistants were willing to tackle. When I went with a raging abcess to our first-class Sudanese doctor, he was distinctly nervous, filled my gums with local anaesthetic until my whole face was half-ache and half-torpor, then tapped a random tooth and asked apprehensively whether that was the right one. I could not tell, and had visions of him going round my jaw, like Front de Boeuf with Old Isaac[7], and extracting molar after molar. It was by good luck that the correct one came out first time.

---

7   In Sir Walter Scott's *Ivanhoe.*

When a colleague in a Southern Province was forced to go to a local medical assistant for an unavoidable extraction, the practitioner borrowed a pair of pliers from a driver and hauled manfully for nearly ten minutes. My friend had made up his mind not to utter a sound and kept his resolution by sheer suffocation until halfway through, when Mathayo made a pause, which gave him an opportunity to fill his lungs. From that moment he did not look back; but what hurt him most was then when at length the molar was extracted, Mathayo danced about waving it and declaring flatteringly that the Moru (the local tribe) did not produce half such fine molars as this.

As a District Commissioner, one made a point of keeping in close touch with all dispensaries. The medical assistant was a useful ally, a valuable Government agent and usually a pleasant and intelligent companion. One could help him in small ways - not least by affording him ordinary intelligent conversation, from which he was sometimes almost excluded in his isolated position. A glance at his books and a tour of the dispensary revealed much. From finding a man with a hole in his thigh through which one could stuff a poker, one might get the first intimation of the presence of an unsuspected pocket of rhinoceros in one's District.

The source and progress of venereal disease in sections of the community could be traced, or at least guessed, and gave some insight into comparative tribal moral standards. The state of sanitation of the local school could be gauged. A slant might be gained on public security, and on the number and severity of tribal fights. The assistant was no more sure than the doctor himself of receiving his compatriot's thanks. I once found a particularly sour-faced and saturnine patient lying in the mud hut which served as the dispensary ward. On my asking the *omda*, who accompanied us, why the patient looked so malevolent and what was his affliction, he laughed and replied, 'Yesterday Hassan Effendi here, our medical assistant, removed a tape-worm from him seven yards long. It was put in pickle as a good specimen. As soon as the patient saw it he leaped off his bed and tried to run to the court to complain that the medical assistant had taken out his entrails and he was a ruined man.'

Ordinary diseases, and operations, are for the expert. It was in coping with scourges and epidemics that any campaign involved administrative equally with medical effort. Some leper-colonies were as much the care of the *merkaz* as of the doctor. Leprosy has from the earliest times exercised a horrid fascination over the human mind. Moreover it was, and in primitive areas still is, the plague which is *par excellence* regarded as the visitation of God for some sin or contravention of the local code of behaviour. Nobody who has seen leprosy and its corroding effects, on the spirit as well as the body, will forget it or treat it lightly, or grudge the effort and expense which have been put into combating it. Yet there are those who hold, with some reason, that this effort is disproportionate to the social importance of the disease. It is an evil which recedes before advancing civilisation; it is very rare now among Arabs, virtually unknown among Europeans, and though I have been told that in certain parts of the Nuba Mountains as much as four per cent of the population is infected, I do not think there can be many parts of Africa where any such proportion is involved.

On the other hand, more than one doctor has told me that he estimates that over a quarter of the inhabitants of the Sudan die of pneumonia (the population as a whole having a great resistance to the streptococci but a poor resistance to the pneumococci); and when a burst of relapsing fever or cerebrospinal meningitis occurs it can, or could before the advent of modern drugs, take its tens of thousands. All one could do with leprosy was segregate the afflicted in settlements where they would not have regular contact with the population, where their relatives could visit them, and where they would be adequately fed and treated with the progressively-successful methods of modern medicine. Discipline at leper villages could be a difficulty. For instance there were times when lepers, who had their own special water-supply, must needs go and bathe in neighbouring villages' Jordans, knowing well that they could not be imprisoned, would not be beaten and had no property with which they could be fined. Although docking their rations was the only feasible punishment, it is one that any authority would be reluctant to inflict.

Cerebrospinal meningitis, or C.S.M. as it was known, before the coming of sulphur drugs was the most regular and deadly of the plagues. It was invariably associated with the hot, dry, stifling weather and dust-laden winds of late winter and early summer, and it would die out rapidly with the first rains. It caused curvature of the spine and neck and produced death – not a pretty one – within a matter of a day or two; and one of its peculiar horrors was that it tended to strike the young and lusty, and to leave the aged and decrepit. Never quite absent, its appearance in epidemic form was periodical, peak periods arriving at intervals of a decade or less. Formerly there was practically nothing that medical science could do. The populace would be urged by chiefs, schools, courts and every other channel of propaganda to avoid crowding, to sleep in the open air, and instantly to segregate suspected or actual cases. Quarantines of infected areas were declared and enforced so far as possible. Intelligence and vigorous administrative action were the only ways of reducing or checking the disaster, and police and district staff joined the medical personnel. To be effective, all measures needed the highest degree of cooperation from local authorities, and among the best sheikhs and chiefs this was forthcoming – but not everywhere.

With the advent of sulphur drugs, the losses from C.S.M. sank drastically. Yet even then their success was not automatic. During a severe outbreak in the Nuba Mountains in 1942 news reached us that things were not going smoothly on one hill, Korongo, whither a dresser had been sent with the new M & B drug. People were dying, and the dresser had been threatened with spears and prevented from working. Inquiry on the spot revealed that the local *kujur*, or witch-doctor, afraid that his stock might fall if Government magic succeeded, had persuaded the neighbourhood that the new drug was a malevolent device intended to make the women infertile, and that there was only one cure for the prevalent complaint – a dose of his own urine mixed with a goat's foetus and some local emetic roots. With John Wellington Wells [the Sorcerer in Gilbert & Sullivan's opera] once under arrest and safely imprisoned, work went ahead and the popular view soon modified. But it had cost a score of lives.

Grim as was the toll taken by C.S.M., people did not seem to fear it unduly. This was because it was a recurrent scourge, was understood and even expected as a periodic but necessary evil. The outbreak of yellow fever which occurred in the Nuba Mountains in 1940 affected public confidence to a far greater degree. Medically, this outbreak was of great interest. Yellow fever was not generally known to be endemic in the Sudan. The Nuba themselves had never within living memory known such an outbreak. Yet when blood was taken from officials and missionaries, several of them were found to have had the disease. Probably it had existed for centuries, but in such a light form as to be neglected or passed over for malaria.

Whatever the obscure cause, the disease struck suddenly in 1940 in epidemic form. Why it chose that year, admittedly a year of heavy rains (for the disease is carried by the mosquito *Aedes aegypti* and possibly by others), is unknown. Why, having struck the Nuba, it did not spread to the Arab districts on either side of them, is unknown. Why it was, as yellow fever goes, a light variety, is unknown. It caused roughly 17,000 cases within a few months, yet deaths were not more than 2,000, and of three British officers who contracted the fever, none died, though two were at death's door. In fact some of the experts appeared to be almost ghoulishly disappointed at its meagre lethal achievements.

The outbreak began at the height of the rains, when the areas with a heavy rainfall are unapproachable save by horse or on foot; and when news came that people were dying rapidly, both doctors and District Commissioners found it puzzling. An Arab medical assistant was the first to assert the true cause, from the clinical symptoms, and the experts who soon afterwards arrived to investigate (and two of whom fell victims) confirmed it. What made the matter a crisis of national import was that, in the second half of 1940, the country had good reason to expect invasion from Italian East Africa. Indian troops were expected, and although the disease was not yet known in India, the vector had been found there; so that if yellow fever became rampant in the Sudan, the Government of India, fearing the incalculable consequences of the plague's entry into their continent, might have declined to send forces. In fact as the survivor of the three investigating experts, who did wonderful work on the disease, put it to me, 'If it were not for the war, this epidemic wad be juist grrrand!'

No vaccine then existed, and though before the epidemic burned itself out with the dry weather, those of us who were working in the area were inoculated, we were afterwards informed that the vaccine had been useless. Fortune had been kind. There was little that could be done for patients beyond such nursing as was possible, and procuring for the afflicted areas all the sugar which the Government could find in wartime, since the fever attacks the liver and a sugar diet was thought to have some slight prophylactic quality, besides improving morale.

What could be done, and was vitally necessary, was to cordon off the infected country and prevent ingress and egress. This was a formidable task and took every available hand, but was effectively carried out. When the dry weather came, the mosquitoes died out and the plague faded.

The other periodical epidemic, relapsing fever, did not, I believe, enter the Sudan until the 1920s. This lice-borne disease was imported by West African immigrants, and its first ravages were very serious. Once again medical science has now found an answer, but in previous years little was possible beyond the usual administrative measures – quarantines, and in schools, prisons and labour lines the boiling of clothes. But extreme cases necessitated moving an entire village population to a prepared site and burning the village itself as the sole means of destroying the vector lice. This sounds drastic, but the cremation of a thatched hut which can be rebuilt with a few days' work is not the destruction of a permanent and solid home, and it was sometimes indispensable for the public weal. Nevertheless it was a distasteful duty.

There might have been an element of poetic justice in such drastic measures, since clean people do not harbour lice. A people known as the Daju, of mixed West African and negroid origins, were possibly the most debased community I had the misfortune to meet. They were not godly, and with them cleanliness came a very long way behind even any pale aspirations to godliness. Theirs was the only case in which I remember feeling an almost Nero-like satisfaction at seeing the flames spread and knowing that the neighbourhood would be not only cleaner and tidier, but safer for mankind.

Modern medicine recognises two sides, the curative and the preventative, and the latter was the concern of the Public Health Service. Our rude forefathers knew very little about public health; they slept seven to a bed, with inadequate cubic space and all the windows shut; they had the midden five paces from the kitchen door and were impervious to the joys and woes of scent; they bred mosquitoes and lived in blissful ignorance that they were breeding death.

It is not surprising that in a country like the Sudan an efficient Public Health Service was a comparatively late development. Nor is it surprising that it met with very little appreciation from the populace, and less support than it deserved from the Administration. For the doctor comes in when he is wanted; the Public Health Officer comes in exactly where and when he is not wanted. The doctor searches for things you wish him to trace and deal with; the Public Health Officer searches for exactly those things which you wish to conceal and with which, after his departure, you yourself will be expected to deal. In fact, the Public Health Officer is, by trade and definition, a snooper, and ranks in the estimation of many officers with auditors and income-tax collectors as a creature not on the protected list.

It must be admitted that a completely hygienic world would not be one worth inhabiting. When a Public Health Inspector was appointed to my Province Headquarters, his first official deed was to demand the draining of the swimming bath on the grounds that it was breeding mosquitoes. Of this we were sceptical. Since the bath was filled by an Emmet-caricature pump, a relic of a mining syndicate which had departed thirty years before, and was liable to blow up if it ever got up enough pressure to lift the water the requisite twenty feet from the river, we considered that, once full, the bath had to remain full. The appearance of newts was the usual signal for removing the plug, but mosquitoes were all in the day's work, and their identification with the malaria-carrying *anopheles* was dubious. The demand therefore had to be gracefully refused.

Two days later the air was full of a penetrating miasma of crude oil; and I found that the edge of the marsh, not 200 yards from my house, where green-sandpipers and stilts and snipe delighted to probe and which was dangerously close to the main pool of the river which affords the best fishing, had a greasy, treacly scum all over it. That trick had definitely been the Public Health Inspector's, and I was only just in time to trump another one, two days later, when I saw smoke arising in front of the house and by a sharp sprint and peremptory orders was barely able to stop a gang of prisoners who had been sent to set light to the grass and turn the area into a charred expanse, on the pretext that mosquitoes might harbour there. Truly they make a desert and call it health.

Yet after discounting a few excesses of this nature, it must be conceded that the Service achieved results and conferred benefits for which they deserved far more credit than they received. Half the physical ills which beset the African and, to a lesser extent the Arab, came from preventable causes - infected water, myriad flies, surreptitious mosquitoes, lethal and dirt-lurking microbes. Malaria, which for a generation had been looked on as inevitable at Province Headquarters and which had filled niches in the cemetery and sent out many a good man feet-foremost, was by the 1950s scarce among those who took trouble to look after themselves. Dysentery likewise was rare. In fact public hygiene had prevailed to improve the efficiency and health of headquarter administration in large measure, and though its interests were still struggling in some districts, and scarcely understood at all in outside areas, it deserved all the support it could get and, if it once prevailed, would halve the population of the hospitals.

The term Public Health covered many an activity beyond the long-nosed investigations of sanitary staff into one's kitchen and water supplies. On one occasion the Central Government decided to call for information on diet in the Southern Provinces. What did the African really eat? What calories did he get and what did he require, in his uninhibited existence? We could not authentically reply. The only way to ascertain was to post clerks, with pencil, paper and weighing machine, in the houses of various typical employees over a number of days and obtain figures not by estimate or by verbal inquiry but by measurement.

Then was exhibited the unconquerable resistance of the African to any attempt at classification and statistical exactitude. At the end of the month (i.e. with pay-day not yet arrived) a huge and muscular ferryman was proved to have consumed in three days nothing but two handfuls of ground-nuts and an unfathomable quantity of beer. Conversely, the day after pay-day, the Sergeant-Major of police, who held a circumcision celebration for his son, was observed, measured and recorded as consuming six-and-a-half pounds of meat, seven pounds of bread and approximately a gallon of *merissa* (grain beer) in twenty-six minutes.

I always regretted that no systematic attempt was made to collect and record traditional medicines and cures, both Arab and African. I am not thinking of the bright ideas of half-trained junior staff, such as that of a particular dresser who tried to get rid of leprosy by rubbing the victim's afflicted limbs vigorously with emery paper, but of the roots, herbs and other methods employed from time immemorial. Many of them were mumbo-jumbo and of more anthropological than medical interest. One such was the demand of an excellent and unfortunate *omda*, who had contracted leprosy, that I should shoot him a hyrax or rock-rabbit, whose flesh chopped up and roasted with the contents of the stomach would cure the accursed disease.

Many other methods had empirically proved their efficacy. Numerous medicinal plants grew, including all the horrors of childhood; senna, colocynth and bitter aloes flourish in profusion in the semi-deserts of the North-east, and I once came near to death when, for want of calomel, I picked a peck of senna pods, boiled them and drank the concentrated essence. Castor-oil grew freely on a sandy soil under a moderate rainfall. Other plants were known to practitioners, but their nature and identification were esoteric secrets and not readily divulged. Cupping was widely practised, and not far removed from the blooding which, in the eyes of our misguided ancestors, was the panacea for all ills. I have watched it performed with the tip of a bull's horn, some six inches long, in the point of which a narrow orifice had been bored and covered with two layers of cobwebs. The operator then cut two incisions with a razor on the patient's shoulder, clapped the 'cup' over them and sucked energetically at the hole, creating a vacuum inside it and drawing a fairly large gob of blood. It was, however, pronounced to be insufficient, which showed that recovery would be a retarded process.

That medical services as a whole were appreciated was shown by the staffing problem. I cannot remember a District Commissioner who was not convinced that his district had been unfairly treated and deserved a bigger quota of dispensaries and medical assistants, nor a province which was not pressing for more doctors and yet more. The Kitchener School of Medicine turned out a steady stream of, for the most part, competent Sudanese doctors worthy of the best traditions of the faculty; but they could not meet the demand; and in latter years, when British staff were thinning out, the Service was a polyglot one, including Italians, Dutch, Egyptians, Swiss, Germans and Persians, some of them men of character.

A Persian doctor was stationed at Province Headquarters, a man of the Bihai faith, who would argue his religious tenets in the middle of a hernia operation, and whose purple character worked some remarkable cures. Unluckily, purple characters seldom take kindly to routine discipline. One day a note from this man was placed on my desk announcing, 'Sir! Unless things change *immediately* I shall have to send in my resignation.' The only possible reply was to invite him to come and lay bare his heart. He was by then removing an appendix and citing the prophet Isaiah, but came later to have tea and explain the symptoms.

It appeared that his superior had refused to place a car at his disposal.

How could he work without transport? A mild suggestion that he might send to the garage for a pool driver elicited a waving fist and a shout: 'Hibernating, Sir! They hibernate winter and summer.' Omitting to press the verbal inaccuracy of this, I soothed him and drove him home. The embarrassing truth proved to be that he had already broken up two medical cars, owing to his habit of dropping the wheel to gesticulate when driving home a point in religious argument, and the Province Medical Inspector had not unreasonably ordered that his metaphysics should not be allowed to jeopardise the meagre remainder of the fleet.

I went to see him the next afternoon and discuss this ticklish point, but need not have bothered. I found him making coffee in the kitchen, clothed in pyjama trousers only, his huge and sweat-beaded torso gleaming through such a cuirass of black hair as I have only seen elsewhere upon a gorilla's chest. He brandished the coffee-pot at me, beamed, bade me enter, and said he would prove from the prophet Daniel that the year of the Second Coming was 1844, the year in which the Great Bihai had appeared. Daniel had done the trick, and the minor issue of the transport problem never reappeared.

To his father   6 January 1944
Nahud 6 January 1944

Rob [then six] continues very uproarious and has even recovered a bit of his Kenya colour, which he lost in Khartoum. One good result of seeing his mother busy with another baby is that it seems to have cured him of any paterphobia (??? try the dictionary) and he now regards me as a most desirable being, which is a great joy, though with the everlasting blitzkrieg of work in Nahud one can't give him half as much time as would be nice.

We have got a donkey, and he goes for miles in his howdah; but the moke is no Pegasus and needs two people to take it. When I tried going out alone with it we found that if I walked in front I had to do all the work by dragging the moke along, which was no picnic, while if one walked behind, to catch it a crack, the sagacious creature scented trouble brewing astern and began to canter, which frightened R, who couldn't hold him back.

CHAPTER TWELVE

Missions

In 1960 all Christian missionaries were evicted from the Southern Provinces by the Khartoum Government. Yet for the first half of the 20th century the missions were such an important factor in one half of the Sudan that any account of the period which did not refer to them would be lop-sided.

I have often heard it said, by both Government officers and other observers who ought to be capable of deeper thought, that missionary effort is a waste of time, and that the African would have developed better if left alone. 'Why try to implant Christianity in these people? They will not digest it. Not one in twenty will take it more than skin-deep. It only gives illusions and upsets equilibrium. The people all have their own outlook and customs and philosophy of life, suited to the conditions under which they live. Why can't we leave well alone?'

This attitude might not carry weight with any believer. But in an agnostic and secular world it met with wide acceptance. Moreover, it was a perfectly tenable view, granted one colossal assumption – namely, that if we refused to introduce a pagan population to our own creed, we should also refuse to introduce them to the motor car, the wireless, the aeroplane, King Cotton, and above all, education. You cannot have it both ways. If we were going to upset African life in one direction, we had to be prepared to do so in all directions. If we did not think it wrong to introduce a man to literacy and the results of applied science (both of which, in two generations, have revolutionised the African mode of life and rendered the traditional outlook hopelessly inadequate), we could not hold it mistaken to offer him the faith which has been the mainspring of our own civilisation for 1,900 years.

Opposition or even indifference to the work of missions could have been fully justified only by a policy of maintaining Africa as a human zoo – a policy never tenable in theory, and now in the light of history seen as ludicrous. A civilisation without a creed for a basis is doomed; and if we will not establish and encourage a genuine faith as a basis for a newly-emerging people, we all know what alternative world outlook is waiting to step in.

Care for the spiritual welfare of the people has never been the responsibility of a government – nor should it be. But such care is the direct responsibility of the civilisation behind that government, and it was the missionary societies who exercised that responsibility on our behalf. The African pagan was probably about as amenable to Christianity as were the subjects of King Penda of Mercia and King Oswald of Northumbria in the seventh century AD, and I doubt whether a modern converter has any greater cause for pessimism than had Saints Augustine and Columba among our barbarous and singularly unpromising forefathers. There was much greater reason for leaving the Briton and the Saxon untampered-with, since their lives were subject to no violent revolutionary process – whereas the whole field of African life has been deeply furrowed and turned over by the ploughshare of technical advances and modern politics.

I have occasionally found individual missionaries obstructive. I have sometimes been convinced of the obtuseness of missionary methods and policies, more because they thwart their own aims rather than causing any embarrassment to the administration. But I believe that if ever History sums up the balance-sheet squarely, the part played by missions in the development of Africa will be shown to have been one of incalculable benefit.

Apart from the headquarters of the Church Missionary Society, and some fine medical work undertaken in the capital, there was practically no missionary endeavour outside the Nuba Mountains, which form a great African island in an Islamic sea. The Southern Provinces, being African and fundamentally pagan, were the area in which missionary endeavour of all kinds was active. Islam does not work by organised societies, but by the personal influence of its adherents. Every Muslim is an unofficial yet effective individual missionary, and there were Muslim nuclei in all centres of civilisation, though comparatively little Islamic development among tribesmen, except in the extreme south-west.

The work of Christian missionary bodies was controlled, as early as 1906, by assigning to each body a sphere of activity. In the early days this wise policy ensured that the various churches had plenty of scope for their efforts without their interests clashing, and without that bickering or rivalry which is a set-back to the societies' work and can be an embarrassment to the Administration, as well as an unedifying spectacle to the sceptical onlooker. The system was highly controversial, and so far as I know it was practised only in the Sudan. It was anathema at least to the Roman Catholic Church, and the development of the country had in some ways lessened, though in others enhanced, the need for it. But it had proved of great value, and in modified form it remained the basis for mission policy up to the date of the Sudan's independence.

The organisation, drive, discipline and very size of the Church of Rome gave it an immense advantage over the Protestant body. Its funds were great.

Its personnel was large and to the layman seemed inexhaustible. Celibacy made that personnel far more effective by avoiding the ties of family responsibility, which were an unceasing handicap to most Protestant staff. To the eye of a well-wisher and an administrator, the greatest weakness of the Protestant missions has always been their ultra-democratic character. A missionary's post is a quasi-military one; yet Protestant staff were far too frequently absent from their field-posts attending a series of conferences. When a firm decision was required, it was often difficult to extract, and sometimes appeared to have been arrived at on the democratic principle of one-vote-per-nob, instead of by a directing and governing mind.

The difference in outlook between Protestant and Roman Catholic could well be seen by attending their services. Both at their best were impressive. The latter, needless to say, was the Mass, and the building probably a fine, red-brick one, erected by lay-brothers and often decorated by some gifted Father with frescoes of angels, more bulbous and Rubens-like than the Botticelli type, but tasteful and pleasing. The service itself was often beautifully taken, the congregation devout and concentrated, and the choir singing those parts which fell to their lot, much as Chaucer's prioress 'entuned in her nose full seemely.' The seminary run by the mission taught the students Latin – and did so effectively. I once found a class studying Caesar's *Gallic Wars*, and in a rash moment asked the teacher why they were not into some author with more literary verve, such as Catullus. This was not well received: war is less demoralising than love – and I left them building walls with Balbur and dividing Gaul into three parts, in preparation for the sonorous and glorious periods of the Mass.

By contrast, a service in a Protestant church was just as full, though the building was humbler, of mud-brick, with big timber beams supporting a thatched roof. The congregation sat on low benches, and there was a certain amount of coming and going, as well as some mild disturbance from small children and women suckling babies. All this was natural to those present, and did not detract from the reverence and genuineness of the proceedings. The service was taken by an African, in the local tongue. When the sermon came, it might have been expected to leave the visitor without a clue, but this was not so. After a few minutes of speaking the preacher produced in one hand a slop-pail full of unprofitable brickbats, and in the other some seedy-looking, withered grain-stalks. A few sentences later, he extracted from under the pulpit a tin jerry holding some even yellower and sicklier stems mixed with *Zisyphus spinachristi*, the densest local thorn. Yet a few more sentences, and with a triumphant smile he displayed a pink vase containing several magnificent stalks of the earliest millet. He had given an effective homily on the Parable of the Sower – and he knew best how to get it across.

The hymns were sung with fervour. The tunes were not all from *Hymns Ancient & Modern*, for wise missionary guides, agreeing with General Booth, founder of the Salvation Army, that there was no reason why the Devil should have all the best tunes, had taken many a secular ditty and set it to verses in an African tongue. The pentatonic scale employed by most African gives something of a twist to the majority of Western melodies, but the originals were clearly recognisable, among them *Il y avait une Bergère*, *John Brown's Body*, and, unless my ear deceived me, *She was poor but she was honest*. The whole performance was African in style and affinities: only the motive power had been drawn from an extraneous source.

If an administrator found dealing with Protestant bodies sometimes difficult from lack of a satisfactory *point d'appui* and central authority, with the Roman Catholic Church the opposite was true. There was always an authority with whom to make contact, and one knew that one was dealing with a totalitarian institution, that no holds were barred, and that any decision reached would be effectively carried out. One's official relations with the authorities were rather like a game of chess, and unless you kept your eyes skinned, red was apt to mate in three moves. In fact I sometimes wonder whether the bishop was not so named as a satire on the medieval Church, for he sticks rigidly to his own colour and always attacks you sideways.

If official relations were occasionally acidulated, demanding patience and diplomatic acumen, personal relations were almost without exception cordial and happy. I never ceased to get pleasure from the society of the Fathers and Sisters of the Verona Fathers' Mission, or to admire their devotion to their work and the varied character and talents they brought to it.

There was Brother Botticelli (I must change the names – so why not resort to the Old Masters?), chief mechanic of the Mission, and a most competent one too. Yet when an occasion required higher cuisine, it was he who was called in as chef, and the hand that could be firm with the spanner was light and persuasive upon the rolling-pin. I recollect a particular luncheon given by the Bishop for the visit of the Governor General. There were six courses, and Brother Botticelli had cooked them all superbly. Not content with that, he even helped hand round the *pommes de terre à la maitre d'hôtel*. The day was Thursday before Easter, and, turning to the Bishop, I queried the propriety of holding such a banquet in the middle of Holy Week. For an instant I thought he was non-plussed. Then, with a perfection of adroit courtesy which won my admiration, he rebuked my ignorance by pointing out that this was Maundy Thursday and was customarily held as a fiesta in order to prepare for the coming rigours of Good Friday.

Then there was Brother Tiepolo, who lived at the station furthest removed from civilisation (207 miles from Province Headquarters, to be exact). He could improvise anything, and his best invention of all was his drink, euphemistically known as 'Raga water', brewed from local honey, white of egg or cream and illicitly-distilled hooch. I always knew that we ought to run him in for producing that liquor, but after being primed with three glasses of it, I never had the heart to enforce the law – and we all loved Brother Tiepolo far too much.

Father Del Sarto was one of the very few Fathers who ever caused trouble administratively. Once, when thwarted in his work, he took bell, book and candle and laid a curse upon the malefactor. The latter, as was not unnatural in a superstitious community, began to wither away, and the Father was compelled to remove the anathema – whereupon the victim recovered with miraculous suddenness. Father Del Sarto narrowly escaped eviction over that incident, for he was of the salt of the earth, a refreshing influence of mild bolshiness, whose one aim was to foster the care of his people.

His hospitality was great. I was once at the rest-house close to a Mission station, with my family, and received an order to come and dine, since they had just killed *un grosso porco*. We went, expecting a nice helping of pork, a banana – and bed. But we had miscalculated. The *porco* appeared in six different guises, as soup, as trotters, as chops, as sweetbreads, as hash, and finally, by some miraculous and instantaneous metamorphosis, as a sausage. The children's night was a disturbed one, but the effects passed off.

Father Coreggio was the greatest living authority on the Dinka language. When a Northern Sudanese or a British official wished to take his examination in Dinka, he was always placed on the board, and no such official was known to fail, because Father Coreggio made sure he did not. Father Salvator Rosa – short and flutter-whiskered – was a really knowledgeable anthropologist, with an unrivalled understanding of local history. His passion was discovering new tribes, and the last one he found consisted of three men, one of them blind, one deaf and the third aged ninety-three. But though colleagues laughed at him, he never resented it, and his erudition was valuable and worth consulting.

In some ways the Sisters seemed to me the most remarkable of all. By the standards of the world their life lacked all the essentials for content – company, exchange of views, creature comforts, variety. Yet you only had to look in their eyes to see the quality the world lacks – serenity. If they came to have tea with you, they would issue afterwards like a section of horticultural harpies, sweep off most of the petunias and then swoop upon the carnations. Three colours especially attracted them: red, purple and pale yellow. One was left looking ruefully at the garden, but since the flowers went to the altar, I could only bless the Sisters, and always felt that I derived a little indirect blessing myself. They enjoyed their windows on the world – literally: for when once they raised an objection to the siting of a new building opposite the Mission, the grounds were that they would no longer be able to watch the football.

Relations with Protestant staff were happy, too. I never ceased to respect the good temper and fortitude of the Church Mission Society padre, who from time to time took services at Province Headquarters, in putting up with Marcus, my parrot. Marcus was the living proof of the doctrine of Original Sin. Not only did his fallen nature automatically choose the lower rather than the higher, and assimilate the more depraved expressions of English, Arabic or other languages; he also had an uncanny and devil-prompted sense of timing.

When a service was held in the big room of the Governor's house, the bird would be placed on the verandah outside, whence he could hear but not view the proceedings. He would sit in model silence throughout lessons, hymns and prayers; but the moment the text was given out and the sermon began, his barrage commenced, usually with 'You talk bunkum, Sir', followed by 'Shut up, yer ba-a-astard.' Two stalwart members of the congregation would have to be requested to remove him to the shade of a mango tree a stone's throw away, whence his blitz could be indistinctly heard but not recognised verbatim. Our padre bore this with perfect sangfroid, and the standard of his sermons never fell. Perhaps the avian emulation gave inspiration.

In their attitude to the African himself both main divisions of Christendom were sound in principle, and normally in practice, and such individual lapses as did occur were usually what might be expected from the background of the missionary concerned. An occasional Italian priest might treat an African in a less liberal manner than is natural to us. On the other hand members of the more extreme Protestant persuasions, with a legacy of Calvin and the Puritans behind them, undoubtedly showed an attitude to the fleshly failings of human nature, and particularly African human nature, which were less than realistic.

I have always thought it would be wise of any institution representing the Church of England to make it clear that it has no connection with advocacy of teetotalism as a doctrine, for the Church is often mistakenly saddled with it. As a doctrine, teetotalism appears to the agnostic and the worldly as a comfortless and killjoy affair; to the thinking Christian it lacks all Gospel support. But as a practical measure, to be urged on individual converts for a purpose, it is another matter. Nobody who has not lived in Africa can conceive what a stumbling-block liquor presents to the African's advancement. The nearest parallel is probably to be found in our own Saxon ancestors. To the great majority of citizens, drinking in moderation is a normal activity requiring no special effort. Among a Muslim community, though alcohol is officially forbidden on religious principle, a proportion of the populace does drink – and though excess is not uncommon, it is the exception rather than the rule. In Africa all that is changed. In the Nuba mountains, during the beano which follows the harvest, I have seen a whole hill – man, woman and child – incapable. Even babies of two or three were rolling around with bloodshot eyes. It was not a pretty sight, and not a subject for mirth. No tradition of moderate drinking exists. Even officials could not always be relied upon to be sober in office hours.

The outlook of the Roman Catholic Church was sound enough. Its staff denounced drunkenness, not drink. Nor did they expect too much of their charges. As one Father expressed it to me, 'I preach against ze dronkenness. I thomp ze pulpit and I tell them dronk man go to 'ell. And zat evening in ze compound I see more dronks zan ever before.'

The part once played by the Missions in education in the Southern Provinces is not a subject to be treated here: it is too big, too technical and too controversial – and in any case it is one of those things in which recent history has brought total change. While the Church of England has concentrated more on medical work, pre-eminently in hospitals, in education the Church of Rome has been outstanding. The training given in its technical schools in carpentry, iron-work, printing and mechanics held the field to the last against anything the Government could show, and has been of the utmost value to the community.

No missionary society can supply the academic needs of a modern educational system; and if they did attempt it, they would be neglecting their primary duty of evangelisation. But in the pride of our up-to-date methods, apparatus and curricula, it is as well to remember two things.

First, the missions were the pioneers of African education. They faced bitter difficulties with inadequate resources, and achieved results long before the state had even made a serious effort – so much so that for long the state regarded them as the main agency of education; and almost to this day the candidates for higher instruction are often from the past institutions of the missions.

Second, I believe with all my heart that any purely secular education, divorced from the authoritative teaching that goes with a Faith, is a false education, and will not breed a civilisation which can stand the test of time. The work of the missionaries has come through the trial of fifteen years of persecution, and it is they who have laid the foundation on which the African civilisation of future centuries will rest.

To Aunt Nora   18 December 1927
as from El Dueim

No mission is allowed in Mohammedan Sudan – and rightly. The fanaticism of the Muslim world is so incomprehensible, and their antagonism to Christianity such, that while political disturbances are no alarming danger, and the efforts of the Bolshie (who has tried to penetrate even here) are negligible, a highly-organised intelligence service has to be kept constantly busy and on the alert from end to end of the country for the least suspicion of a religious rising. One mad *fiki,* one initial success of a rebellious sheikh calling himself a *Mahdi,* and the whole country might be up, from Kassala in the east to Darfur in the west. So one has to be careful.

To Elisabeth   15 July 1951
Wau

I visited one of the Roman Catholic missions *en route* and found them just sitting down to their lunch. They filled me up with a rather heavy brand of wine, and when I reminded them I had got to drive the car after it, quite seriously observed, 'Ah – but it is consecrated wine. It cannot possibly hurt you.' Anyway, the strength of their faith or my head averted disaster.

They eat immense quantities of spaghetti, these Italians. It is odd how other people's eating always seems gross to oneself. They do seem to shovel it down so. I suppose one of the more notable differences between civilised man and the barbarian is the former's dependence on regular meals and inability to fast or feast to excess, while the latter can stuff and starve with equal impunity.

To Elizabeth   15 December 1951
Wau

We have been having the usual stream of visitors and look like sitting down to Christmas dinner about forty-six strong, an unprecedented number. We have just been having our bishop, Allison, the one who always sings and whistles in his bath. I wouldn't even mind him doing that if he didn't stay so long in the bath and keep other people out of it …

He told me that in an examination in one of his mission schools not long ago the pupils were told to draw a picture of the Flight into Egypt; that one of them produced four figures in an aeroplane and when questioned as to who the fourth was, replied that it was Pontius the Pilot.

To Elizabeth   9 February 1952
Wau

We had a very anxious period when there was reason to think that the Foreign Office, in dutiful obedience to the Yanks, was going to go bad on us and sell us to Farouk [King of Egypt] in return for Suez. Luckily we have some good friends in high places, and even more luckily some of the Sudanese gave out that if that happened, they'd fight, and Howe and the CS laid it on thick and told the Foreign Office it would take three British divisions to keep this country quiet. Thank goodness it *was* this [Conservative] Govt. and not its predecessor. Is it a stale one by now – what I heard the other day? That someone has proposed erecting the Skylon[8] in Whitehall as a memorial to the late Govt., because it pointed nowhere, had no foundations and was kept in place by wire-pulling.

To his nephew David Lyon   17 March 1952
Wau

Near Juba we ran into a party of hunters who are going to the Bahr al-Ghazal, and I shall meet them on the return journey. He is a Belgian millionaire called de Bruyer; arrived at his camp, we found that Mrs de B. was resting. As she has had eight children already, at the age of thirty-three, and obviously dislikes travel in Africa intensely, she doubtless had need to rest.

However, Mr de B. was there, with sixteen servants, six tents and the biggest refrigerator I have ever seen, and cordially offered us champagne, Guinness, Amstel or any other drink we liked, stating his own preference for champagne always and at any time – and was a little disappointed when I plumped for a Guinness. These millionaires are nearly always kind folk, but I can't help finding something slightly nauseating about them, and can't breathe quite freely until a mile away from them.

---

8   The futuristic structure built on the South Bank for the Festival of Britain in 1951.

CHAPTER THIRTEEN

Education

The subject of education was a dismal one, and we groaned when the mail brought educational circulars, and groaned even more audibly when, as was always happening, the local school was the site, and its welfare was the occasion, for some ceremony, entertainment or function to which the public was invited, and attendance at which we felt to be incumbent. In fact 'Education' became, at least in the twenties and thirties, one of those slogans which one inwardly loathes while outwardly cheering and loyally doing all one can to foster.

When the educational drive gathered way and no longer needed administrative boosting, a District Commissioner's duties towards it became less vital; it became less of a slogan, and his distaste for it diminished accordingly – for its importance to the nation's emergence was immense and undeniable. This fact could be turned to good use: when creating the annual Province budget and particularly anxious to secure the approval of some proposal or other, the surest path to success with the Central Government was to point out that the said proposal has important educational significance.

This was a high trump, and, judiciously played, usually took the trick.

One's duties were of course mainly concerned with elementary education. The so-called Sub-Grade schools (elementary or preparatory establishments, often sited in mere villages, aiming at the rudiments and widespread literacy, and usually financed by local government) were largely under the District Commissioner's control for staff, discipline and maintenance. The siting and distribution of all types of school within a district were largely his concern, in consultation with the local government and any other authorities involved.

The annual entry into elementary schools was an interest he could never neglect, for, in any rising country, when the demand for education is greater than there are resources to meet it, it is vital to see that the right people are educated; and unless the entries are rigged – or at least guided and directed – it is usually the wrong ones who get in. Above all, it was a duty to visit every single school in the district whenever possible, to keep in touch with the headmasters, who were important men, and to know something about every subordinate master, to watch over their welfare, and to take up with the educational authorities any transfers which seemed necessary in the public interest.

In the Southern Provinces elementary education was principally in the hands of the Missions. In the north, all schools, apart from a very few private ones in the big cities, were Government-run. The Arab headmasters were picked men, and the majority of those with whom I had the privilege to serve were personalities of exceptional character. They were disciplinarians and diplomats combined, and I conceived a great respect for them. The masters were mostly the product of the big Training College near El Dueim on the White Nile, and I can testify that most Sudanese boys had more skilful and better-qualified teachers than those under whom I sat in England. The Sudan's reputation with neighbouring countries stood high, and the educational system in the Hadhramaut was largely founded by seconded Sudanese staff.

The most outstanding headmaster I knew was the leader of these. Sheikh El Gaddal was in charge of the school at Sinkat, among the Hadendowa, biggest of the Beja tribes of the Red Sea Hills. It was difficult for any foreigner to win their confidence or to learn their tongue, yet he did both. There was only one trouble with Sheikh El Gaddal – and that was that he was a difficult man to live up to. Thucydides makes some character in a set speech say of the Athenians that 'they neither rest themselves nor permit anybody else to rest,' and the phrase might have been coined for Gaddal. He was eternally having bright ideas (not the irritating kind, but constructive conceptions), which needed, and deserved, vehement action.

Only once did his enthusiasm lead us into a seriously false position. The Gordon College had advertised throughout the provinces that it was prepared to send round a magic lantern with sets of slides of suitable Uplift Value for showing in schools; and on the urgent prompting of

Gaddal, in an incautious moment, we applied for the apparatus to be sent. It duly arrived, and we laid on a showing to which the public were cordially invited and turned up in force, for a small entrance fee to go to the Propagation of Learning. My colleague, more skilled than I, nobly sacrificed himself by consenting to work the contraption, while I had the easier task of standing and giving the traditional thump with a billiard cue for the next picture, and explaining it in Arabic for the general edification.

We chose a set of slides marked on the outside 'Dwellers in the Desert', as being certain to be easily comprehended, relevant to local conditions and easy to expound. We had not had time to make a thorough examination of the slides beforehand, but we gave out the subject and waited. I thumped, but there was only some black smoke and a word of blasphemy from the direction of the contraption. We waited again (fortunately an Arab audience is far more patient than a European one) – and patience was rewarded amply, for at last there was an exclamation of triumph from my colleague, and there appeared on the screen, upside-down, a magnificent silhouette picture of the Albert Memorial. It was quickly reversed on to its bottom, and we told the audience that it was the tomb of a *fiki*. We passed on to the next slide with trepidation – and this was justified, for up came some Patagonians sitting round a pot.

We had to stop and examine the slides, only to find that they had been wrongly packed and labelled, and we had got a miscellaneous lot. When we switched hastily to a set of animal studies, the first slide revealed an ibex – and since that was the finest animal in the District, and was the Province badge, we knew we were all right. But it had been a narrow squeak.

In the early days education had been suspect, and in many parts of the country, we had had to force it upon people. By the late 1920s that stage was long past in all the more advanced areas, but in less developed areas such as the Hadendowa, suspicion of the pen, as rival to the sword, was still rife. This passed, and in late years the cry for schools and the competition for admission to them became remarkable.

One problem was, and still is, the nomad. He is traditionally conservative and averse from enlightenment. A boy taken from Bedouin surroundings and subjected to the static hell of school existence would be unlikely to endure it for long; and if he did, he would be likely to return a changed man, out of touch with his fellows. The experiment was made of attaching a teacher to the entourage of the head of a great nomad tribe, so that there might be a circumambient school, and learning might flit with the camel-herds through the desert. But I do not think it was an unqualified success. Education must have a fixed centre, and now the nomad boy must either seek enlightenment at the cost of his freedom or remain unfettered and ignorant.

Another besetting problem was how to ensure that a young, rising, educated generation should not grow up to look down upon its benighted parents. Youth, in comparing itself with the previous generation, is not over-inclined to humility. The Pierian spring produces heady wine as often as cold douches of water; and the scorn of child for parent, and conceit in its own superiority, is neither pretty to behold nor socially beneficial. The evil could not be entirely avoided, but on the whole it was much less rife than one might have expected.

I am inclined to think that education bred conceit more in the African than in the Arab. The latter's immemorial tradition of respect for age and honour of parents had a stabilising effect on character, and smoothed the transition from an illiterate to a literate state of society. It is true that not many boys who had once tasted the sweets of learning would return to hoeing fields or herding cattle, but such a phenomenon was well known, and exhibitions of intellectual snobbery were rare.

This could happen with Arabs also. I once entered a Dinka cattle-camp, and seeing a stark-nude young man, covered with ashes, sitting and hammering a tent peg, I addressed a question to him in halting Dinka. It was a surprise to be answered in ready and high-class English, and to find that the lad was on holiday from an Intermediate school.

When paying a visit to a school, a tour of the classrooms was difficult to escape. This was a penance; for the instruction of the young in elementary mathematics, geography and composition is not an activity to stimulate the onlooker, and I have never felt envious of the tedious existence of a school inspector, who is paid to suffer from it. Yet it showed one a great deal about every individual on the teaching staff, taught one to distinguish the teaching genius from the mere hack, and made clear what was the local material of boys and (by enquiring about the boys' homes) where the biggest demands for education lay.

I used at first to try to join in, show the masters how to stimulate interest, test the boys' general knowledge and make happy suggestions. I was rash enough once, in a geography lesson, to attempt to explain how an eclipse occurs. I was armed with an orange and two tennis balls (unfortunately this demonstration requires three hands), and after a few agonised moments trying to remember how an eclipse *does* happen, I gave a very convincing exhibition. I then turned to the most attentive and intelligent-looking lad in the class and asked him, 'Now, can you repeat exactly what causes an eclipse?' The answer came straight: 'Yes, Sir. The devil eats away a chunk out of the moon.'

Plays, entertainments and shows were common in all local schools. They tended to follow a pattern, and the singing items were the ones to miss, if this could be arranged. Western music appeals to few oriental audiences, though jazz and its allies are now current coin in the Middle East, at least as a form of drug, just as they are in the West. Conversely, to the European ear, the chromatic cadences and nasal intonations of Eastern singing are normally incomprehensible and generally unpleasing.

The African, if not the Asiatic, appreciates the Salvation Army type of honest, thumping, brass-band melody, and Africans make fair instrumentalists, at least on the weapons which answer to a ham-hand and a lusty lung. The Roman Catholic missions were the first to find this out and exploit it. Father Giotto with his band was a joy to watch, if not always to listen to. Pride in his team struggled with the demands of a fastidious ear. As the euphonium ground out more and ever more discordant moos, you could see him biting his lip, and his baton became jerky and spasmodic until, able to endure the discords, he would cast the baton away between the cornet and the French horn, rush at the offending euphonium, pluck his instrument from the player and boo several valiant bars to show him how it ought to be done.

He would then thrust the piece of ordnance back into the stupefied offender's hand, recover his baton and his dignity, and with verve and suavity regain control of the orchestra. Twenty bars later, you could see him casting black and malevolent glances at a trombone who was dismally braying a semitone flat in the back row. His foot began to tap out of time with the music – and five bars later away went the baton again, and away he went to pep up the trombone in person. But he did get results.

Plays, serious, comic and moral, were frequent, and in many cases

162

strikingly good. Both the Arab and the African boy have qualities which the European lacks: a natural gift for memorising, which renders a prompter almost unnecessary, and a complete lack of self-consciousness.

This last extends to the audience, and hitches or contretemps which in England would cause consternation to the cast and derision among the audience are accepted as all part of the game. I recollect a performance, at a town club, in which a famous lady singer and *danseuse* – the Gracie Fields of the country and the first woman to appear in public in such a role – had been persuaded to take the stage. It was a big occasion for the town, and all the elite and most of *hoi polloi* were in attendance.

When all was ready, the signal was given for the curtain to be pulled. The top began to draw nicely, but the bottom remained stuck on a nail, until the whole curtain rent diagonally with a loud sizzle. The lady was quite undisturbed, and began to sing. But although the *donna* may not have been *mobile,* her clothes were, for her transparent, silken veil-cum-shawl slipped from her head and shoulders and floated on the night-zephyr over the footlights. An onlooker – a senior official – recovered it and handed it back with the composure of a parochial sidesman handling the bag. She received it with equal *sangfroid,* re-draped herself and proceeded with the dance. But at her first considerable stamp upon the flimsy boards, all the lights went out. We sat patiently in Stygian darkness until an electrician from among the audience righted matters – whereupon the performance continued without a tremor of discomposure to a brilliant climax.

This quality stood the boys also in good stead. The plays themselves were sometimes set-pieces in classical Arabic, which rouses the admiration of an audience that respects a parade of erudition more than it does ours. Sometimes frank comics, in which the stock harlequinade figures – the fat man, a pantaloon, the simple policeman – were played with gusto and skill; and sometimes the plays were of the boys' or masters' own designing. These shows usually pointed some wholesome moral, and bore a striking resemblance to the pattern of the stock fairy story.

When, in a play at a local school, the aged father's beard came off as he was admonishing his two wayward sons, it was the sole occasion on which I saw an audience show ribald symptoms. However, they had not done with the father; for after he had died and the two wicked sons had committed crimes which brought them before the judge, the proceedings were held up to enable the father's ghost to appear, beard and all, in a white sheet, and, apparently unseen by judge and warders, tell his offspring what he thought of them. This interested me, since although djinns, ghouls, revenants and even vampires appear in Arab demonology, I never elsewhere encountered an honest, conventional spectre, either in literature or in conversation. Also, do ghosts wear beards?

The education of girls unavoidably came later than that of boys. Among a society by whose tradition, as in Athens, 'she was considered the best wife of whom least was heard either for good or ill', emancipation of women does not come promptly or easily, and it speaks both for the forwardness and the balance of the Northern Sudanese character that it began so early, has progressed so rapidly and has had a beneficial but not yet visibly disrupting effect on society. By the middle 1920s schools for girls were usual in the advanced riverain areas and the bigger towns. By the middle 1930s they had spread to all considerable centres; tribal leaders were regarding an education for their daughters as a natural thing; and the capacity of the schools was seldom equal to the demand made on them.

Few classes of Government servant won my admiration more than the headmistresses. They were pioneers, carrying a light to a people who in the earliest days of the movement must have been suspicious of their activities. To win support for their novel gospel, they had to display to the full the traditional virtues of respectability – deference, self-effacement, subordination and the most perfect courtesy. This difficult combination they achieved, and girls' education advanced through elementary to higher levels. One was always welcome at the local girls' school – and with a foreign administrator the mistresses had fewer inhibitions and restraints that when in the presence of Sudanese gentlemen.

In the south, the first big venture in my province was among the Dinka, who formed the bulk of the populace, as well as its most conservative element, and it was commonly known as Dinkdean. For such a pioneering departure a British headmistress and assistant were needed. Further assistance was difficult to find, for among the primitive and progress-resistant Dinka there were no sufficiently-educated girls at that date.

A Syrian teacher was sent from the north, but did not last long under the inclement conditions. On my first visit I found her – a voluminous and jellyish creature, lying on an *angareb* and groaning, pretending to be recovering from a terrible attack of fever. Poor thing, she had no one with whom she could associate; she could speak no word of Dinka, and only limited English. Owing to a failure of the steamers, there was no flour and no ghee – the latter a necessity to anyone of her kind. She had seen three snakes, and three scorpions had dropped on her (though mercifully not stung her) from the roof.

The two British mistresses therefore had to launch the venture unaided, with only a short time to acquire rudimentary Dinka and with buildings incomplete, their only close support a difficult but valuable matron who had already served at Dinkchester, the boys' school nearby, and knew how to discipline local children.

As to the girls – it was not easy to muster a satisfactory nucleus for an experiment foreign to the people's nature and beyond their comprehension, and pressure had to be put upon chiefs to produce a quota. The necessary intake did arrive, however – wide-eyed and naked little girls utterly ignorant of what awaited them or what it all meant. Anybody with less ardour and less sense of discipline, combined with less love of the children, than the two mistresses might have quailed.

The first cause of trouble arose over sanitary matters. The girls, thinking that the neat P.W.D.-built earth closets put up for their delectation might be some form of trap, insisted on making their after-breakfast pilgrimage to the bushes in front of the headmistress's window. This was, of course, intolerable, and after an order to desist had been disobeyed, several of the offenders were severely spanked. As soon, however, as it was appreciated that the earth closets had nothing sinister about them, the boot was on the other foot. Girls would hold up their hands in class for permission to 'leave the room', and were reported to be draping themselves with rolls of Bromo until they looked like the statue of Laocoon.

The school never looked back. The only serious trouble I heard of was a pupils' strike, caused by distaste for the new uniform; but this was suppressed after some executions by the headmistress; and Dinkdean went on its steady way towards changing the face of Dinka life. As Mark Twain observes, 'Soap and education are less sudden than a massacre, but they are more deadly in the long run.'

In the north practically no European teaching staff were necessary below the level of the Gordon College in Khartoum and the big central

Teachers' Training institution. Sudanese masters possessed the ruling, administrative and tutorial qualities needed to run the whole great educational edifice. In the south, with its later start and inadequate resources, British headmasters and mistresses were needed to get under weigh the more important institutions.

Curious sects have a habit of turning up in Africa, though of course not in Islamic surroundings. When Seventh Day Adventists gained a foothold in a secondary school, rumours of the Second Coming began to affect the pupils' attention and to be an embarrassment to the staff – until the wise headmaster posted a notice saying that 'By Order of the Headmaster, the Second Coming will not take place until the completion of this term's labours'.

To his father   October 1939
Rashad , Kordofan Province

Baggara wrestling is interesting. The youths are stripped save for a brightly-coloured waist cloth or drawers. They are blotched all over with grey ash and sometimes have an ostrich feather stuck in their hair. They wear a leather belt covered with small bells which tinkle when they run round the circle and waggle their haunches or leap in the air.

Bouts are between members of different sections of the tribe, and there is a good deal of feeling; if a Goliath from one side walks round the opposing ranks challenging, they are rather careful about choosing an opponent for him for fear he should be beaten. One of the umpires has a kudu horn, which gives a monotonous but rather musical bellow, and which he blows over the head of a competitor, who kneels to receive it, during the intervals, to give him more strength and guts for the next round.

A number of chorus girls on either side keep up an encouraging paean throughout the proceedings, and when a wrestler throws his man, all his women supporters rush into the ring, execute a triumphal ballet round him, pour scent and water over him from a rather seedy-looking kettle and carry him off.

CHAPTER FOURTEEN

Communications

I have already mentioned the dictum of a Governor under whom I served, that there should be only two forms of travel in the Sudan – the aeroplane and the camel; and it was surprising how often the two extremes were in juxtaposition. You might be among the pastures and morasses of the Arab Dinka close to the White Nile, with the plumed hats of a cattle camp to the north of you, naked, spear-bearing herdsmen around you, a herd of elephants on the horizon to the south, and half a day of plowtering and bog-trotting to the nearest big stretch of firm land, yet with the sound of aeroplane engines in your ears every half hour, for you were below the direct Cairo-Johannesburg air route.

In recent years the air system of the country had developed into an efficient service of the highest value. The contrast between old and new, tradition and progressive invention, nature and science, was in evidence everywhere and gave piquancy to the whole. The train hooted its way across the desert, and beside the track rode the villager on what looked like a small, moving hay-rick – a donkey twinkling along almost hidden beneath its load of grass and fodder. The train itself might be completely stopped by a swarm of locust hoppers, whose bodies, crushed on the track, so grease the wheels that they skid round and cannot bite upon the metal. The lorry jolted along its *via dolorosa* from irrigation canal to railhead with a load of cotton, and vast Lahawin camels plodded the same road, each with a load of nearly 1,000 lbs, on the same errand and only one degree slower than the truck. The official covered the map complacently at 35 mph till he came to a waterway or boggy patch, where petrol gave way to muscle, and fifty happy, shouting locals had to be mustered to man-handle the vehicle through. As the aeroplane streaked overhead, the carrier bore his head-load at a brisk 4 mph beneath it. The telegraph carried a message 600 miles from Khartoum in half an hour, but it took two days for the despatch to cover the last twenty miles – if at all – borne by a leisurely messenger carrying a piece of paper stuck in a cleft stick.

Even a form of transport as modern as a river-steamer may depend more than the passenger realises on the sheer weight of hand labour. Wait until the steamer grounds (as it frequently does) on a sandbank, and, while hawser and donkey-engine pull upon one side, watch the crew and any other labour available heaving and pushing against the other side of the hull. Such an occasion gave me my one and only meeting with a caricature Guards officer, moustache, monocle and all. We were travelling on a steamer in Upper Egypt, and had stranded on a sandbank within sight of port. For more than an hour the crew had been manfully hauling, up to their waists in the river, with little result. Our friend had maintained a stony silence for two days; but now he turned round, looking on at the proceedings, and opened his mouth. 'I say, pretty beastly jolly watching these fellers push the boat – what?' With which he relapsed into silence.

If you leave the main channel of the Nile and poke up the side rivers, particularly those of the Bahr al-Ghazal, you may find the labour at work on which the steamer's arrival depends. It will consist of a Northern Sudanese officer, a foreman or two and an unspecified number of Dinkas. Their only implements are ropes and a few cutting instruments, and they are engaged in hauling out from the main waterway the huge blocks of floating papyrus or *sudd* which surreptitiously encroach and build up until the whole passage is choked and no large vessel can penetrate. On their primitive effort hangs the arrival of the steamer; on the arrival of the steamer hangs the arrival of trade goods for the bigger part of a Province, of grain supplies to cope with famine conditions in a district, and of petrol without which the Province fleet of vehicles cannot run, and administration breaks down.

Even the main channel of the Nile, in which a hold-up is now almost unthinkable, needed the same clearance by man-power a mere two generations ago. After the battle of Omdurman, Colonel Peake was sent with a gang of 500 prisoners to clear the barrage which had blocked the channel some hundred miles south of Malakal. The task proved herculean. Finding his resources insufficient, he sent back a message by telegraph to Khartoum requesting further supplies of labour. The answer from 'K' returned swiftly: 'Arrest 500 suspicious characters and complete the work.'

Travel by rail through the deserts of Northern Sudan, in a shade temperature in May of 116 F and with a dust storm blowing, was not a joy, even in retrospect; yet it was an experience. No officer will forget his first rail journey from Port Sudan to Khartoum, the country growing flatter and more desolate as the Red Sea Hills give way to the Atbara desert, the circular red furnace of the setting sun, and, for mile after mile, every telegraph pole crowned with a vulture, each huddled in a different but always grotesque attitude like that of a Nôtre Dame gargoyle, and all starkly silhouetted against the glare of the evening sky.

The discomfort of such a journey was not the fault of the Sudan Railways. I doubt whether any country in Africa or the East was better served by its railway system; and the difference in comfort, cleanliness and efficiency was soon marked when one travelled on the Egyptian State railways or even in East Africa. Real discomfort came only when travel by first-class coach was for one reason or another impossible. Some Provinces through which the railway ran had a Province saloon. This was used at the discretion of the Governor, and by kind cooperation of the railway staff could be attached to a goods train for a journey from point to point. The saloon of Kassala Province – the only one in which I travelled frequently – was to be avoided, and a camel hurriedly to be obtained, if possible. Known as Black Maria, she boasted octagonal wheels. Your servant would lay the table and bring the soup while the train was standing at a station; but as soon as motion began, you saw the knife, spoons and soup bouncing and jittering towards the edge of the table; and even if saved and consumed in time, the soup contained a flavour of gritty *je ne sais quoi* from the miasma of desert sand which churned up through gaps in the floor-boards.

The alternative to using the Providence saloon, when no passenger train was available, was to ride at the back of a goods train. This type was known as *ala keifak,* or 'as you like it', because it was not due at any point at any time, but travelled when it felt like it, stopped when it wanted and arrived when it happened to. The terminal van had a cell inhabited by the guard, a large centre compartment for luggage, and a second condemned cell with one hard bench on which a mattress might be spread. There was no communication with one's servants, and no sanitary facilities: all one could do was make for the skyline at the next station. If the train started while one was busy (which was unlikely, for the guard knew all about one's difficulties and shared them), it could be caught after a vigorous chase. This type of travel was to be recommended only to those who wished to mortify the flesh, but five times I perforce endured a journey of nearly 200 miles.

The all-round management of the railways was of a wonderfully high standard. Our only criticism was of a certain tendency to centralise. Every little matter seemed to have to go for decision to Railway Headquarters in faraway Atbara, and it was always difficult to extract action or decision from the man on the spot. Once, in a fit of unusual and misplaced sanitary zeal, I poked my nose officiously into some railway property in the Red Sea Hills, and, led unerringly by the stench, unearthed a large dump of rotting donkey manure and night soil, buzzing with flies and already forming a sizeable pyramid. I mildly asked the official responsible what he proposed to do with this delectable pile. 'Sir,' was the reply, 'it will be referred to Atbara.'

A number of hotels and rest-camps were run, and well run, by the Sudan Railways, including the rest-camp at Erkowit, some 3,300 feet up in the Red Sea Mountains, and the nearest thing to a hill-station the country boasted. In days gone by the lovely view over crag and gully to Suakin and the wine-dark sea beyond it had been beloved by Lady Wingate, wife of the Governor-General, and was affectionately known as 'Kitty's Leap'. Then a notice from Atbara appeared on the notice-board of the little Erkowit hotel bearing the instruction for visitors and tourists: 'Out of respect for a celebrated lady the beauty-spot hitherto commonly known as "Kitty's Leap" will be referred to in future as "Lady Wingate's Seat".'

As for the roads, on which most of the ordinary officer's sufferings took place, it is difficult to sum up. Over much of the Northern Sudan there were no roads, only tracks. There was neither any need of a made-up road nor the wherewithal to make one. Lorries could travel with ease over hard sand, and through softer sand with difficulty, sweat and digging. Over dry cotton soil (if not too cracked) they could pass at high speed, but over wet cotton soil they could not pass at all. In the south, and wherever rainfall was heavier or hills abounded, permanent roads had to be maintained, the trunk routes by the Public Works and minor roads by the district or local government concerned. Road upkeep was one of the few things in which the African is superior to the Arab; the Nuba in particular made adept and vigorous road-repairers.

Samuel Johnson once remarked, 'Sir, a woman's preaching is like a dog walking on his hinder legs. It is not done well; but you are surprised to find it done at all.' Much the same might be said of travel on many of the Sudan's roads. Grisly as was the passage of them, when one recalls the inadequacy of the labour and the perennial meagreness of the funds doled out by a thrifty Central Government, the surprising thing is that it remained as possible as it did. Only on the major southern roads were permanent labour camps employed, under northern foremen who often showed great skill, not merely in engineering, but in managing the local labour and getting the best out of it.

There was always a difficult period towards the end of the rains, when the year's damage had been done and the time for systematically tackling it had not yet come round. I have travelled twenty miles along a track covered with four-foot-high grass and studded with the low hills of termites. If one went confidently, blindly but not too rapidly, Mr Ford always won and shaved the top off each ant-hill like cutting the top off a hard-boiled egg. Had one, of course, encountered a granite boulder … but we never did.

The termite or white ant was the scourge of every traveller and most house-holders. When trekking by camel I once incautiously camped on ground riddled by white ants. In the morning the sides of the tent, the saddlery, the cook-boxes – everything was covered with their clay tunnels. Yet they had eaten nothing except the heart of a rolled-up *Observer* containing an article by Mr J.L.Garvin, the Editor.

Of a lorry, or any vehicle, on these roads, all one could say was that it was never quite full enough, but always too full. To the populace I do not think that the concept of overloading had any meaning at all. No vehicle ever had a fixed capacity which barred it from carrying further goods or passengers. If a vehicle was there, it could be got onto, and the springs, tyres, chassis and engine had to look after themselves. Overloading was a

primary cause both of mechanical breakdown and of serious accidents –
but experience brought no change in custom.

I was once about to set out along the series of sand-drifts and ruts
which form the main road westwards to El Fasher and French Africa, on a
truck which was already overladen, and to which several aspirants for a free
ride had been denied access. As we were on the point of starting, an Arab
woman came up. She was in a sad state. She was with child illegitimately,
her time was not far off, her people had disowned her and cast her out.
There was no one to deliver her baby: none of the local Gamps would
help her because she could not pay the customary dues. I looked at the
groaning truck, then at her, and remembered that if the jolting precipitated
affairs, we should have only a screwdriver, two spanners and a tyre-lever
– which are not the correct medical instruments.

But in an emergency risks must be taken, and I decided to pile her
on, hazard a breakdown and take her thirty miles to a dispensary to
which a trained midwife was attached. Once again we were on the point
of departure when the *omda* hurried up, dragging an evil-looking old
harridan who practised as a midwife and had consented to take the case
if dues were paid. I produced the small sum, thankfully unloaded the
unfortunate sinner, and set off gingerly along the shocking surface. A few
days later at a different centre I met a man who had been present on
the previous occasion. He beamed at me. 'You remember that girl you
handed over to old Fatima the midwife? She had a lovely little daughter
just twenty minutes after you'd left: both doing finely.' I thought of the
tyre-lever and shuddered.

Rail or road – they must both cross rivers, and rivers can be crossed
only by bridges or ferries. A bridge is normally a subject for professional
engineers, and when on a big scale must be so. Yet even up to the 1950s
minor bridges of stone and timber were left to the administrative amateur,
and more than a few sizeable waterways were bridged with timber alone,
the result of amateur enterprise, local skill, prison labour and a grudging
few score of pounds to finance it all. In 1946, when returning to the
Province in which I had started work twenty years earlier, I was gratified to
find that a timber bridge I had helped to erect in 1927 had been scrapped
and superseded by a permanent one only in 1942.

The demand for bridging was always beyond what the professional departments could meet. I spent seven-and-a-half years trying to obtain a bridge over the river at Province Headquarters – a structure first proposed by the Governor in 1910. All we ever succeeded in eliciting was an improved ferry, which was hauled across the river on a steel hawser (at the height of the rains the stream was 120 yards across and sixteen feet deep, with a four-knot current). Even that had its limitations, whether due to fate or to human weakness. A forestry lorry once arrived, to cross the river, the driver being heavily in beer. The ferryman, observing his condition at the last moment, did his best to dissuade, but with a cheery wave and an optimistic foot on the accelerator, the drive whooshed straight down the incline onto the gangways, onto the ferry, onto the gangways at the far end, and, like a victim walking the pirates' plank, off them and into eight feet of water. By some subaqueous miracle he not only came up, but came up sober, and ran fifteen miles home. The lorry was extracted by a chanting choir of Dinka prisoners under the skilful conductorship of the officer in charge of the Province mechanical transport.

The same chorus was again in demand shortly afterwards, when a wild-eyed orderly rushed into the office to say that the ferry had sunk with the loss of two lorries and a dozen people. The mendacity of rumour is one degree greater in Africa even than in Europe, and when we had doubled to the river-side, to save life or at least recover corpses, it was only to find that with a heavily-loaded lorry too much on one side, the ferry had tipped up in five feet of the stream, and lay up-ended and immovable, owing to the floats having filled with water. The casualty was easy meat for the prison gang, but if the accident had not occurred in a rapidly-falling river, which enabled salvage within a week or two, half the province and its headquarters would have been cut off from the outside world. We felt that with this disaster in our pockets we could scarcely fail to obtain the long-sought bridge; but all we could win was an obscure place at the bottom of a five-year development programme – and after five years the bridge was still not up.

Nearly all the ferries in the southern provinces were Government concerns. When people wished to cross a waterway, they must do it by wading, swimming, canoe – or not at all. The Nilotic's dug-out canoe, in which he might spend quite a large part of his life, could vary from a rickety section of palm-trunk which would tip over at a wink or a nod, to a

solid and serviceable mahogany trunk which could weather rough storms.
Of the former kind was a canoe in which I once threaded a waterway
in Dinka country, and when in a burst of ill-justified confidence I asked
my ebony Charon to hand over the paddle so that I might have a try, his
laconic and crushing rejoinder was, 'I cannot swim.' Of the second kind
was the craft in which I once joined some West Africans in a nocturnal
crocodile hunt with torch and harpoon. For half an hour a fourteen-foot
crocodile towed us up and down, and at one point his jaws closed on the
gunwale with a crunch which sounded as if it would have crushed steel.
Yet later examination showed the mahogany to be hardly dinted.

These mahogany canoes were liable to be dangerous only when they
were past service but still in service. After an inter-province meeting
my wife and I once started home across a fifteen-feet deep waterway in
a canoe which had been commandeered as a ferry. Near the prow was
something like a termites' nest of mud sticking up from the bottom. We
had gone half way and were exactly over the deepest part of the river when
our ferryman suddenly dropped his statuesque attitude and lethargic
movements and burst into feverish strokes with his paddle. At the same
moment we became aware that our seats were wet. Screwing round, we
could see that the white ants' nest – a lump of mud bunging up a sizeable
rent – had disintegrated, and a flood was pouring in through a gap a foot
long by eight inches wide. With seven strokes the ferryman propelled us
forty yards towards the shallows until with a gurgle the canoe sank with
all hands in four feet of water. Luckily our baggage had gone ahead – and
damp clothes are soon walked dry in the tropics.

The ferries of the north were a different affair. Under a powerful
north wind Father Nile can create waves such as few who do not know
him would believe. The privately-operated ferry boats are made from
acacia planks sawed lengthwise. The sawing itself is worth watching, for
the method must be the same as that used by Noah for the timbers of
the ark – the expert standing on a platform and holding the great double-
handed saw from above, while his mate stands below, and together
they saw accurately down a fifteen-foot baulk of timber. The planks
are roughly though stoutly pegged together, and the resulting craft may
be seventeen feet overall, with a beam of twelve feet; but when loaded
with three camels, five donkeys, a bull, seventeen goats and thirty-seven

humans, there is only a foot of freeboard. The oars are logs shaped rather like hockey sticks, each pulled by a separate man. The helmsman steers with an equally unwieldy-looking tiller; and in place of the Dinka's lump of mud, the Arab uses old clouts and rags to bung up leaks. I have seen a colleague sea-sick on such a crossing, and have more than once felt grateful that I could swim. Tragedies occurred somewhere or other nearly every season, but nothing seemed to alter the craft or the fortitude and skill of its operators.

'Communications' included the postal system, with the telegraph and telephone. Postmasters were always the men to be courted. In the old days many were Egyptians, later nearly all replaced by Sudanese; but whatever the nationality, I do not remember one who was disobliging: the majority were helpful and were valuable friends. To the overseas officer in a far country all mails are slow, yet when I look at the Sudan postal services in perspective and compare them with others, I know that our mails were as rapid as in any other country, and more reliable.

As to the telephone – it became more and more necessary and more and more of a burden. I was inclined to think that the system connecting small police posts and other outstations was as dangerous as it was useful; for although its occasional advantages in an emergency could not be gainsaid, under normal conditions it tended to kill that spirit of initiative and responsibility of which the Sudanese N.C.O. was so capable, and to make men ring up and bleat for instructions when they might otherwise have used their common sense and taken action.

It was, however, in the use of telegraph and telephone that the genius for distortion found its full bent. When the military authorities in Khartoum, who were proposing to conduct manoeuvres in the flat, waterless area between the capital and Kassala, wrote to ask the Governor of Kassala whether one of the political staff might attend the operations, he wired back: 'Am sending Cooke who will make all arrangements.' The reply came, 'Noted with thanks but troops bringing own rations and camp kitchens.'

More often, however, the perversion emanated from the telegraph clerk or other intermediary. Before the days of wireless sets, when the summary of daily news came in a Reuter telegram sent to all province and district headquarters, the evening message was handed to a member of the

Club, and we were astonished to hear him read out: 'Rome. January 24th. The Pope has been in bed with the goat and passed a disturbed night.' His Holiness had been suffering from gout.

It was names that particularly foxed the transcribers. When in 1950 a departmental officer named Mr Small visited my province, we were apprised by telegram of the advent of Mr Smell. This was particularly unfair, since he was a sanitary inspector. Similarly, when Sir James Bowker, then Minister to the Embassy at Cairo, honoured us with a visit, the Post Office warned us of the coming of a Mr Porker.

The railways, however, could go one better than the Post Office. There is a drawing-room game for which everybody sits round a table. A thinks of a message and whispers it to B. B whispers what he thinks he has heard to C, C to D and so on round the table until the last person enunciates the metagrobolized message as he has received it. The same game was played by the railways, with messages passed along the line from one station-master to another. It was much safer to use Arabic: English might be employed, but at the sender's risk. On one occasion the Governor had gone to visit the headquarters of the big cotton scheme some forty miles north of Kassala, and while he was there his tourer gave trouble. It was a Friday (the weekly holiday in a Muslim country), and no telegraph office was open – but the courtesy of the railways was at his disposal. By the time the message had gone from a British Assistant District Commissioner, through some other official, to a garage superintendent enjoying his Friday morning beer, thence to a senior mechanic, so to a junior assistant and finally to a raw clerk, its content had altered drastically. The original opened with the words 'Please send us tool for grinding piston parts of Governor's car,' but the plea read by the officer holding the fort at Headquarters ran: 'Please lend up too for grinding pisspan parts of Governor's cat.' Poor puss!

To his mother   14 January 1944
Bahr el-Arab

This from down on the Bahr el-Arab, having a trek by pony, with bulls for baggage, along the river among the Dinka … Deing Majok, the Dinka Chief, is trekking with me, and his chief vizier Grfur, an old gent who slew several of his many brothers and lost an eye in the duel and was left for dead, but has survived to be No. 2 in this little kingdom of 20,000 Dinka, and to have twelve wives and I forget how many children. The graph of a Dinka's wives rises with age and wealth (about twenty cattle being the average price to pay for a new wife) up to middle age, and then falls again as he gets elderly.

Yesterday three canoefuls of hippo-hunters came by, and had they not been going afar off for their quarry, I should have gone with them for the fun of it. How they tackle a hippo, in those craft, is a mystery; they do sometimes get upset and, occasionally, killed. The harpoon itself, a thing like a telegraph pole with a barbed spike stuck on the end, looked enough to sink the ship.

The river has crocs in it, big ones in the deeper water, but one can find safe backwaters and shallow bits to have a bathe; and the Dinka, being themselves starko, think it no impropriety in one (as Arabs would) to doff clothes and take a wash *coram populo*. In fact they rather admire a white skin, and one may go for a quiet dip and find oneself the embarrassed object of admiration from a group of young men and maidens.

To Father   Feb 44
Nahud

Rob shows a very real appreciation of music, though no ability to produce an air, and will listen indefinitely to the gramophone. He squinted down as far as he could into the bowels of the machine while Caruso or Tauber or some vocal nib was bellowing, and then observed, 'If I was down there, should I be able to sing like that?'

He was saying his prayers the other day, and when he began 'Our Father ...' turned to Margaret: 'Who *is* our father, Mum?'
       'Well – it means our *heavenly* father, Darling.'
       'Mmmm ... Daddy isn't heavenly, is he?'

CHAPTER FIFTEEN

The Official

Nobody can understand the nature and life of a country unless he knows something of the machine which runs it. A machine of this type is comprised of human beings, the officials great and small, from the driving-belt to the tiniest screw, who make the wheels go round – or in some instances prevent their revolution. It is significant that the Arabic word for a governor, *mudir,* means literally 'one-who-causes-things-to turn-round,' and the word for administration is derived from the same root. In the last decade before Independence in 1956 Sudanese were rising rapidly and steadily towards the higher posts, both in the administrative and the technical services, as the right and inevitable step towards self-government. But in the formative period of the 1920s and 1930s the *cursus honorum* for a Sudanese officer did not normally rise above middle-grade posts, which often entailed great executive responsibility but did not involve decisions on policy and higher political considerations. That was still to come.

The material for officialdom depended on the out-turn of the educational system. Many officials in those days had had only an intermediate education, though the product of the Gordon College, now Khartoum University, was becoming increasingly available. In the Southern Provinces there was no material of so high a standard. With public security and firm administration not universally spread until decades after the North, with no productive economy which could justify the expenditure of large sums on social services, to the detriment and deprivation of the more productive North, the South could turn out little beyond mission-trained lads to man the still-simple machinery of Government.

The Sudanese official showed at his best in active, day-to-day administration, whether in the field or in the station. The corroding effect of bureaucratic employment in the rabbit-warren of a central government or a department is proverbial. There are few individuals, and no races or classes, who are immune from that corrosion. The only shield against it lies in the qualities of independent thought, sense of responsibility, imagination, humanity, and habitual promptitude. These are the qualities of individuals, not of communities. But they are rarer in the Orient even than in the West, and the Sudanese therefore made a better autocrat or man-on-the-spot than he did a cog in a large and complicated departmental or secretarial machine.

The running of a ministerial system and of the biggest departments cannot be carried on without a bureaucracy, and the fact that an independent Sudan is now doing this speaks for the resilience and the coefficient-of-expansion of its people's character. But in the second quarter of the 20th century it was on the executive side that the Northern Sudanese genius was at its best, and was the *sine qua non* for the country's political and economic progress.

We are dealing with the humdrum affairs of daily life, and in the ordinary humdrum district the indispensable parts of the machine throughout the Northern Provinces were the following: the *mamur*, with or without a Sub-*mamur*; the translator, or clerk, with or without subordinate clerks, according to the size of the *merkaz*; the accountant, again with or without subordinates according to circumstances; and the *sarraf* or cashier, who kept the safe. Those were the pillars without which the edifice could not stand. In any sizeable district there would be a police officer. Where there was a prison of more than minor dimensions, there would also be a prison officer. Any big district would be likely to have a *kadi* – though he was a member of the Legal Department. Schoolmasters, doctors, dressers, agriculturists, veterinary officers, postal staff, foresters - some or all of these, and many others might be found in any district; but their direct allegiance was to the heads of their departments, and though contact with all and direct dealings with most were essential, they were not the District Commissioner's own men. Of employees, unclassified and not on permanent terms of service, the range and variety was of course enormous and differed with the circumstances and needs of the area.

First the *mamur*. As Independence approached, and finally came, the *mamurs* were the cadre from which most naturally and most fruitfully the District Commissioner and Assistant District Commissioners and finally Governors and Deputy Governors were drawn. Right well they had earned their new responsibilities when they came. It is only in retrospect, and after obtaining a comparison by seeing other territories, that one can realise the full value of the *mamurs* as pieces on the executive chessboard and the immense debt owed to them as a class.

In the first quarter-century *mamurs* were mainly Egyptian. It was not until after the abortive and Cairo-inspired mutiny of 1924 that Sudanese men replaced Egyptians in all save a few of these posts. Chosen for character even more than for education, the *mamur* was the assistant to the District Commissioner in running his district. Although he might go on trek, it was not his foremost duty to deal with the tribesmen from outside, or the political affairs of the district at large. Rather, he was the link between the District Commissioner and his official staff, the premier Sudanese representative of the Government, the hub of the headquarter machine and guardian of good administration in the *merkaz*.

But his activities and his value went beyond this. A great burden of routine activities could be safely left in his hands. His counsel in all matters of personalities and politics was to be sought – and more often than not to be followed. He was the *éminence grise* to even the most brilliant District Commissioner, the man behind the throne, on whose sagacity and loyalty one could always rely. I think the keynote of the 'old *mamur*' type was dependability, that cardinal administrative virtue; and later generations of *mamurs* added higher educational qualifications to this without losing the bed-rock character of their predecessors. I cannot personally recollect ever being seriously let down by a *mamur*. Once, when the books of a certain Greek merchant licensed to sell liquor and suspected of contravening the licence-laws were submitted to a snap check, the *mamur* came head of the list of clients, having up to that date consumed one bottle of brandy and 975 large bottles of beer. Yet whatever might happen after dark, he was always abroad, neat, sober, mounted, impeccably dressed and on duty at 6 am the next morning.

Many a raw and ignorant young Assistant District Commissioner was trained and supported by his *mamur*, to whom he could always turn in trouble or in need. When I struggled through my first public speech in Arabic, making goodness knows what ludicrous blunders and in danger at any time of breaking down, whenever I paused to say, 'Er...' I could hear the whisper of the *mamur*'s voice in my ear behind me, '*Wallahi,* that's grand,' and the inspiration bore me triumphantly through.

When I arrived on first appointment at Province Headquarters the immediate question from the rather formidable Governor was, 'Young man, do you know anything about vines?' My reply, intended to be deprecating and disclaiming, must have misled him, for he said, 'Oh, I see you do. I will put you in charge of the vine in the Headquarters garden. Go and produce grapes.'

I found a measly and shrivelled wisp of a plant hanging dejectedly from a couple of staggering poles. It was to the *mamur* that I turned as a friend and guide. He knew all about vines. Next day two four-gallon petrol-tins full of bull's blood arrived from the slaughterhouse and the vine was given a sanguinary douche. The following day a donkey which had judiciously died was hauled up by prisoners and carefully interred beneath the roots. Admittedly the flies encouraged by the blood and the maggots engendered by the moke killed the vine, but after all that was the best thing possible for it, and it was patent even to the Governor that prompt action had been taken on his instructions.

Some *mamur*s were men of many parts. One with whom I worked was brilliant in his way, and I always felt that he had missed his true vocation, for within a few months he invented a substitute for coffee, a new kind of soap, a method for clarifying water and a trap for bugs. The latter had something of that simplicity which is the hallmark of true genius: a section of wood, with a groove on one side of it and holes bored through from the outer wall to the groove on the inner side, was fixed up on the wall of the prison (always a hot-bed of bed-bugs) with the groove on the inside. At night the bugs, which love crannies and holes, after biting the prisoners would climb the wall and go through the inviting little holes into the groove behind them to roost, and in the morning you took down the block of wood and shook them into a pail of water. Elementary, my dear Watson.

Bless the *mamur*s! They were a great race. If they occasionally feathered their nests, it was the custom of the country, and they did such things by measure and knew when to stop. They were loyal, wise, and trusty, and I pay my tribute to them.

The *mamur* was traditionally the 'father of the nation.' The *kadi* was of a rather more aloof and Olympian type but shared with him the chief place in the official hierarchy. The *kadi* was the judge of the religious Shari'a law to whom went all cases involving marriage, alimony, divorce, inheritance and suchlike matters which fell to be judged under the personal law of Islam. The *kadi* was, by virtue of his office and his learning, always accorded great respect. He was not always a popular figure, and it is possibly to his credit that he was not so. The typical old-fashioned *kadi* was conscious of the aura of piety and erudition which attended him. He tended to be a Pharisee. He was academically minded, unyielding, a stickler for the letter of the law, more interested in the details of the Shari'a than in the humanity to which it was applied, conservative and suspicious of devolution of judicial powers to the unlearned *fiki* and the tribal authority which followed upon a policy of decentralisation.

Tribal elements as well as British District Commissioners found it difficult to appreciate this type. On the other hand, I never heard even a remote suspicion of a *kadi*'s integrity, and the learning of Sudanese *kadis* was ranked high, for Nigeria at least borrowed several of them to establish and improve its system of Shari'a courts. Even to the Pharisaic tendency there are exceptions, and a younger generation of *kadis* began to arise with a more modern and liberal outlook. They lived a rather less puritanical life, had a refreshingly practical view of the law and of humanity, and gave invaluable aid and instruction to the semi-trained *ulema* attached to Arab courts as experts in the Shari'a to sit with them in all such cases. There were a number of this type of *kadi* for whom I conceived a high respect and a personal friendship.

It is curious what a ribald joy humanity takes in deflation. There was one particular *kadi* who was definitely unpopular. He was a Pharisee of the Pharisees. One eye looked at cover-point, the other at mid-wicket. You could never be certain which you were bowling to, and he was known as the wall-eyed *kadi*. On one occasion he was visiting me in the house over a particular case which was going on in a native court and which looked like becoming a *cause célèbre* and giving a good deal of trouble.

Over a cup of coffee we entered into an inquiry about certain laws of inheritance arising out of the case and involving the share of a daughter in some property. The *kadi*, ensconced in a cane-seated chair, was at his most erudite and pursued the ramifications and intricacies of the law with tedious gusto until my head swam. As he was in the middle of a particularly involved exposition, I heard a deep and nauseous gurk, and looking towards the door I saw Marcus the parrot appear round it, with that peculiar crab-wise gait and upward, sidelong leer which I knew to presage his more flagrant acts of aggression. The *kadi* continued his discourse, and it appeared that if there were a surviving son by the father's first wife, then the daughter would inherit only a sixth: on the other hand if there were no son, and if only one other daughter survived and she were married and …

At this point, with a stifled gasp and a sternward clutch, the wall-eyed *kadi* rose vertically a foot into the air. Being sceptical of levitation, I looked for a more mundane cause and found it in Marcus. He had sidled unobtrusively under the chair, inserted his beak upwards through the cane seat, grabbed whatever he could between those powerful mandibles, and compressed them: and he now uttered the particularly vulgar chortle of triumph with which he reviewed ill deeds successfully done, and fell to preening his feathers.

When Marcus had been whisked off to his cage, and the *kadi* had preened *his* feathers, we agreed that although Holy Writ, which has uncomplimentary things to say about the pig and the dog, contains no specific reference to parrots, they are undoubtedly evil and birds of Iblis - the devil. The wall-eyed *kadi* bore no grudge, and I always liked him better after that. But I have never learned what the daughter's share would be.

The Sub-*mamur* was, as his title implies, an assistant to the *mamur*, a young man and generally a product of the Gordon College, who entered the administrative service at this lowly rung and had the whole range of its hierarchy before him. The able men in their ranks had the advantage over the old-type *mamur* of an up-to-date education, and there are men who were sub-*mamurs* fifteen years ago and are now worthy Governors of Provinces. The sub-*mamur* learned his trade from his senior, the *mamur*, assisted him in all routine matters, and was often an expert in legal investigations, and was detailed to do specific jobs for which the experts did not exist or for which nobody else had a taste, and to take particular tricks when a knave would suffice without playing a king.

When, in my first district, a large and fearsomely-horned, ownerless bull of vitriolic temper took to wandering round the environs of the *merkaz*, invading the cultivations, to their owners' vociferous wrath, and chasing any would-be captor, it was the sub-*mamur* who was cast for the role of matador. By the ingenious deployment of some attractive cows, the enemy was enticed into the *merkaz*, where the sub-*mamur* awaited him with a police .303 rifle. I followed him, not too near, while the *mamur* stood behind my right shoulder brandishing a huge two-handed sword and with the stated intention of hamstringing the furious beast, should it attack me. With the van thus formed, the main body of several hundred sheikhs, minions and people followed – at a respectful distance. The problem was (a) to get our quarry by himself, so that none of his wives need die with him; (b) to get him against the river so that if the highly-excited hunter missed him, the bullet would be innocuous and none of the onlookers would die with him.

The bull seemed to sense our efforts to mate him and kept making sideways bishop's runs across our front, or direct castle-like attacks across the board and then retiring behind his pawns. He was cornered at long last and as he began his charge the sub-*mamur*, with a bullet intended for the chest, succeeded in severing the top of his spine, while the *mamur*'s sword whistled past my ear as he swept it up in preparation for the onslaught.

The Head Clerk was in charge of the correspondence, typing, filing and any necessary translating; the latter grew less as a District Commissioner became competent in Arabic script. I do not think Sudanese abilities were at their highest in this line, for the records were in English, and though many officials spoke and wrote good, and sometimes very good English, imagination and method did not always come easily, and idiom was apt to entrap them - as for instance when a volume of correspondence about expenses and arrangements for the visit of HRH the Duke of York, later King George VI, was filed under the heading, 'Financial,' sub-heading 'Royalties.' But many clerks were competent and clear-headed and what they lacked in method they made up in memory. If the Clerk had been long enough in the District, you could say to him, 'Hamid Effendi, would you let me have that correspondence about the well-digging at Um Gadein?' and it would appear on your desk like magic. No wonder a District Commissioner always strove to retain a trusty Clerk. When in due time Hamid Effendi was wafted elsewhere, his successor would find no key which would guide him to Um Gadein, and after a week of rummaging, the business of the well would at long last be run to earth in a file about ivory poaching or rabies precautions.

The Accountant's duties extended beyond the actual keeping of revenue and expenditure records. Tribute and all taxation affairs, market fees and figures of sales and many other kindred subjects with a *soupçon* of relevance to finance were dealt with in the accounts office, and when the District Commissioner came to his annual Gehenna of producing a district budget for the next financial year, it was to the Accountant that he looked for comparative figures and for the statistics upon which all good estimates are based. A competent Accountant was a jewel, and many of them were very competent. Many of the books and records were in Arabic, and though no man could rise to the top of the tree without ability to keep books in English, many of the most reliable and valuable dealt in Arabic only to the end of their career.

Such a one was Babikr Effendi, who was my accountant in the first three years of the war. He was limited, entirely reliable, fatherly, pear-shaped and very religious, never missing his prayers at the standard hours and busy telling his beads even while adding up a column of figures without, apparently, his arithmetic being upset by the ninety-nine attributes of the Almighty. He always said you could do anything with prayer; and he was right.

In 1940, when invasion from Italian East Africa was expected, the officials of the district asked that they might be given shooting practice on the police musketry range so that they might defend the country against aggression. I acceded readily to this request, not because our volunteer squad would affect the issue of the final battle, but because it showed the right spirit. To the musketry range we therefore trooped in the early morning (when visibility was best) and spattered the unoffending hillside with bullets, in lying positions at one hundred yards. When Babikr's turn came, he was unable to lie, owing to his spherical contours. He squatted instead, groaning and telling his beads. At length he raised the rifle to his shoulder, pointed the spout towards the target, closed his eye tightly, ejaculated, '*Bismillahi!*' and fired. There was spurt of gravel ten yards in front of us. The next moment the markers signalled a bull. He had put a ricochet through the centre of the target, and I have never met soldier, hunter or ballistic expert who had seen it done. Babikr's true greatness then showed: for, unlike some, he knew where to stop. He smiled benignly, mopped his brow, and said, 'That's enough . You see what prayer can do.'

The *sarraf* or cashier was the man in charge of the Government safe and responsible for handling all cash that went into or out of the chest. This was a circumscribed job, requiring only moderate ability but fastidious accuracy and absolute reliability. Of all possible jobs it was the one I would most have avoided, for handling specie is not an employment welcomed by most men. I never met a habitually inaccurate *sarraf.* The only manner in which they occasionally gave trouble was through their fear of being held responsible for bad coins and their refusal to accept any coin remotely defaced or severely rubbed. Any such refusal, made to a simple people who believed that they were proffering legal tender, could affect the populace's faith in the coinage, and if one wrote to the Treasury often and long enough, one could always get the sarraf overridden: but it took much time for small matter.

Sarrafs' posts used traditionally to be very much the perquisite of officials with Egyptian blood in them. They had a natural aptitude for handling specie. Similarly in earlier days most of the higher accounting jobs appeared to be in the hands of Copts, who were peculiarly fitted for this type of work. For centuries a depressed Christian minority in Egypt, they had been as Goering said of Schacht, 'unloved, unwanted, and indispensable,' surviving by their unrivalled capacity for painstaking, persevering, laborious, unobtrusive control of the grimy details of routine administration and the tortuous ramifications of finance with which other brains were disinclined to encumber themselves. Centuries of depression – oppression would be an exaggeration – combined with this type of work have rendered the typical Copt expressionless of emotion, literal-minded, fatalistic and rather timid. As one senior Sudanese officer said to me, 'Sir, all Copts are afraid all the time.'

This is, of course, hyperbole and I have known many exceptions, but in essence it was true. The fatalism was there all right. When a Coptic doctor of my acquaintance produced a fifth daughter, he appeared lachrymose but resigned and informed me that her name was to be Iqbal – 'Acceptance.' As to the literal-mindedness, it could attain ludicrous proportions. New instructions once reached us about the siting and construction of petrol-stores. They were to be built on certain specifications, with certain cubic space and window area, and must have 'a fire-line cleared of thirty yards' width'. I set out to find a suitable site in company with the Coptic Registrar of Lands. The surroundings of that particular *merkaz* consisted of baked cotton-soil for as far as the eye could see. Yet my companion tried to turn down site after suitable site with the query, 'But, sir, how would you clear your fire-line?' He wished to find somewhere where grass, vegetation and combustible material flourished so that at expense of much money and time a fire-line could be cleared and prepared, as the instructions said that it should.

Nevertheless many of our Copts were most cultivated and highly educated, as well as able men. A particular Chief Accountant at Province Headquarters, an admirer of Western civilisation, preferred to write his name of Ramzi as Ramsay, and when once asked what he did for recreation replied, 'Sir, I lie upon my bed and I study the works of Dr Marie Stopes.'

The officials of a province headquarters were the same in principle as those of a *merkaz*, though rather more diverse and running higher up the hierarchical ladder. The Chief Accountant and Head Clerk were men of substance, ability and experience, and after seeing other territories in Africa I realise how well we were served. Much routine drafting and hack-work was done for one by a Head Clerk, and many a false step was I saved from by his producing relevant letters or previous decisions in the nick of time.

The Chief Accountant did all the preparatory drudgery for the bugbear of the annual budget, producing an efficiently-constructed framework on which one could operate. In routine affairs his motto, whenever one was in a dilemma, was that of Cervantes - 'Patience, and shuffle the cards.' A Governor or head of department had the power to move a surplus from one account to fill a hole in another, and if money were wanted for helping a District Commissioner to build a bridge, the Chief Accountant would brood, shuffle, and rummage in all the budgetary cupboards, and find that there was a sufficient saving on the items for Prisoners' Rations and the Upkeep of Graves. It may have been doubtful finance, but the work went forward.

At the time when I write [the 1960s], in the southern provinces tragedy is writ large and all is flux. In the post-war years the higher headquarter posts were nearly all filled by northern officials. Districts were staffed by southerners. I am of those who believe racial doctrines, *Herrenvolk* and 'blood' theories to be pernicious and belied by history, and I look to a time when the African will have overtaken the European and the Asiatic in the essential qualities of civilisation. There are already individuals who exemplify the process. But in the 1940s the value, purely as a chessman on the board, of a southern official was seldom that of a northern. The South, uneconomic and un-unified, had started years behind the North. A crash-programme of education, the keystone of administrative responsibility, was in its early stages. Dependability and sobriety, now developing over the continent, were then harder to find, and the traditional standard of living was lower. Rightly or wrongly, the southern official was on a lower scale of pay and conditions than his northern counterpart.

A strike of southern officials, who simply left their posts and absented themselves for several days, gave the clearest example I can recollect of the difference between the African and Arab temperament. When the Arab feels aggrieved, he organises himself much as does the European. There are agitators, there are ringleaders, there is vocal and articulate protest and planned action. With the African the reverse was the case. Anybody interested in wildlife in Africa has seen the reactions of a herd of antelope; there is no visible sign, command or suggestion, yet a wave of curiosity or fear may sweep through the herd and all individuals act together in concert. So it was with the African staff. It was scarcely possible to pick out a leader and certainly not an agitator; nothing was planned, nothing articulated; yet they acted together as if at a word of command. This type of hostility is harder to deal with than the other, for it is blank, negative and sullen; there is no focal point, no *pointe d'appui* with which to get in touch, no representative with whom to negotiate. Only time and patience could and did restore the position.

In dealing with one's officials, it was essential to share their private lives, and it was among the advantages of the country that one could do this. One of the great Sudanese qualities is the ability to be official in the office and human outside it, to drop shop, to drop formality, and to be perfectly natural. The official tea-party might be a ponderous duty, but the whist-drive at the club or the gathering round one's own dart-board was a pleasure. You could often get an insight into a man's character from his technique at the dart-board. The cut-and-thrust head mechanic of the garage would fling his missiles like six-inch shells, the first into a window-frame, the next into the bull's-eye and the third through the pantry door – followed by the subtle police officer, who would sidle up like a trained assassin about to use his stiletto, and surreptitiously flick his dart into the triple-twenty.

It was also important to maintain liaison with the local doctor, to keep a check on the health of one's province staff and to visit them in their affliction. The main motive for this was, I hope, pure humanity, But one also learnt quite a lot of useful history . The sojourn in hospital of poor X, an Arab official, with an abcess on the ear, is an Act of God. The entry of Y, a Southern clerk, with a bad dose of malaria, is an act (or omission) of the P.W.D., for on inquiry and investigation we find that the mosquito wire on the verandah of his house had not been repaired despite constant plaintive appeals – with the natural result of a dose of fever and an official off duty for five days.

Then here is Z, a rather light-coloured Copt, with a black eye and a badly cut crown. His explanation – that he tripped over the cat in the dark – we receive politely and inquire the real reason from fellow officials, who are not loath to supply it. Z's wife is a woman of far from irreproachable morals, and on being unflatteringly addressed by the wife of another semi-Coptic wireless-operator in the Post Office, she had set about the lady with a snatched-up gridiron and a fairly effective set of nails. The husband of the worsted lady, vowing vengeance, had hidden in the dust-bin provided by the Public Health authorities and, emerging suddenly from that shady retreat, assaulted Mrs Z with a rolling-pin as she returned from visiting a friend after sundown. Z had gallantly but unwisely intervened, and had received the honourable scars which brought him into the ward. The assailant is to come before the District Commissioner tomorrow. That means he will be sentenced to a month's imprisonment, and that will mean a visit from his fat and weeping wife who will turn on the hysterics and paint a harrowing picture of poor little Georgy and Juju who will have no Easter-egg in April unless their Daddy is let out in time. For the sake of peace, that will mean remitting a little of the sentence and tactfully asking the man's department to transfer him elsewhere.

In the next ward is Henry Mabrouk, one of the Southern clerks in Province Headquarters. He has broken a bone in his knee. He dreamed that the *mamur*'s horse had gone rabid and was going to be shot; he was there watching the process when the horse broke loose and with mouth agape and luminous eyes came straight at him. He was rooted – and with a screech and a convulsive leap had awoken, clasping his knees together so hard in his fright that he dislocated a small bone. This is not the first nightmare that has put Henry *hors de combat,* and when I later look up his confidential reports, I see under the heading 'Habits' my predecessor has entered the single word, 'Bacchanalian.'

Officials' families had always to be taken into account. Family ties are strong, and events within the home could gravely affect the performance of a man in the office or in the field. A feud between wives more than once upset the balance of a headquarter or district machine; and confinements, births, deaths, sicknesses and the minor affairs of children gave one many a small problem and many a peep into home-life.

An accountant, Tewfik, of Egyptian origin but (rather curiously) of Protestant upbringing, once insisted that I attend the christening of his ninth child. A rather coy message reached me in the evening to say that his wife had just presented him with a sweet little daughter that morning and would I bring the C.M.S. padre (who was sojourning with us) to officiate the following afternoon. It was slightly disconcerting to find so young an infant awaiting so patiently the sacrament of baptism, but when we arrived both mother and infant seemed in good fettle. Godmother No 1, the voluminous wife of a foreman, in a light plum-coloured dress (the temperature was 104 degrees) and looking like a captive-balloon straining at its moorings, was standing on tiptoe cutting up the carcase of a sheep at the bedroom door, for the post baptismal rejoicings. However, she rinsed her hands perfunctorily and came in, smiling, to officiate. We stood beside the bed whilst three young Master Tewfiks leaned over it and gazed with solemn eyes at the padre, and the cat played about under the bed or with the boys, and the penultimate Miss Tewfik sat on her pot in the corner. We had proceeded as far as renouncing the World, the Flesh and the Devil when there was a crash, announcing that the cat had eluded the Masters Tewfik, dashed into the next room and upset a bowl of goldfish. Godmother No 2 scuttled out, to shoo and pick up the fish, at which time the penultimate Miss Tewfik came tottering over from her pot, undressed, and tried to stuff two semi-masticated sweets into her mother's mouth. It was all a great success – and I trust the baptism was valid.

Among departmental officials one was in only slightly less close touch. For all their loyalties and professional variety, they still formed a province team. Duty and friendship apart, it paid to know exactly to whom to turn in an emergency. When all the lights in the town went out, as they frequently did, and telephone inquiry elicited the stock explanation that a bat had hung itself upside down on the wires and caused a short-circuit, it was useful to know to whom and in what terms to address remonstrance or stimulus to ensure the extrication of the corpse (if it was not mythical) and restoration of the current. When no telegrams could be sent because the wireless transmitters were out of order, and the expert sent to mend them had gone into hospital with hallucinations that he was being assaulted by the daughters of djinns, and the rest of the staff had tried to mend the transmitters with a cold-chisel, it was well to know and to be a friend of the amateur-expert in the P.W.D. who might providentially solve the crisis. Postal staff were particularly important friends, for in a far country prompt delivery of mails counts much towards one's sanity and perspective.

Technical officials were of course in constant demand as advisers and experts – foresters, agriculturists, veterinary officers, engineers and doctors; while wandering comets who dealt in obscure diseases, ceramics, trade unions, geophysical data and other occasional subjects, would sometimes pass through our denser provincial atmosphere before their orbit took them back to Khartoum. On the whole, we generally felt that our departmental officials on the spot were the goods, and doing their level best, while their Khartoum Headquarters were scandalously neglectful of our interest and ignorant of the local conditions. This was doubtless quite unjust, but it is probably the same the world over.

I usually found that, when called as expert advisers, senior Sudanese were practical and purposeful. They were also less verbose on their subjects. I shall not readily forget a meeting of the Province Council (an advisory body to the Governor, drawn from all sections of the community, chiefs, and intelligentsia, officials and residents) at which the conservation of soil and avoidance of erosion were discussed. Discussion was to be opened by the expert, a much-valued but dour Scot, who proceeded to read his thesis. After he had spoken for twenty minutes, in a rich amalgam of Doric and dog-Arabic, I began to become restive. It was all being faithfully but flatly translated word for word into unmeaning Dinka by an uncomprehending translator for the benefit of a somnolent quota of chiefs, and there seemed no obvious reason why it should ever end.

I interrupted to suggest that the Scot should come to the point and produce his practical suggestions, but the only response was the grisly threat, 'Aye, Ah'm ga'en on tae that laterr.' I then glanced at the sheaf of notes under his hand and counted twelve closely-written sides of foolscap, from which the tail-end of two sentences was just legible – '...the interdependent ecological factors of soil and vegetation...' and 'under present circumstances of global economics...' That settled it, and he had to be tactfully led to a close, which he accepted with the final Parthian shot, 'I hae still a muckle lot to tell ye, but the Governor says ye can no underrstand it.'

I felt a beast, and have done ever since. There are few things a man more hates than to be robbed of his own verbosity.

To his father   12 May 1944
Nahud

We had one excitement before I left Nahud – a visit from John Wellington Wells. He was an Egyptian conjuror called Immanuel, a little man, not more than 5'2"or 3", with black, prominent hypnotist's eyes which I didn't like a bit when he came to pay his respects in the office on arrival. He gave us a lot of straight conjuring to begin with, which was very well done – and I never get tired of seeing rabbits (chickens in this country, where rabbits don't grow) produced out of hats, and eggs out of people's noses, always with the hope that I shall one day be able to spot how this is done.
After a long programme of that, he produced his hocus-pocus turns. He had a young man assistant, a pale and rather sensitive-looking

youth, whom he first hypnotised and then bound his eyes with a napkin and left him sitting on the stage while he descended into the audience. He first came up to me and took hold of my gold signet ring and looked at it; the young man could at once tell him not only what he was holding but the exact Arabic figures and letters of the date and my name engraved on it. He went round the audience asking sotto voce questions, or taking hold of things, and in every case his medium could tell him the name of the person he was speaking with and what they were thinking about ... doubtless everyday stuff in hypnotist circles, but certainly very queer to watch.

Finally he produced three swords and had them stuck, point up, in the stage. His lady assistant, a rumbustious young Egyptian with a black and roving eye, whom I liked a lot and who must have weighed twelve stone, was produced. He first hypnotised her, and then had her laid flat on the points of the three swords, one sticking into her neck where it joins the back, one into her behind and one into her heel. He then first removed the middle one, leaving her on the two swords, fore and aft. He then gently removed the one from under her heel, leaving her with the one point sticking into the back of her neck, and the whole of her body and legs projecting (obviously with great muscular effort on her part, in spite of the hypnotism; and he kept her there for half a minute before having her lifted up and removed.

How such levitation is performed I can't divine. You can rule out all trickery with wires. Wires would have had to be attached to the stars; we were in the open. But I'm pretty certain that Mr Immanuel would have been burned 300 years ago. Certainly there was something Mephisthelean about him. When he came to pay his respects in the office, one glance at him was enough. I felt that in another few seconds I should either have to slog him over the head or succumb to those black eyes.

To his father   25 May 1944
Nahud

We had a big fire in Nahud, in the Native Lodging Area (i.e. the suburbs, built all of grass)... On riding to the place, I found that about nine acres had been completely cleared, forty-four families burned out and nearly 200 grass buildings burned. Luckily there were no very serious human casualties, though one or two poor animals had been killed.

Now one has to decide between the claims of the Holy Charity, which dictates raising a subscription fund to help out the homeless, and the Devil in the guise of Common Sense, who whispers, 'Those blankety fools had gone and built a warren of grass houses packed far too close together, and it's their own damned fault. Let 'em learn from their own disasters.' Holy charity wins, but we aren't going to have the warren rebuilt, and a lot of them will have to go and live elsewhere.

CHAPTER SIXTEEN

Servants

It was a wise man who first remarked that 'No man can be a hero to his valet.' Whether or not the dictum is true, I am not sure; but it is certainly true that no man can *feel* a hero in front of his valet. You cannot feel a hero in front of anybody who knows the state of your underclothes or sees your false teeth standing in a tumbler. But can a valet be a hero to his master? He can, at his best, be at least an object of regard and affection, and at his most sinister perhaps of veneration. Well I realise how memory can lay a film of gilt paint over a blotchy, or even a black, scene. Yet experience elsewhere gives a sense of proportion, and I know that, by the standards of most countries, East or West, we were ably and faithfully served.

On first appointment one was allotted a body-servant. A junior officer in the secretariat would interview a job-lot of applicants, select the less obviously villainous, and divide them among the newly-arrived batch of young district commissioners. It was customary to get rid of the man thus arbitrarily dumped upon one after a few months, to select one's own and to stick to him. Having taken this course, I kept my body-servant, Saeed, for the entire period of my service in the country. Two syces saw me through twenty-seven years. The only reason why I had three cooks was that after ten years the first died, and that after another nine the second went sick. Such figures were in no way unusual.

Although cooks and body-servants might come from several parts of the Northern Provinces, the great bulk of them came from the riverain population living south of the Egyptian border, the people of Halfa and Dongola. These were the mine from which the best servant material was quarried, and you may find specimens of its products not only in the Sudan and north to Cairo, but in Soho, in Paris and for all I know by now in Moscow. If you travel by steamer down that part of the Nile, you may well wonder how the villages which line the river exist, for apart from a narrow fringe of date-trees and a narrow belt of cultivation, laboriously watered by creaking, bull-powered water-wheel (nowadays sometimes by pump), there is only harsh desert and no visible means of subsistence. To no small extent the inhabitants live on the more able-bodied among them who are absent and working anywhere in the Sudan, or maybe beyond it, as servants.

The Dongolawi provides not only the best servants, but many of the leading merchants. In former times he had a somewhat sinister reputation. According to an old Arab proverb, 'a Dongolawi is a devil done up in a man's skin'; and it is undeniable that, particularly as a trader, the qualities which make a successful predator were strong in him. But he had other and better qualities as well, and the calling of a servant brought them out.

Above all he had loyalty, along with a strong sense of prestige and of 'the honours of the house.' He identified himself with his master's fortunes, and even if he was a rogue, as most of them at heart were, unlike so many rogues he had his own code of roguery, knew when to stop, and did things by measure. One's cook carried out the daily shopping in the *suk,* or market. There were several ways of controlling expenditure, but the normal way was to make him keep an account, give him £1, look at the account daily after breakfast (many Dongolawis were literate in Arabic) and dish out another £1 when the last was finished.

But a busy official, especially one not blessed with the tutelary genius of a wife, is not going to inquire in the *suk* about the precise price of pawpaws, to weigh the carrots recorded as bought and make certain they *did* weigh 2 lbs, or to examine the refuse-heap to see whether it was true, as the cook claimed, that three of the six eggs bought yesterday were bad and had to be thrown away. This fact the cook knew and played upon with the skill of a virtuoso. If the usual comment on rising prices, his pains to select the best meat and the egglessness of the local hens were wearing thin, he always knew how to touch a more poignant string. Should you remark that he had charged you two piastres (five pence) for pepper three times in the last week, and that you loathed the stuff, he would give a deprecating smile and rejoin: 'Ah, but your Honour's *guests* like it.' Did you remark that the price of meat seemed appalling, his suave but icy riposte would be that the *best* meat *was* expensive, but that he had heard it said that the Province Medical Inspector and the Governor were noted for *never* having tough meat.

The daily war over the *suk* bill was thus one protracted and losing rear-guard action, from which I knew that the cook was making a steady ten per cent profit which I could not prevent, at least not without a degree of trouble and nastiness which I was too weak to incur. But I also knew that he would never turn a ramp into a scandal and go beyond his steady cut. A wife would very likely reduce this to five per cent – which was why some cooks preferred to serve with bachelors.

If your man had no conscience about making a steady income out of his master, he would protect his master's interests against anybody else; and this was not merely a case of keeping poachers off his own preserves. It was therefore a commonplace that one's own servants were always paragons, while Smith's and Jones's were a set of unscrupulous crooks carrying on all sorts of surreptitious knavery behind their half-blind masters' backs. The odd thing was that Smith and Jones were never grateful, as they should have been, for the information.

A rake-off on transactions was all part of the code. Positive dishonesty with one's property was against it, and in the higher elite of servants – though not among the lower ranks – theft was rare. When a servant did decide to steal, he usually observed the Law of Progressive Abstraction. In accordance with this, the object selected would be removed from its normal resting-place and put somewhere out of immediate sight, but where it could be instantly pointed out if you noticed its absence. If you did not notice its absence within about a week, it would be placed somewhere further off, say in a different room – where, however, it could be rapidly found if called for. The next and penultimate stage was to remove it to the back premises, whence it could still be produced, after a simulated search, if by any ill luck its absence had struck you. Only after a convincing period of un-notice had gone by, giving opportunity for confusion of tracks and dragging of red herrings, in the unlikely event of later inquiry, was the object finally removed and disposed of. There is art in all things, even abstraction.

Protection of one's prestige and honour was automatic. Once I had got out of a lorry and was walking into a local *suk* to chat with the people when something made me look back, and I beheld Saeed coming after me and making cryptic but agonised semaphore gestures. I turned towards him, with my back to the wind – which immediately told the shocking truth. Clapping a hand to the rear, I discovered that my shorts had split right across the seat. Saeed's sense of propriety, on that occasion perfectly justified, could sometimes be almost excessive. On a sweltering day in the Nuba Mountains we once encamped not far from a fresh, running stream. The chance was too good to miss; so, taking off clothes, I found the deepest pool available and submerged myself in it. When I lifted my head above the surface, I saw two beady and evil black eyes looking fixedly into mine, and the head, hood and a foot of the neck of *Naja haje,* the Egyptian cobra, raised above the water a bare six feet away. He, too, was visiting the stream, probably on a quest for frogs, but he was not a congenial bathing companion. With a convulsive leap I exploded from the pool onto the bank and roared to Saeed, 150 yards off, to bring the shotgun. Quick as ever in the uptake, he sprang for it, rammed in two cartridges and raced towards me – but over the last twenty yards he slackened his pace and started walking with his face averted. His master had no clothes on, and cobra or no cobra, the proprieties must be observed.

Such servants had a great feudal quality, in that they took the keenest human interest in the family and in all one's affairs. To the children they were indulgent to a degree – far too much so, in fact. By our standards Africans do not discipline their offspring, and harshness to a child, even when well merited, is repugnant to them. The only occasion on which Saeed fell out with my wife was when she had very properly chastised one of the children for disobedience; he would scarcely speak to her for two days. Why their own children grew up with such natural good manners was always a mystery to me; they must be of a different temperament, more imitative, less resistant to instruction, and less in need of discipline.

In addition to loyalty, the best Sudanese servants had the other great advantages of presence, *savoir faire* and sheer competence. If guests arrived in your absence; if the Public Health Officer came prowling round to snoop for mosquito larvae in your water tank; if the wife of some imprisoned scallywag turned up and wanted an interview to plead for her husband – whatever the occasion might be, the head servant could be trusted to do the honours and know how to treat every person in a manner proper to their degree and their mission.

As to competence, facts are the best commentary. At the Christmas gathering the party might number anything from a minimum of thirty to a maximum, on one occasion, of over sixty. Yet, under the supervision of the lady of the house, cook and head boy would direct and execute all arrangements – the marshalling of other servants lent for the occasion, the apportioning of jobs, the borrowing of extra cutlery, the placing of furniture, the table decorations, the use of neighbours' ovens for roasting the several turkeys, and the collection of the birds and etceteras when ready and done at the same moment – altogether a feat of organisation worthy of a quartermaster and an adjutant combined.

Servants had a strong sense of the proper way of running Christmas festivities, and the traditions had to be observed. One was that the turkey or turkeys must be made very drunk before being killed. For this purpose we kept a bottle of the most lethal Greek fire-water. I do not think the tradition is pure superstition; the old saying that 'no harm comes to a drunk man' has foundation, in that the inebriate, when he falls down a flight of thirty stairs, falls loose without tightening up his muscles in anticipatory apprehension, and therefore escapes serious hurt. Perhaps Clarence realised this when he chose his means of exit. [9] It is at least tenable that the turkey, if sufficiently intoxicated, dies loose and without tightening its muscles, and is therefore tenderer. Any suspicion that the brandy comforted the cook rather than the turkey was unjustified, for the dose was administered in public.

Similarly, the plum-puddings must blaze correctly when brought in. Tradition demanded it – and if they would not blaze the right way, then they must blaze the wrong way. We used the same Greek fire as for the turkeys, and never had any trouble. But a colleague who had refused to dish out brandy for this outmoded and archaic custom incurred retribution. The pudding came in blazing magnificently like a Guy Fawkes pile, with lurid flame. But just as our host was about to congratulate his servant, in spite of himself, on the pyrotechnic display, one of the guests sniffed,

---

9   The Duke of Clarence, brother of King Edward IV, was executed by being drowned in a butt of Malmsey wine.

then another; and as the pudding passed behind him, he distinctly caught the acrid odour of paraffin. Denied his brandy, but loyally determined to maintain tradition at all costs, the cook had done his best with a good douche of the only alternative available.

If the Christmas festivities included any acting or charades, you could be certain that every servant in the station would be present, with his face glued to the windows to watch the proceedings. The games interested them intensely. What they thought of the veterinary inspector clad in a waterbuck skin as Robinson Crusoe, the doctor's wife in a suit of armour made out of old petrol tins as Joan of Arc, or the Governor as a prisoner in a broad-arrow suit and a clanking chain borrowed from the province prison, I never discovered – and Saeed at least was too well bred to divulge; but the spectacle held a fascination. Perhaps it merely corroborated what the servants must have always suspected – that their masters were deranged.

The best Dongolawi servant, in addition to the stock professional qualities, often possessed unusual gifts. Saeed, for instance, was a competent masseur. Many of the riverain Arabs are brought up to the art of massage, and you may see an elderly man lying on an *angareb* while his son or grandson works away at his limbs and muscles, rubbing out the rheumatic effects of age and reinvigorating his flesh. Saeed was an expert at this process, and although his methods were probably cruder than would be approved by a Swedish practitioner, they were effective. My back frequently gave trouble, the result of an old polo injury. When it grew unusually painful, I would submit to a *dilka,* or massaging, which consisted of lying flat on my face while Saeed pummelled, pounded and chafed my back for twenty minutes with a sweet-smelling of sesame oil and some herb known only to him. The process left him panting and in a muck sweat, and me feeling like a ploughed field, with the breath knocked out, but the aches and pains were materially relieved for days.

Another faculty which he possessed to an almost uncanny degree was that of carrying a clock inside his head and waking at any time according to orders. If a start had to be made in the small hours while on trek, or for any other reason it was necessary to rise at an unusual hour, he could be trusted as well as an alarm clock to awaken one – with tea, too – within a minute or two of the time stated. He would rouse one by the common Arab method of taking hold of one's big toe through the bedclothes and gently waggling it. This is in order to ensure that the waking process is a gradual one, since the soul leaves the body during sleep, and if the body should be roused too peremptorily, the soul might not have time to climb back into it.

This capacity to waken at need at any time of night was the more odd in one who, under ordinary circumstances, slept, as did most of his countrymen, like the dead, impervious to sound or sensation. I was once staying at an isolated rest-house and was about to go to bed. There was a full moon, and just as I had donned pyjamas I heard a slight noise. Looking out from the verandah I saw a hyena emerge questingly from the bush. A second hyena followed it. The first walked slowly towards the *angareb* on which Saeed lay, his head enveloped in a blanket. The animal sniffed at his feet and then right up to his head before turning away and beginning to look for scraps and garbage around the kitchen door. Hastily putting-together a 12-bore shotgun – the only armament available – I sneaked out, slipped up behind the kitchen block, and suddenly emerging round the end of it, gave the hyena both barrels at point-blank range from a position within six feet of Saeed's ear. He never even stirred in his sleep.

The good Dongolawi servant studied his master and knew him inside-out. This was not wholly altruistic, but neither was it merely Machiavellian. It was part of his tradition and made him invaluable (which was what suited Master) and indispensable (which was what suited him). A generation ago a District Commissioner was posted to one of the most forlorn and lonely stations in the country. He was one of those characters who suffer from a pendulum-type series of fits of excess and fits of abstinence. For a month he would drink heavily. Then for a month he would become a tee-totalitarian maniac of a grim, Puritan type, before the tides of his nature brought another Bacchic cyclone. The onset of the maniac month was always marked by a ceremony, at which he would make the necessary resolutions and avowals, line up his whisky bottles in a condemned rank, then fling defiance at the Devil, and the bottles over the wall of his compound. His faithful and honest servant, who knew that they would be required again roughly one month hence, as soon as he heard the first thuds of bottles falling into the soft ground, would scuttle round behind the wicket, collect them in the slips as they fell, and return them to the store-cupboard – to be duly rewarded with his master's thanks and a possible pay-rise a month later.

Many of the best cooks, like head boys, came from the lower Nile stretches. Their cuisine differed, and other people's food usually tasted nicer than one's own, probably because variation from routine is the best sauce. At their worst they fed one on tough mutton and a monotonous succession of caramel puddings, the latter the standard resource of most bad cooks, and its appearance held in many households to be an indictable offence. At their best they were really good chefs; but what strikes me in retrospect is less their actual cooking than the conditions with which they put up. Stray guests and unexpected arrivals were common, and a cook might easily be told at an hour's notice that there would be three or four extra guests to dinner. Yet it never seemed to cause undue discomposure or materially to affect the menu, though it might give unrebuttable excuse for an inflated *suk* bill the next morning. No European cook would have endured for a month the inconsiderate treatment a Sudanese received, both as regards the number of mouths to be fed and the irregular times of meals.

The most remarkable performances were probably those put up when on trek. However long the stage, however shambling the camel, however bony the mule, jolting the lorry or stony the foot-trodden path; be the country water-logged or desert, with a little scanty scrub for fuel, the cook on alighting would extract from his baggage his portable grid-iron, assemble tins, supplies and fuel of some kind, and in an unbelievably short space produce a very tolerable hot meal.

On trek, moreover, the cook might be without support. In the station few cooks would work without a scullion or 'marmitone' (derived from the French *marmiton*), a lowly-paid boy, whom as a rule the cook was allowed to engage or dismiss as he pleased. He washed the saucepans, plucked the fowl, swept the kitchen and did all the menial jobs in the back kitchen, besides, in many cases, a little pedestrian cooking under supervision. Many a good cook started life as a marmitone – and though good cooks were worth the price of rubies, marmitones were three a penny, and one ran through a good many of them, the number varying according to the cook's temper, digestion, exactingness and habits.

My third and best cook, Osman, was normally sober, though less dutiful and meticulous than Saeed in his Islamic obligations. Occasionally, however, he would throw sobriety to the winds, and I always knew when he was in beer because the permanent mild cast in his eye became a temporary, acute-angle squint of surpassing intensity and malevolence. One evening he appeared in the middle of company, his straight eye piercing me like a gimlet and its wayward companion darting daggers at a guest sitting on the starboard side of the verandah, to announce that the marmitone must be disposed of immediately. The lousy little minion had shredded the onion into the fruit salad. What would my guests think?

I certainly wondered what my guests were thinking, so I shepherded him away and sent for the marmitone. He did not appear, and it was some time before Saeed and the second boy found him cowering in the shed wherein slept the guaranteed prisoner who worked in the garden. The lad was obviously scared, and blurted out that he had chopped up some onion for the soup and had merely put it down on a table beside a bowl of fruit salad – whereupon Osman seized him by the scruff of the neck, dragged him towards the stove and forced his head into the oven, vowing that it should be served up to the Governor in lieu of the roast chicken. In the end the chicken, not the head, came up, and it was very good. Osman never let us down, even when in liquor. But the marmitone had to go.

With occasional exceptions, Africans did not make servants of this calibre. There were a few really good ones in the Southern Provinces, but they were hard to come by. As a rule they either lacked the necessary sense of responsibility and professional zeal, or, if they had it, lacked the poise, the *savoir faire* and the personality of their northern counterparts. The most constant fault was perhaps that of misplaced zeal. This is the most frustrating of all sins for the master; for you cannot bring yourself to show real anger with a man who has honestly done his best in the hopes of pleasing you. Yet zeal can play more havoc and cause more annoyance than slovenliness or neglect. I once saw Khaddam, my *secondo* or No.2 in the household, holding my favourite walking-stick – a carved and poker-worked piece made of the best ebony, of which I was very fond – and lustily flogging the ground with it. I shouted at him, but he continued to thump with the full power of his ham-like forearm. He then rose and came towards me beaming in pleasurable triumph and obviously expecting congratulation, with what was left of the walking-stick shattered to fragments in one hand, and a three-foot sand snake of a completely harmless species in the other.

On another occasion I was staying for a night with a colleague before proceeding on leave. We had arrived and unloaded, and on going to my room twenty minutes later I found that his servant, Arama, had already displayed his zeal by unpacking every box, including those destined for travel to the United Kingdom, and had concealed all the clothes most wanted in the most unlikely places – in the bathroom or under the bed or in the drawers of the writing table. Even in opulent houses it has always been a bugbear to me to be unpacked-for by a butler, and a Zande *secondo* lacks the acumen and the imagination of a Jeeves. The next day was a Sunday, and I wore long trousers to attend divine service. On coming back, I wished to change into shorts, but neither in the drawers nor in any other place could a pair be traced. Finally Arama had to be called for, and it proved that he had taken all six pairs of shorts which I had with me, all save one of which were still clean and pressed and unworn, together with all my shirts and stockings and underwear, whether dirty or clean, and was busy washing them assiduously. It was Talleyrand who used to give his disciples and subordinates the solemn warning, '*Mes enfants, n'ayez pas de zèle.*'

This mistaken endeavour to please, to rise to the occasion, was a commendable and yet a plebeian trait, and could extend to regrettable extravagance of dress. Poor Khaddam, deputising for Saeed who was ill for a season, would give of his best, but you could see his huge paw shaking with nervousness as it grasped the sauce-boat, with one big finger over the edge and in the gravy – which, on one occasion, he tipped down the back of the Senior Veterinary Inspector's shirt. It was very hot gravy, too. The inspector bore it with cheerfulness and fortitude, but the lapse exacerbated Khaddam's nervousness, and something, even if only a token or symbol, was needed to boost his ego. When, after mopping-up operations, he had reappeared with the sweet, we noticed that the smart white cap with which my wife had fitted him out was adorned with a large red insignia on the front. When told to bring it for closer inspection, he did so with an outsize grin of *amour propre* and displayed a big circular label of pillar-box red culled from a consignment of lamps and bearing the legend BRITISH MADE THROUGHOUT.

This sartorial exuberance, almost unknown to the Arab, who has quiet, traditional and excellent taste in dress, appeals considerably to the African, and perhaps tribalism adds to its terrors. A colleague's servant, Rabih, a most faithful retainer of singular ideas, who would generally prefer to lay a fork for the soup and to replace it with a spoon for the beefsteak, used to appear on State occasions wearing a deer-stalker of the shape patronised by Sherlock Holmes but coloured a gruesome yellow-and-black Macleod tartan. This was the less excusable, since these were not even his master's true tribal colours.

Such points were doubtless difficult for them to understand, as were many of their masters' ways and words. One of the 'Bog Barons' – the early, ex-military District Commissioners in the south – had a servant who was trained to make certain responses as a matter of discipline and good breeding. On his first appearance in the morning his master would say, 'Good morning, Hezekiah. A fine day, isn't it?' To which the well-drilled answer came: 'Yes, Sir. Bloody sweaty.'

Arab servants had a more effective freemasonry than did African. When crockery or cutlery was needed to cope with a large party or meeting, they could be trusted to pool resources and sort them out afterwards, and the loss of a spoon or a mixing-up of plates was surprisingly rare. Southern servants were less adept in this field, and zeal for master's interests could, as usual, lead to trouble. I even remember it once leading to medical treatment at an inter-province meeting in the bleak marshes of the Upper White Nile. Spoons had been pooled, and Kor Jock, the faithful and zealous Dinka servant of one of our party, apprehended Kor Bill (many Nilotic names have a strong Anglo-Saxon ring), the Nuer servant of a neighbour, in the process of abstracting one of his master's table-spoons as the meeting was breaking up.

Kor Bill had objected, and a tug-of-war with the spoon ended with Jock getting possession and hitting Bill over the head with it. Bill then seized a brand from the fire and coshed Jock on the crown. But Jock had, in turn, snatched up a shillelagh, chased his opponent to the edge of the marsh, laid him out and left him on his back in the mud, returning both righteous and victorious with the spoon. The damage was considerable, but luckily not beyond the powers of iodine and plaster, and a start an hour before dawn ensured that there would be no opportunity for a second round.

Other servants depended on the nature of the station and the demands of the work. A camel man, for instance, was employed only in districts where riding and *hamla* camels were kept and used. It was wonderful, however, what could escape routine scrutiny. In about 1927 an auditor discovered that the sum of £5 per month was being paid to the Governor General's camel man. The ensuing audit query was, for once, justifiable. It was put to the Civil Secretary's office, which, after scratching its head, correctly sent it on to the Governor of Khartoum Province, who naturally knew nothing about it, and passed it on to the Deputy Governor. He had never heard of a Governor General's camel man, so passed it on to the District Commissioner of the municipality. The D.C. was equally in the dark, but handed it to his young assistant for investigation. The assistant had never a clue, so asked the *mamur*, the fountain of all knowledge. Even the *mamur* held no key to the riddle; but after discreet enquiries he unearthed an elderly and decrepit fellow, who was brought tottering into the office.

'Are you the Governor General's camel man?'

'Yes, your Honour.'

'But the Governor General hasn't got any camels.'

'No, your Honour, but His Excellency Wingate Pasha used to ride often when he was Governor General. In 1906 we once rode all the way from Kassala to Tokar. Ah! Men were men in those days. True the present Governor General has no camels *as yet,* but I am ready and waiting to take over His Excellency's stud the moment he sees fit to acquire new animals. They must be of the best Bishari breed; and I shall be honoured and happy.'

After this bravura performance (I was told), even Finance showed a heart, and the old man remained in receipt of his emolument for his few remaining years.

Syces might come from any part of the country, and some of the best haled from Darfur, the westernmost province, which was a land of horses. My own syce, Khamis, was a southern Muslim, perfectly honest except where the bottle was concerned. When sober, he was reliable, and drunk or sober he was faithful. He was with me for the first ten years of my service – until I abandoned horses on transfer to Khartoum – and he later rejoined the firm to see out my last eight years. Unlike most Africans, he had a soft spot and good hands for all kinds of creatures, not horses alone. He was one of the only two or three persons who could handle Marcus the parrot without risk of losing a piece of finger, and the virulent old bird was devoted to him.

Once when I visited the communal stables, I found them running over with guinea-pigs. Inquiry among the other syces revealed that they were the property of Khamis. He admitted that they were his, and assured me that he had no thought of enlarging his meat ration or of starting a trade in guinea-pigs, but said he simply liked to have them around him. Charming as this was, he was bidden to remove them from the stables and keep them in his own quarters. The day after the next pay-day I noticed that he seemed unusually downcast, and asked him if anything was the matter. The guinea-pigs were the matter. The day before, he had collected his wages and gone back to his quarters, but then had dropped his jacket on the floor when he went outside on some small errand. When he returned, he found that the guinea-pigs had rootled all over his clothes and had chewed up a pound note in the pocket. He held it up, an Egyptian £1 note, hopelessly savaged, with nothing left save the inscrutable smile on the Sphinx's face and a trifle of Arabic script. In his anger he had turned the despoilers out of the house; but he was offended when I suggested that they deserved eating, and two days later they were back in his room again.

To his mother   26 January 1944

Another pleasant thing, when staying among Baggara, is to get good, fresh, frothing milk to drink. I suppose the idea of drinking milk direct from a cow, unsterilized, unpasteurised, unpeptonised and whatnot, is almost shocking to the modern hygienic mind – probably there are a good many million urban dwellers who scarcely realise that milk comes from the udder of a live cow ... but with beer unobtainable, there's no other drink to touch fresh, warm milk.

To his father   3 March 1944
Nahud

At a lunch party with the Nazir of Kawahla, they were very free with the merissa, the Kawahla being famous for their particularly good brew, and it so loosened the tongue of Wilson that he tried to tell the assembly all about a rowing tour they did on the Rhine, from Cambridge. But as the Kawahla have never seen a boat or heard of the Rhine, I am not sure what they made of it. The Arabs have a saying that beer puts a man through three stages – first it makes him a peacock, then it makes him a lion, and finally a baboon.

To his mother   24 September 1944
Nahud

I took a toddle up the jebel in the afternoon with the .22 to look for guinea fowl. The only fowl seen made for the horizon at once, but it was an enjoyable climb, and there were some fine caves and rock-stacks at the summit. Coming down, I was walking a contour along the hillside when suddenly, from a fold in the ground a trifle downhill of me, walked a full-size leopard. He never saw me, and was actually walking past, thirty yards away. By ill luck the rifle was unloaded, and as I opened the bolt to load he heard the click, took one glance and was off up to the caves like a streak – a most graceful sight, but a chance missed, as he had been doing much execution among the village goats.

CHAPTER SEVENTEEN

Recreations

There was a type of officer who was intensely conscientious. He did his hours of work, and then did some more. He always had some duty which prevented him from joining in any lighter activity. He gave his nose to the grindstone and lived for his leave – if he did not break down before it came. Worthy and excellent though he might be, I never found that he gave the best value; and the reason was that he never had his heart wholly in the country. The best value of all was given by the man who had his interests all around him, his hobbies ready to hand, and got his kick in life out of the country itself and the daily round.

There is no word in colloquial Arabic to translate 'hobby.' The correct term might be found in literature and would be understood by any man of the intelligentsia, but to the Sudanese populace as a whole it would be unintelligible. The hobby is in the main a European conception, the individual interest and activity by which a man recreates himself and maintains that zest and perspective which are the ingredients of any good creative work. In a country like the Sudan, a man with hobbies could always be happy: without them, he was lost.

The country was rich in pastimes and it offered great variety: riding, polo, big game, bird-shooting, mountain-climbing, sailing, fishing, swimming, anthropology, tennis, archaeology, botany, ornithology, bridge, chess; you could not get all everywhere, but you could get some anywhere.

I start with the horse. In the old printed forms for the confidential reports which had to be rendered from time to time on every administrative official, after spaces for 'Judgment,' 'Tact,' 'Power of Command,' came a space labelled 'Horsemanship.' We were never quite certain whether this was meant to be taken literally or figuratively – *i.e.* referring to one's 'hands' in dealing with people. Since the compilers of Government forms are seldom allusively or metaphorically minded, I think the literal sense was intended. At all events the stock entry under this heading was 'Sufficient,' which was less than justice to the expert fraternity, and a benevolent pass-mark to those who sat on a horse only as long as it stayed still, and then only because they had to. When this space was altered, about the early 1930s, to 'Office Work' (previously omitted) I think that even the least hippocratic officers felt that the Service had lost tone.

There is no denying that in earlier days hippocracy was carried too far. This was a pity, not only because it was slightly absurd in itself, but because it tended to lead, as happy feudalism gave way to prosaic and pedestrian modernity, to a swing of the pendulum and a relegation of the horse to a less honourable and prominent role than it deserved. It is strange that a golden mean could not be struck. It has always seemed strange to me that the two best games in the world – Bridge, the finest sedentary game, and Polo, the finest active one – should produce more envy, malice, hatred and uncharitableness than the rest put together. Perhaps it is not odd at all, for any game of absorbing splendour is apt to produce devotion of an almost religious type. I have seen lasting enemies made both at the bridge table and on the polo ground.

I do not think any sport gives quite such concentrated enjoyment as polo, when it is treated in the right spirit, as a game and not as an article of faith. Most ordinary province polo was taken in this spirit. Grounds differed, from the hard red surface at Omdurman, where a good hit would travel half the pitch's length and a fall was a dangerous thing, to the grounds of the east, north of Kassala, where if a stiff wind were blowing all eight players might at times be gathered together searching for the ball amidst an impenetrable pall of dust and waiting impotently till the cloud blew away before again setting to work to hack it from bunker to bunker.

Personnel in polo teams could be, and should be, as varied as possible. Polo was a great leveller, and there was no such thing as *lèse majesté*. One particularly plethoric and heavily-built Governor, when ridden off the ball, roared at me for 'crossing,' which was an untrue charge, and spent the rest of the chukka pursuing me and attempting reprisals, regardless of how the game was going. Eventually I got away with the ball, closely ridden into by him as he leaned further and further sideways in an attempt to elbow me off it. I succeeded in dribbling the ball through the goal, and at that critical moment he overreached himself in a last desperate effort, clutched wildly at one of the goal-posts, the horse proceeding smoothly from under him and he was left clinging to the post like a man hanging on to a punt-pole when the punt has slipped away beneath him. It was a wonderful sight; and no physical hurt done; but feelings are more important than bones, and I left on trek early the next day.

My own Waterloo came a trifle later, when I was riding a borrowed pony. It was named Pegasus, an unhappy misnomer, for a less airy and volatile quadruped could not be found in the Tropic of Cancer. He was hard to move out of a phlegmatic and plodding shuffle, but if he once did move it was direct for Cairo or the Cape. The ball had been struck upfield and an Arab sheikh, half-brother of the Nazir, riding ahead of me had struck at it and missed. Instead of riding on, he pulled up on top of the ball, and coming up behind I struck in turn. The head of the stick, on the follow-through, caught in the long, flowing matted tail of his country-bred. The loop was round my wrist. At that moment Pegasus decided to turn back to Rhodesia while the sheikh's horse suddenly made a bee-line for Suez. I was jerked from the saddle and found myself being towed behind my opponent like Hector behind Achilles' chariot. Luckily the ground was one of the softer ones, and the loop parted before serious harm was done.

Then there was Sheikh Ahmed Fadlalla, who was excitable and had a wooden leg but played a most valiant game and usually kept his head and his leg until about the third chukka, when the latter generally came off, especially if in trying to hook his stick you accidentally hooked his leg by mistake. The onlookers were keenly on the watch for that, knowing that it must occur sooner or later.

Sheikh Yusif, the head merchant at Province Headquarters, was another redoubtable player. He rode sixteen stone, and under his flowing robes the little ewe-necked screw he bestrode was sometimes barely visible. Yet he could make that screw go like a gazelle. The effect was apt to be spoiled only by his habit of pulling up sharp on the ball, winding himself up, and smiting. If smitten, the ball travelled 150 yards and the game began again apace. If missed, his horse usually trod it into the soft surface and the players gather round, raking and thumping, in what he genially described as a *katl dabeeb,* or 'like killing a snake.'

When numbers needed making up, one could put a syce into the field, but it might be risky. My African syce, Khamie, was as faithful and likeable a retainer as could be desired, but was not immune from the weaknesses of the flesh. I once ill-advisedly put him into a chukka at short notice. He had looked a trifle abnormal before the game and was not standing very steadily, though the horses were as well turned-out as ever. As soon as the chukka opened he smote the ball hard towards our own goal, then roared after it, shouting obscenities at its father and mother and waving his stick, twice dangerously crossed the District Commissioner and Veterinary Inspector, and having reached but missed one of the goals (it did not matter which) slid comfortably off on to his back and lay with his face to the sky while the pony went home.

For ordinary hacking there could, in the more unattractive stations, be little incentive beyond the mere need to exercise. Among hills and in the verdant green of the early rains, with the smell of freshly rained-on earth all around (surely one of the half-dozen best smells in the world, to rank with gorse, heather, a bean-field and newly-ground coffee) it could be a delightful recreation. But there were other objects for riding.

One unusual one was hyena-hunting. Wherever there was a rocky *jebel* or kopje, hyenas were likely to lie up in its caves and recesses by day, travelling long distances at night in quest of food and sometimes doing serious damage to flocks and herds. A run after hyena was both difficult to secure and difficult to bring to a successful issue. The spotted-hyena can go at a pace which will hold the average country-bred for nearly two miles; he can jink, he will take to the most villainous terrain; and even if he has had a full feed he can lighten ship in no uncertain manner and go on unencumbered.

The strategy is simple - in theory. You kill a sickly cow and lay it out a mile away from the *jebel.* The spears then assemble long before dawn, ride quietly out and place themselves half way between the corpse and the *jebel.* The theory is that the replete hyenas will be returning to the *jebel* at dawn, and can be intercepted and ridden away from their lairs. This would be excellent if (a) the hyenas always found the bait, (b) they did not sneak away into the bush, very unfairly, after their meal instead of making for their bedrooms, and (c) those that did make for bed always waited for the spears to place themselves before completing their journey. Even so, runs did result.

There was considerable thrill in moving silently out in the rather eerie stillness, with the chill of the false dawn on your cheek, and peering into the dusk ahead of you as visibility increased with tantalising slowness. Every bush seemed to move, and every rock took on a hyena-shape. Nothing? No, nothing: and then there came a wild shout from the left and the whole line swung into motion and was off in the direction of the view-halloo. As likely as not, on dashing at full speed over the crest of the intervening sand-dune one would find two or three other spears ignominiously pulled up and looking at a chalky-faced donkey, which would then bray its derision. If a hyena it were, a good point would be assured, and the odds were on the quarry. I never secured a first-spear myself, but from time to time a skilful rider scored.

Hunts were few and mostly ephemeral. The Dongola Hunt, recorded in Kipling's tale 'Little Foxes,' was a real phenomenon but a matter of ancient history. We did, however, run a hunt for a short while in the heart of the Red Sea Hills, under the auspices of an Irish regiment stationed there. Mounts were limited: I possessed two horses, the Assistant Commissioner one, the regiment three between them. There were two donkeys which pulled the rubbish-cart and a sinister, wall-eyed mule which pulled the night-soil cart. Anybody else had to follow on camels. Hunt uniform was a polo helmet, jodhpurs and a bottle-green coat with buff facings. The pack consisted of some six couple of pi-dogs, and the quarry was provided by gazelle, which could give the pack fifty yards in a hundred; jackals which usually went to ground among boulders, and desert hares which jinked deliriously from bush to bush.

Meets were held soon after dawn, but were seldom punctual, since the pack on being loosed from the kennels was apt to go off in full cry after the first attractive bitch which flaunted herself across their path. The pack eventually came to a bad end by setting about the goats of an elderly Fuzzy, who disposed of two couple with a spear and laid out the careless whipper-in with a brickbat. But sport while it lasted was good, though unremunerative, and on that stony and risky terrain justified Mr

Jorrocks's definition of it as 'the image of war without its guilt, and only five and twenty per cent of its danger.'

After huntin' come shooting and fishing. But I cannot go deeply into them, since this is neither a sporting handbook nor a treatise on natural history. Of the pursuit of big-game with a rifle, or with camera (which was my particular hobby) I say no more here than that it was one of the most valuable hobbies of all, partly because it took you so completely out of the milieu of grinding routine, partly because for body and nerves it was strenuous and beneficial, and partly because it taught the geography of the country and threw you into touch, by means of guides, trackers and hunters, not with the governing class – the sheikhs, chiefs or intelligentsia – but with the ordinary man, be he Arab or African, and gave a chance both to study him and, indirectly, to learn his point of view and to hear both rumour and truth which would seldom be dropped over a cup of coffee and never be confided in an office.

In scatter-gun shooting, any sheikh or leader was always glad to share, whether it was with his own armament or with a borrowed gun. Such weapons would not always have passed an armourer's test. An *omda* took me once to a spot which he said was excellent for sand-grouse. It was; but I started with misgivings, having seen his fowling-piece which displayed, when rattled, a quarter of an inch's play between stock and barrels. This did not deter him; the gun had been good enough for his grandfather and his father so why not for him? I sighed and took up a good position and enjoyed some excellent shooting: but when I looked round to see how he fared, I saw him 150 yards off on his knees, holding his head in his hands. At the first shot a large sliver of the brass cartridge-cap had emerged through the chasm ready for it and taken a big strip of skin off the front of his forehead, mercifully just missing the eye. Six months later he still had the scar – and the gun, but was not using it.

Another young sheikh who came with me after duck was of unusually pious disposition. Now to be eatable under the law of Islam a creature must be slaughtered, *i.e.* have the life-blood released from the jugular. Some hold that anything killed in the chase is *halal* (lawful) whether slaughtered or killed dead on the spot. Others hold that it is *halal* only if, before firing the shot, the huntsman thrice ejaculates, '*Bismillahi*' – In the Name of God. Once when a shoveller-drake arose from a pool by the Nile and took a line straight overhead, up went his gun and as the drake approached I heard my friend exclaim *sotto voce*, '*Bismillahi!*' But he had underrated the speed of a frightened duck. It was not until the bird was perpendicularly overhead that the second pious pronouncement came out; further and further backward bent the aiming figure, and as the third '*Bismillahi*' triumphantly escaped him – so did the duck, and the gun discharged into the blue as he collapsed upon a wet mud-bank. This did not deter him; he was as keen as mustard and secured a duck before the afternoon was out.

It was on such an outing, with an excellent *omda*, that I learned the Arab cures for snake-bite. We were hunting guinea-fowl, which were plentiful, with a .22 rifle, and had secured three and were returning to the village and within calling distance of it, when he gave a little hop and exclaimed, 'A snake bit me.' Looking down, I was just in time to see *Echis carinatus*, the saw-scaled viper, the commonest lethal snake in the Northern Sudan, glide into a bush. We rushed the mere two hundred yards home and I cut the bite, which was over the instep, open with a razor-blade, squeezed, rubbed in permanganate and put on a tourniquet for a while. The *omda*'s own supporters and family then took over the care.

First he was seated on an *angareb* or bedstead; a hole was dug in the ground, the afflicted limb placed in the hole and the earth packed tightly round it. This was to 'prevent the poison going up the leg,' and may have served as a subsidiary tourniquet. Second, a handful of fresh limes was brought, and the patient sucked and absorbed all he could. Third, four eggs were broken, the whites separated, and were swallowed raw 'to dilute the poison.' Fourth, a cup of ghee, or clarified butter, was brought for the same purpose; that went down well – and stayed down. Fifth, some powdered roots, (*randia nilotica* a narcotic plant also used by African tribes for poisoning fish) were fetched, mixed with water and drunk. Sixth, a tiny piece of rhinoceros horn, a precious heirloom in the family, was sent for, a little portion filed into a cup of milk and the potion quaffed off. Seventh, a *fiki* was called in. He wrote the appropriate Koranic texts in heavy sepia ink on a wooden board, washed off the ink with his own spittle into a little water, and ink, water and spittle went down the *omda*'s throat.

Lastly, the women of the village came to me and demanded the snake. It seemed most unlikely that the offender would have awaited our vengeance, but luck was in. On tracking back our steps, we found the enemy still coiled in the bush where he had taken refuge. He was slain and the corpse handed to the women on the end of a stick, whereupon they rolled it in cow dung, baked it, and buried it. This was because 'if the body was left out after sunset, the patient's leg would swell and he would die.'

When I inquired after the patient's chances, I was told that if once he were sick he would live. Thinking of the ghee, the eggs, the limes, the ink, the horn, the roots and the spit, I felt that I would lay six to four on the *omda*. He was not allowed to sleep, but was kept awake by a sustained charivari of beaten tins and singing and about midnight was gloriously sick. Though severely ill for a week and laid up for three weeks, he recovered, for which I was thankful; he was an excellent *omda* and a good friend.

Of the birds which provided sport and food – bustard, sand-grouse, guinea-fowl, francolin, snipe, pigeon, geese and duck – there is no doubt that duck gave the greatest fun. Many a small lake or set of mere well-holes flooded after the rains, as well as big sheets of water, held duck into the dry season even far northwards across the Sudan. I sometimes wonder whether the expert shot, who is a perfect marksman by nature, ever gets quite so much satisfaction as the second-rate and average performer. I shall not forget the satisfaction of securing three Garganey teal with three successive shots as they whistled down wind, single, over a well-field in the semi-desert; for if one lived to be ninety it would be unlikely to be repeated.

Sport fishing was limited to the Red Sea Coast and to some riverain districts; but the two mainstays, the Nile perch and the tiger-fish, could give most enjoyable sport in reward for spinning or trolling. The club-book at Province Headquarters held records back to 1908, and in addition to perch which ran to 132 lbs (the rod-and-line record, from the Jebel Aulia dam above Khartoum, is over 270 lbs) contained the entry 'one Ford radiator' which was hooked and landed after a dour fight of twelve minutes. The weight was unfortunately not recorded.

The river provided a great refuge from daily cares, and one easily taken advantage of. Angling is absorbing and as a rule promotes nothing but friendly feelings. The only hazard which brought a spice of risk to it, at least at Province Headquarters, was Hermann. He was a very large bull hippo, so named from his resemblance to the late General Goering, who during the dry-weather, when the river sank to a trickle with great pools at long intervals, took up his residence at the head of the long pool which fronted the town and cantonment. Here he spent the winter months in morose solitude, occasionally attracting one of his harem to solace his existence. A rival bull once appeared and the townspeople were kept awake for an hour and more by the noise of battle; next day they consumed the rival who lay, lacerated by his opponent's ivories, dead at the bottom of the pool.

Normally Hermann remained semi-submerged in a shallow, growing skittish only towards sunset. To approach him then in the boat was asking for trouble, but only once did he make an attack on us. At twenty yards he faced round and suddenly charged the dinghy, hooshing along the top of the water in a most aggressive manner. I dropped my rod and snatched up the shotgun, brought for close-quarter protection only, but after covering twelve yards he swerved and dived. It had been only a demonstration. Next day he repeated the performance with the Province Medical Inspector, and nearly received a bullet. When later he was still ruder to the O.C. of the local company of the Sudan Defence Forces, and chased him off the river, patience was exhausted.

Even then there was reluctance to execute such a character. The wily O.C. therefore waited until his stern was exposed on a sand-bank, and then fired a well-directed thunder-flash under it. A winged hippopotamus has not yet been recorded by Science, but Hermann very nearly achieved this distinction. He flew a mile upstream to a pool where his primacy and privacy alike were unchallenged, and remained there for the rest of the season.

Diary 17 March 41

The troops round Keren are clothing native soldiers in baboon suits and sending them to photograph our lines; there is an army order out that any baboons seen with cameras will be at once forwarded to HQ.

To his mother   November 1942
Nahud

One of the minor unpleasantnesses in Western Kordofan is the haskaneet grass, a ubiquitous growth which carries horrid little spined burrs (something like the iron 'crows' feet' which Bruce, most unfairly, strewed about for the English cavalry at Bannockburn) which cling to your legs as you walk through and are most painful and inflaming.

I remember in the Secrtariat a solemn despatch arriving from the Embassy, covering a solemn despatch from the Foreign Office, covering a letter from a female with some name like Flavia Flabbe who confided that she was engaged in painting a series of plants representing the national emblems of all countries, and would we be gracious enough to inform her what was the Sudan emblem. I drew a heraldic design and suggested that the emblem should be a haskaneet, with *UBIQUE* written over the top and *Nemo me impune lacessit* [10] underneath. We very nearly sent it – but decided in the end that the proper answer was 'A Lemon'!

To his mother   January 1943
Nahud

The man began to poke gingerly with the butt of his long Baggara spear. Next moment there was a grunting roar and a rush and out came the lion! We had all four ridden within ten feet of him where he lay up. The horses stood on their hind legs and the Arabs shouted, and Saeed & Co, not 150 yards off, began to run up, and the lion disappeared over the bank. At last I got the horse still and could dismount and load.

We ran after, and very soon I saw him, through a thin screen of thorn, walking sedately. On seeing we were after him, he quickened, and when I got beyond the thorn he was 100 yards ahead and going strong for some long grass twenty yards ahead. So I drew a

---

10   No one provokes me and gets away with it: the motto of Scotland and various regiments.

bead (remembering to aim a foot low as this 1928 ammunition flies anything up to that high at 100 yards!) and blowed if I didn't take him clean through the loins. He swung round roaring, and we thought he would charge, but he couldn't move much, and we could close in and finish him clean.

The sequel was interesting: sure enough, he was a big lion, but scraggy, yet so far from being old was obviously in his prime, with perfect teeth. But on skinning him they found a porcupine quill embedded in his mouth. Clearly he had had the worst of a bout with a porc, had been sick and fasting for long, was now getting better, and being weak had to start off with humans and sheep till fit again. A good riddance.

CHAPTER EIGHTEEN

Colleagues and Government

A territory in Africa which is half-way from the primitive era of local autocracies to the ministerial system and responsible self-government cannot hope to be free from the ills of bureaucracy. A central government must be organised by secretariats and by departmental headquarters under them. Those headquarter organisations must have a nucleus of permanent officials, and a hierarchy through which it is not always easy to trace the thread of personal responsibility; and there is no guard against the corroding effects which follow.

The Sudan I knew was not free from the maladies of a centralised bureaucracy. The understanding between the head and the limbs, the Central Government machine and the provinces, was never perfect. To the dweller on the Olympus of Khartoum, the antics of provincial officials were apt to look irregular and anomalous (a word beloved of most secretariats, and often covering anything which does not comply with the orthodox rules laid down). To the man on the spot, in the heat and the dust and the crux of prompt decision, the action or inaction of a far-away government frequently seemed unsympathetic, impersonal and unrealistic.

Yet I know that in fact the relations between centre and perimeter were better, and the comprehension of the former more lucid and realistic, the loyalty of the latter deeper, than in most territories. The first reason for this was that, although the country was vast, its official British personnel was small. Nearly everybody knew everybody else, at least at second hand and very often at first hand, so that personal touch could never be quite squeezed out by officialdom, and many a matter was really decided not by the bleak official correspondence which passed through the correct channels, but by the demi-official or private letters which passed behind it, between man and man.

The second reason was the admirable policy of staffing a secretariat or departmental headquarters with men seconded from the provinces, who were brought in to serve for two, three or four years at the hub and then sent back to the circumference. Some stuck, it is true, and a period of more than a few years in the central machine certainly had a dehydrating effect, which began to dry up the juices of humanity. But for the most part dehydration was avoided, and the system ensured that a steady flow reached the provinces of men who understood the central machinery and could appreciate the difficulty of taking decisions at that level. *Per contra,* new blood constantly reached the heart – men who were fresh from the *Sturm und Drang* of provincial affairs and had not lost their contact with day-to-day realities or with the people themselves.

The third reason was the quality of the men recruited, and particularly of those at the top. Sir Douglas Newbold, as Civil Secretary, under the stress of one of the most anxious periods of the war, could maintain personal contact with every part of his command, insist on that personal touch throughout the secretarial warren over which he presided in Khartoum, and write in a personal letter:

> *Après la guerre* I propose to found a school of the Higher Dynamics, run by a governing board of Churchill, Montgomery and the ghosts of Coeur de Lion, Alexander and Cromwell, to teach vigour and decision to wavering, fusty bureaucrats and the dubious denizens of Embassies and Foreign Offices, with *Vae Vacillantibus* inscribed over the portal.

It was he in person who taught me my first salutary lesson in drafting official correspondence. As a junior secretariat officer I had been bidden to prepare a letter of instruction to a number of province governors on a rather tricky subject. I duly turned out something which appeared to me a fairly serviceable *passe partout* for all the provinces concerned, written from an impersonal angle and full of the standard office clichés – 'It is regretted …', 'Cannot see his way to implement the proposals adumbrated …', and 'If it eventually transpires that …' I was summoned and asked to which governor this draft was addressed. I innocently replied that I thought it would do as a circular for all. The answer was an injunction to take it away and produce a different draft for each governor. 'Remember the personality to whom you are writing. Is it X? Mix him a gentle and soothing bromide. Is it Y? Make doubly sure of every littlest fact and reference, or he will nail us on the least inaccuracy. Or is it Z? Give him a kick in the pants.'

The maintenance of personal relations, which might be obscured but never wholly overlaid by official procedure, ensured that the Central Government never became excessively pompous. It was the spirit, not the letter, that mattered; and provided that an officer was loyal to policy, and was a whole-time worker, he could criticise, fire squibs at or lampoon his higher powers with impunity, or even, who knows, with salubrious results, for criticism or lampoon can lead to a sense of perspective in the shot-at, and is a powerful purgative of the darker humours in the shooter.

I can remember only once getting into trouble for undue levity. Two ladies, Miss Smarts and Miss Beam, were entering the country to join a missionary society. This simple matter involved routine work, which need not go above the heads of juniors, on two sides of the secretarial system, the Personnel branch, concerned with passports and personal details, and the Internal branch, which dealt with the educational and administrative aspects, and in which my billet lay. Having written a minute dealing with my side of the routine, I sent the file through to my opposite number in the Personnel office to do the same on his side. In pencil underneath the minute I idly scribbled, purely for the eye of my peer:

> *Miss Smarts and Miss Beam*
> *Are a missionary team.*
> *I wish they were tarts,*
> *Miss Beam and Miss Smarts*

and gave the file to an orderly to take through. Being new, bone-headed and hard of hearing, the lad took it to the office of a highly-placed and more serious-minded superior, where it was laid upon his desk and duly perused. That one was not passed off easily.

Service in the Secretariat, provided it was not too prolonged, was of priceless value to an officer, deepening his understanding, giving him balance, and showing him from within the chinks in the armour of a

Central Government through which he could then successfully poke them after he had gone back to the provinces. But it involved life in the metropolis and a life out of regular and constant touch with the Sudanese themselves, and was therefore unpopular with the majority. Social advantages the capital certainly had, but even in the social field there were penalties as well in the shape of formal functions, of which the periodical official *levée* was the most galling.

I have often marvelled at mankind's capacity for continuing to hold events which everybody loathes, because each individual thinks that some other individual likes them, and nobody has the initiative to stop them. Moreover, the *raison d'être* for the *levée* lay in that lowest stratum of human nature, the proclivity for snobbery. Had such a function been dropped, nobody would have lamented its disappearance. But so long as it existed, and so long as old Mahmoud or Mr Kyriazis or Ramzi Bey or young Gubbins were on the list, it was necessary for the boosting of one's own *amour propre,* whatever one's race, that one should not be omitted from the élite.

The Briton probably resented the function more than did others. For one thing, it involved the expenditure of good money on a white kit sprinkled with golden odds-and-ends, which made him look a cross between a Portuguese admiral and a seedy commissionaire, with a sword appended which might have served for toasting an unbelligerent slice of bread. His self-consciousness was increased by the fact that, under his comfortless black boots, the trousers were secured by elastic, so that he was hamstrung and static, unable to bend and able to walk only with stiff legs, like a wooden marionette.

In fact there were only two joys at a *levée.* One was to wait in hopes that His Excellency or some other Olympian would drop a handkerchief or a glove, whereupon one could watch the frustrated gymnastic antics of the ADCs as they attempted to stoop down and pick it up. The other was to observe the physiognomy of the guests as they filed past – bored English officials and short-tempered officers; slimy and perspiring Egyptian faces surmounted by the *tarboosh,* with stomachs protruding under tight black frock-coats; patient Sudanese notables – the most poised and courteous part of the human *mélange.* Besides all these there would be a deep-bearded Greek Orthodox priest, followed by a couple of sallow Armenian merchant-princes, with that unmistakeable high forehead and sloping head, and the resigned yet subtle look which seems to say: 'I know you have massacred my forebears and can even massacre me. We are used to being massacred. But we shall get the best of the bargain in the end.' The Second World War is to be blessed possibly for one thing only: it killed the *levée*.

The Sudanese is, like the Briton, on the whole not a lover of ceremonial and formal display. His informality and natural manners are one of his most engaging characteristics. When a party of notables visited England in 1937 for King George VI's coronation, what struck them most were (a) the informal friendliness which they found reciprocated to them, and the willingness of the people to help without pestering them beyond their needs; (b) the law-abidingness which seemed part of the public nature; and (c) the age of things, especially the colleges at the universities. The idea that such institutions might have been running for 500 years, or that a college lawn had taken three centuries to bring to perfection, gave a sense of continuity staggering to men whose history had been one of insecurity and unstable fortunes.

Secretariat service did not mean total interment in a clerical rabbit-warren. The Government wisely sent its secretarial staff on periodical visits to the provinces, to maintain their sanity and sense of perspective. One might be engaged in many interesting side-lines – in lecturing to Sudanese training schools, in contacts with the Gordon College, in liaison work with some film company shooting a picture in the darkest wilds of Africa (a few miles out of Khartoum city), in acting as secretary to the annual meeting of Governors or in presiding over or sitting upon examination boards.

The work of a secretary at a Governors' meeting was some of the most exacting that a young man could be called upon to perform. No stenographer was available, and the strain of maintaining unremitting attention, of sorting the wheat from the chaff, of omitting the clouds of irrelevance and faithfully following the few rays of decision or illuminating suggestion, followed by the effort of producing a finished draft within twenty-four hours of the sitting, was considerable. How much little touches count! When one hawked the draft minutes round to the Governors individually for correction, one felt a glow of gratitude to the man who made a single, small emendation and scribbled 'Good work' in the margin. One felt weary exasperation with the one who had maundered *sotto voce* and semi-audibly at the end of the table and then appeared hurt and peevish because his gist had not been correctly caught, and now substituted a draft of his own containing all the trenchant and opposite things which he might have said but hadn't. Again, one felt rewarded by a third man whose only marginal criticism ran, 'Do not spell "loath" "loth". This is biblical' – and appended his own comment on the meeting in the form of a Recessional:

> The speeches and the cars are sped,
> The Governors and wives take flight,
> Returns to each official bed
> The old impermeable night.
> Gods of the East, our meeting bless
> Lest we progress, lest we progress.

Working on examination boards was seldom popular. In the provinces it had its moments of joy when one surveyed the general knowledge papers of a promotion exam for junior southern clerks, and learned that 'General Weevil was created Archibald,' or that 'Philip Mountbatten was emperor of India before it became a country. Last year he married Queen Elizabeth and was made Duke of Edinburgh by King George V.' But in Khartoum the penalty for an interest in the Arabic language was to be placed upon the annual board which conducted the Arabic examinations and to have to deal, in this sinister capacity, with one's fellow countrymen.

I came to the conclusion that Torquemada's task must have been more exhausting than is commonly admitted. Any inquisitor may quail at having to correct 150 long papers and to hold sixty orals, especially if he is expected to have the results out (in addition to his ordinary duties) within a week – an expectation which involves sleeplessness and overtime, with no trade union to enforce extra emolument. Orals could be harrowing when the candidates were nervous. Only the most hard-bitten examiner could have remained unmoved opposite a nursing-sister whose pay-rise and confirmation in her post depended upon her passing, and who was

so un-strung that she sat speechless, unable to utter even in English –
until one of the board slipped out and engineered a sham casualty. Its
appearance galvanised the marble statue into activity, and into a flow of
Arabic proficient enough to cope with the supposed practical problem.

We were a motley crew, the British servants of the Sudan Government,
with a wonderful variety of idiosyncrasies, failings, aptitudes and tastes.
But no man need ever fail in his job or lack satisfaction in it, provided he
had the humanity to like, and elicit the liking of, the people themselves.
Indeed, many of the best-loved and most remembered officials were
those whose affability or eccentricities imprinted them upon the public
memory, and who were not rated, in the official confidential files, as aces.
Among such was the Governor who used to sit nearly naked on the deck
of the province steamer, playing the flute; the District Commissioner
who armed and trained a brass band and presented them with a silver
bugle to toot him home from daily office; the officer who, in his cups,
used to kick his servants – until one day he kicked a servant who was
not there and broke his own leg; the other District Commissioner who
presided over some of the morasses of the upper White Nile, and who,
donning the uniform of a Turkish admiral, would board the post-boats
and hold them to a ransom of whisky; the agricultural inspector who
so impressed the Nuba that when a fine stud boar arrived to improve
their piggeries, they gave it his name as an honour; the other, fearless
agricultural inspector who played the cornet and who, when the intake
pipe of one of his irrigation canals became blocked, dived into it at the top,
cleared the obstruction subaqueously and came out of the spout riding
like a water nymph on the crest of the flood.

The Sudanese, in fact, appreciated a character, and would accept
almost anything from one. A senior P.W.D. officer was persecuted by one
of the large, grey goshawks common over much of Africa, which took to
raiding his fowl pens, and carried off three chickens on three consecutive
days. When, on the fourth, the marauder came and perched on the wall,
bold as brass, the official fetched his fowling-piece, loaded it, poked the
end cautiously out of the dining-room window, drew a bead on the top of
the wall and discharged both barrels. The pick-up included what was left
of the hawk, a luckless chicken, an Arab artisan and three Dinka labourers
who were resting in the shade of a tree. That did produce a temporary

226

strike of Dinka workmen, who thought that the outrage had been deliberate and intended to spur them to unwelcome activity. But even then the sight of the perpetrator dangling the few feathers of the hawk as evidence was enough to persuade them of his harmless intentions, and we had a renewal of slightly less lethargic labour the next day.

It was partly personal character which counted, and partly the prestige of belonging to the *hukuma*, or Government. In sophisticated areas and in later political times the prestige of being in Government service might inevitably and perhaps not unhealthily wane. But over the bulk of the country and the bulk of the half-century, attachment to Government did carry with it an aura of importance and authority which reflected the respect in which Central Government was held. When a party of visiting sheikhs and notables were being shown round the charming and friendly little zoo in Khartoum, my eye was caught by one of the retainers – a simple, rather bucolic Arab with a broad smile. He was standing in front of a Whale-headed or Shoebill Stork – that curious, gargoyle-like apparition from the papyrus swamps which suggests the continued existence of pterodactyls or the materialisation of an opium-smoker's dream. The man stood silent and spellbound for a full minute, then shook his head and ejaculated half to himself: '*Wallahi*. Mighty is the Government.'

Government prestige in fact extended beyond the confines of our ken into the spirit world. When the servant of an anthropological expert working among the Dinka became possessed by a spirit (as is apt to happen among that people) and fell into a state of catalepsy, an exorcist had to be brought in to deal with him. After making the customary preparations and dispositions, the practitioner apostrophised his adversary: 'Spirit, come out of that! What do you mean by assailing a man who is far from his home, and moreover one who is working FOR THE GOVERNMENT?' The spirit came out like a lamb.

The advice of Sir Douglas Newbold – to treat everybody differently – stood one in good stead in every kind of dealings. The individual always had to be studied. There was the Governor whose special failing was for Roquefort cheese, or failing that for some really green and noisy species, and if one could but lay in the necessary, any visit of his would assuredly be a success. When a professional statistician arrived on a mission to garner information about some current problem, the correct procedure was to put two strong gins into him, and all the facts and figures into his mincing machine. It did not seem to matter what the information was like, since the statistical sausage which was eventually churned out in the form of percentages, graphs and comparative columns seldom bore much relation to reality.

When an auditor came to carry out an audit, the right thing to do was to treat him as a man and as a friend. He was usually most helpful. But when the audit *department* from faraway Khartoum began taking long shots at one, their remarks often showed a sublime ignorance of local fact, and were best answered by the Retort Direct or by reference to plain common sense.

Bureaucracy drove many good men to distraction. When a junior British official dislocated his neck in a motor-bicycle accident, and was brought into hospital in Port Sudan, the doctor who treated him feared that he might never recover, and felt that he might – like a man about to be hanged – have the choice of his last meal. The patient thought for a while, then whispered, 'I suppose you couldn't find me a bit of asparagus.' Asparagus does not grow in Port Sudan, either in May or in any other month, and the various coverts drawn were all found blank until at last the kindly and pertinacious doctor ran to earth, in a grimy little back-street shop kept by a Greek trader, and bought for the sum of two shillings and three pence, a tin of that asparagus which is one of the few things that seem to grow better and more luscious in a tin than in Mother Earth.

The patient enjoyed his last meal – and then miraculously his neck mended and he eventually issued from hospital a remarkable cure. Months later an audit query filtered through to the doctor, emanating from Khartoum and demanding to know, by return, the full and cogent reasons which had rendered necessary the apparently unjustified expenditure of 2s 3d on asparagus, a vegetable which did not appear in Column 7 of Schedule III of Chapter IV of the Regulations governing hospital diet. The doctor, over-worked as he was, decided that a clean breast was better than subterfuge, so wrote a straight account of the accident and concluded with the moving peroration: 'I feel certain that under the circumstances you will see your way to approve this trifling if irregular expenditure, in the name of Humanity and in satisfaction at the miraculous recovery of a valuable official.' The letter was typed, and he signed it. Underneath he appended a postscript: 'If this gives YOU a pain in the neck, TRY ASPARAGUS.'

I suppose we all have our potential murder tucked away somewhere, the peculiar circumstances under which we might be provoked beyond endurance. In the case of Sudanese, the man who came nearest to giving such provocation I found to be the policeman or junior employee who asked why he had not been promoted 'since I have never done anything wrong.' The oriental finds it difficult to comprehend that the way to promotion is not to sit tight, and by avoiding initiative, to avoid making blunders, or to appreciate Napoleon's dictum that the man who never did anything wrong never won a battle.

With our fellow countrymen, I was perhaps most nearly moved to a breach of the Sixth Commandment by a zealous engineer who put gelignite in our favourite fishing pool. But that was an isolated instance. The *type* which excited lethal feelings was undoubtedly the time-waster. He assumed different forms. There was Smith, the eighteen-stone North Country Steamers' engineer, who would walk into one's office while a case was in progress, deposit himself on a groaning and inadequate government chair, produce a wad of photographs and show one pictures of Smith front-face on a horse, Smith side-face on a horse and Smith backside-view on a horse, before asking for the loan of a pony – to which one acceded in order to get rid of him, despite the knowledge that he would ride the poor beast into a lather. There was Robinson, the doctor, whom one respected and admired but whose standards were so exacting that at meetings he could allow no challengeable point to go unchallenged and no detail to go by default, so that you wearily knew that his final objection would never be reached and allow you to get home for lunch.

At least Robinson was business-like and produced results – which could not be gainsaid and was far more endurable than Jones, one of those officials with a diffuse mind and an almost Irish genius for false trails and red herrings, in whose presence a meeting would start off upon the plain troubles of coping with an epidemic, only for everyone to find themselves listening to an engaging exposition of Jones's views on the preparation of hides or his experiences of coping with lice in prisoners' clothing.

Close behind time-wasting came vagueness, actually another embodiment of the same proclivity. It was not frequent or encouraged in the service, and was therefore notable when it occurred. I recollect a youngish man appearing unheralded in the office and saying that his name was Potter. I said, 'Yes?' He said he had come from the Ministry of Education. I said 'Yes?' He said that he represented Arts and Crafts. I said, 'Yes – what particular craft?' He did not reply, but said he thought he would visit a particular mission station among the Dinka called Kwajok. There was no reason why he should not visit that insalubrious spot, though no very evident one why he should. Was he not going anywhere else? He said, 'Yes' – he had been told to go somewhere else, but could not remember the name. I asked if he had not been given a copy of his itinerary. He said he had, but had lost it. He thought the name had an R in it. I suggested Raga, 205 miles west-north-west. Yes, he thought it probably *was* Raga. Could it perhaps be Meshra, 107 miles east-north-east, in a bog? Now that he thought of it, perhaps it might have been Meshra. There was also of course Busseri, twelve miles due south. Well, now that I mentioned it, the name did seem to ring a bell … He was quite prepared to go there if advised to. I then asked what he hoped to do. That produced something quite definite. He said he had three objects: (1) To see whether anything could be made of local dyes, (2) to teach the Africans to make their pots a nicer shape and with different wiggles round the edge, and (3) to see whether the Dinka, together with the Banda, Bongo, Belanda, Mandala, Shatt, Goolygoolies and the rest of the twenty-six tribes who lived out west, could be imbued with artistic sense. It was very tempting to send him to Hofrat el-Nabas, where some intelligent baboons and a few buffalo lived in the bush. Actually, it did not much matter where he went – as long as there was an R in it. Perhaps his towering mind was obsessed with oysters.

This rare type of negative vagueness was not to be confused with the more purposeful disordering of wits, which was usually a definite pathological symptom, sometimes the result of loneliness. Really isolated, single posts, common enough in the early days, were few in the fourth and fifth decades of the century, and suicides and lesser casualties of loneliness were very infrequent. One man who partially succumbed was an officer in charge of a company of the Equatorial Battalion of the Sudan Defence Force. When accorded a visit of inspection by the *Kaid* (the major-general commanding the force), he survived the ordeal fairly well and entertained his distinguished guest and staff, laying on a very tolerable dinner.

The meal over, and conversation having eventually flagged as the night advanced, people began to look at their watches, and a move was about to be made when the door opened and the host's servant appeared with a bowl of steaming porridge which he placed in front of his master. The officer solemnly took up a spoon and got down to business. There was total silence – the silence of non-plussment – while he schlooped cheerfully away until eventually, noticing the silence, he turned to his chief guest and laconically observed, 'I say – I hope you won't mind this, Sir. I find it saves me so much time in the morning.'

The odd fish, the eccentric, the memorable figure, the purple character – there were more of them than in most territories. They were not confined to a bachelor society, but they flourished in that milieu, and as conditions fit for married life spread, so, I think, did the galaxy of 'specimens' tend to wane. When communications improved, and public health services grew, married life and even family life became possible, if not always advisable, in the furthest stations; sanity and humdrum virtues tended to prevail, and memorable individualism to recede.

There was both gain and loss in the process. When I was on the path to marriage, all that my Arab friends wanted to know was (a) Was my bride nice and fat? (the willowy European figure does not appeal to the Arab, nor, Dinka apart, to most Africans), and (b) how much bride-price had I had to pay for her? I do not think the populace realised how much they owed indirectly to the great corps of wives who devoted themselves unselfishly to the country and maintained the sanity, perspective and welfare of its administrators and public servants. Not that there were no purple characters among that corps. I recollect ... but it might be ungallant to proceed further.

Diary 23 April 1953

At 9.30 took a salute from the police and SDF guard and said goodbye to everyone. One cannot be unmoved, and feelings are too deep to be recorded. If only we can be of those of whom Kipling said:

Let us now praise famous men,
Men of little showing,
For their work continueth ...[11]

We have not failed, for all the political disasters.

Diary 2 June 53
Coronation day in England

God save the Queen... We listened on the wireless to the whole thing up to the end of the Abbey service. It was impressive, fine and clear. Cantuar very good. (Where was Ebor? No sign of him.) Music good; how barbaric the trumpets are ... Just as the Queen was going in to the Abbey a telegram arrived congratulating me on a CBE. It does that SG credit, considering I've been as much in opposition as a man can be and serve loyally.

To Elizabeth   2 May 1953
en route to Kenya

I've just boarded the *Lord Lugard* at Nimule, and in an hour we ought to be off up the Albert Nile, and goodbye to Sudan territory. It has been a very big wrench, this last week, saying goodbye to the Province, and to the whole country, and it's no use pretending one doesn't feel it. You leave part of yourself in a place after more than quarter of a century there. But perhaps the greatest privilege of service here has been the people one serves with. In all my time I can remember only one man I really couldn't have worked with – and he was legal, and a crook. There are so many good friends one leaves behind, not only British but Sudanese – and politics can make no difference to that.

---

11   *Stalky & Co. A School Song.*

POSTSCRIPT

Note written on 25 November 1952

In 1947 a crucial decision was taken about the future of the Southern Provinces. Many of us felt that a black, non-Muslim, backward South could never hope to amalgamate in one independent country with an Arab, Muslim, advanced North, and that the right solution would be to tack the South on to Uganda or get H.M.G. to declare a protectorate, or at least appoint a British Lieutenant-Governor and run it separately.

It is very likely that none of those alternatives would have been successful; at all events, I and others agreed to try to forge a united Sudan – but on the specific understanding that in the new constitution there should be special safeguards for the South, and that at all costs British administration must continue for many years. On any weaker terms I would have resigned, rather than become Governor of the Province.

In the last five years my faith has been sorely tried on many occasions. But I have forced myself to continue to believe in our power to carry out our promises. We had got certain safeguards into the constitution, and there was no intention of lightly removing British staff from the South. Southern MPs in Khartoum were fairly impressive, and the horizon was not without hope. But I remained convinced that union (as opposed to mere absorption of a black helot community by a dominant Arab majority) *could be achieved only under British leadership.*

In the Sudan as a whole, with great patience and endless skill and trouble, a constitution was drafted, and almost became reality – a Sudanese government, power within a year or two to choose their future, a steady Sudanising of administration but retention of British advisers and key administrators, safeguards for the South. H.M.G. agreed, but Egypt would not play. Therefore we were going to go merrily ahead with the elections, and damn Egypt.

Then came the manoeuvres of Egypt's President, General Mohammad Neguib, who, with a most astute approach, upset the whole apple cart. He knew that if he could once get British influence out of the Sudan, Egyptian money, wire-pulling and the urban mob of Atbara and Omdurman would get the country under his thumb. The *effendis* could be bought; the tribal heads who hated Egypt could be relegated to insignificance; the 95 per cent of the people who wanted merely good administration (and the Southerners who wanted the British) just wouldn't be heard.

His plan, therefore, was to outbid H.M.G. 'The Sudan wants independence? Why – of course. Take it! Get on with your constitution. I won't oppose it. In fact I've got a few suggestions that will make it even more democratic …'

Those suggestions included (i) having a sort of board of Sudanese, Egyptian and possibly Indian representatives to control the Governor General; (ii) Sudanisation of the Police, Army and administrative services within three years; and (iii) removal of Southern safeguards, on the grounds that Sudan is all one country. With a lot of soft soap and persuasive blarney he came to an agreement with most of the representatives of the Sudanese parties. The British press, blind as the Gadarene swine, welcomed the new and helpful attitude of Egypt and her readiness to bargain. Nobody bothered to stop and consider that (i) would turn the Governor General into a rubber stamp and remove his power either to step in in an emergency, or to protect the South; that (ii) would mean the ruination of fifty years of work and the reduction of the country to chaos; and that (iii) combined with (ii) would relegate three-and-a-half million people to neglect and exploitation, and in time (have no doubt) to the recrudescence of the slave trade.

Actually Neguib's proposals to the Sudan parties were different from his proposals to H.M.G., and the proposals to all the parties differed from each other. Some Sudanese party men are already getting cold feet and beginning to doubt their agreements. Meanwhile, the legislative assembly is dead, and since the new parliament is not yet elected, the main body of Sudanese opinion, including the Southerners and the big tribal heads, has no vehicle of expression and no representative body which it can consult.

Everything depends on H.M.G. If they stand firm, the various intrigues of parties, Egyptians and self-seekers may well cancel each other out; sensible Sudanese opinion may consolidate, and the new constitution may go through. If H.M.G. fail, the Sudan is lost and ruined, and we have committed the most contemptible renunciation of responsibility in our history. I feel that nothing less is at stake than my faith in our nation. If H.M.G. were to let us down now, England is rotten at the heart – and it would break mine.

Second note, written on 18 January 1953

The agreement of January 11th between Salah Salim [Egyptian Minister of State for Sudanese Affairs] and leaders of the Sudan parties has darkened the situation and produced a crisis, but has not altered the issue.

The parties agreed to various Egyptian terms, including the removal of H.E.'s powers to protect the South, together with Sudanisation of the administration in three years, in return for Egypt's recognition of the Sudan's right to independence. There is no love of Egypt. Salah thinks he has double-crossed the parties. The parties think they have double-crossed him, and that once the magic independence has been achieved, they can go back on anything they said and kick Egypt in the pants. So everyone (for the moment) is happy, and there has been a wave of emotional unity among the Northern parties over achieving the one common goal before they split and start scrapping again.

The result is that H.M.G., already under pressure from the military authorities, Egypt and the Yanks (as the *New York Times* correspondent said to H.E., 'Don't you think we Americans care a damn if eight million niggers starve or are slaves?') to accede to the Egyptian demands in order to get a deal over Suez (and God and the Foreign Office know the value of any agreement with Egypt) – H.M.G., I say, are now under the additional pressure of having all the Sudan parties united for the moment in favour of the Egyptian demands. The one snag to everything is the South.

These were the circumstances under which H.E. and the Colonial Secretary summoned the three Southern Governors on 13 January. The matter was put to us thus:

H.M.G. must have a treaty, for strategic purposes. If we agree, the new constitution can start and a treaty will be obtained. As to the South – it will have nearly a quarter of the seats in parliament, as well as two Ministers, and by playing a skilful game may be able to look after its own interests. If we stand out on the grounds of fulfilling our pledges to the South, and maintaining safeguards and British administration, we may wreck everything. Bang goes the treaty; the new Sudanese constitution gets postponed *sine die*; and we may drive the parties into Egypt's arms, and even have non-cooperation, civil disobedience and chaos in the North – which must reflect on the South too.'

These are powerful arguments, and great pressure was put on us by superiors and (I am sorry to say) colleagues to admit them, and to consent to go back and persuade the South to accede and cut its own throat in the public interest, and perhaps in the long run in its own. We could only answer (in more parliamentary language) that we were ------d if we would: that a constitution without the safeguard of H.E.'s special powers and above all without prolongation of British administration was something we could not persuade the bulk of Southerners to accept, even if we tried, and that in any case neither we nor most of our district commissioners would consent to try to put it across.

There was an exchange of shots with Cairo and H.M.G. (an average of 150 pages of cypher wires coming into the Secretariat every day; and as we left it today:

1. *H.M.G. have been advised to stand quite firm against rapid Sudanisation of the service, in the South at all events.*

2. *H.M.G. have been advised to stand firm about H.E.'s safeguarding powers.*

3. *Provided (1) is assured, but if agreement cannot be reached over (2), we might induce the South to join in the elections, granted a protocol to say that the first thing to be debated by the new parliament must be Southern safeguards.*

4. *Failing this, we advise H.M.G. to break off negotiations. H.E. would then have to declare a state of emergency, a conference of all Southerners would be called, and if agreement with the North could not be reached, the whole future of the South will have to be reconsidered (Federation with the North? British mandate under United Nations?)*

That is as we left it today. What the next move will be, I can't tell you. In general, from all the secret and open stuff I saw, things improve the farther away you get. Our Cairo embassy is contemptible, the F.O. a bit shady, H.M.G. apparently sound, the British press good. I don't much like *The*

Times, which is untrustworthy, but *Telegraph*, *Manchester Guardian* and even the revolting *Mail* have been worthy. The *Mail* had a glorious picture of Salah at Rumbek, with nothing on but his underpants, joining in a Dinka dance and leaping like the priests of Baal. The Gippies themselves had taken it and used it for their propaganda; the *Mail* somehow scooped it and used it for ours.

PASTURES NEW

A year later, when the British Government gave in to pressure from Egypt, the author resigned. After leaving the Sudan, he moved to Uganda and became Deputy Head of the Game Department, based in Entebbe, where he continued until 1960. In 1961-62 he took on a short-term job for the Government of Northern Rhodesia (about to become Zambia), in charge of the evacuation of animals from islands in the Zambezi river as the lake behind the Kariba dam was filling up. Then he retired.

The Sudan had become an independent republic on 1 January 1956, and soon Owen's worst fears began to be realised as parliamentary parties split into factions, and corruption became endemic, leading to a military coup in 1958, Communist infiltration, and later to civil war. As he wrote in 1970, 'The last decade and a half have been years of tragedy, oppression, revolt, racial hatred and horror.' He lived long enough – until 1982 – to witness the disintegration of the country which he had spent his career striving to unite.

ACKNOWLEDGEMENTS

Publication of this book has been made possible by the generosity of the author's son Robert Owen and nephew David Lyon. The family presented Owen's letters and diaries, together with a draft of his memoir, to the University Library on Palace Green in Durham, which now owns copyright in the papers.

The Editor would like to thank Jane Hogan, keeper in charge of the Sudan Archive at Durham, for her expert guidance, and Dr Ahmed al-Shami of St Antony's College, Oxford, for encouraging us to proceed with the project.

INDEX